Economies and Societies in Latin America:
A Geographical Interpretation

R.

2 ?

Economies and Societies in Latin America:
A Geographical Interpretation

Peter R. Odell, *Professor of Economic Geography and
Director, Economic Geography Institute,
Netherlands School of Economics, Rotterdam*

and

David A. Preston, *Lecturer in Geography,
University of Leeds*

A Wiley-Interscience Publication

JOHN WILEY & SONS LTD
London New York Sydney Toronto

Copyright © 1973 John Wiley and Sons Ltd.
All Rights Reserved. No part of this publication may be reproduced, stored in a retrieval
system or transmitted, in any form or by any
means electronic, mechanical, photocopying,
recording or otherwise, without the prior
written permission of the Copyright owner.

Library of Congress Catalog Card No. 76—37110

ISBN 0 471 65258 X

Printed in Hungary by Franklin Printing House, Budapest.

Preface

various aspects of the spatial structures of Latin American economies and
societies.

This is not a book on the regional geography of Latin America or even
one which describes and explains the locations there of particular sets of
phenomena. Books which attempt this already exist and reading at least
some of them constitutes an essential prerequisite to understanding what
this book is trying to say about Latin America. (See the bibliographic notes
at the end of each chapter.) But nor is this book a problem-orientated polemic
concerned with presenting, in the usual apocalyptic terms, all that is wrong
with the economies and societies of Latin America and recommending
either bloody revolution and/or more technocracy as the only possible
solutions.

Rather is it a book in which the authors have sought to present the
essential features of the spatial organization of economies and societies
in Latin America. It must be understood that the two authors have contrasting interests in Latin America with respect both to the areas they know best
and to those aspects of its spatial structure with which their studies have
been mainly concerned. These contrasts are reflected in their separate
contributions and it is hoped that this diversity of interest has led to a book
with a broader scope than any single author could hope to achieve and
which will, therefore, be of interest not only to their fellow geographers,
but also to other social scientists—in particular, economists, economic historians, sociologists and social anthropologists—who may well find useful,
as a background to their own studies, this consideration of Latin American
economic and social phenomena from a spatial point of view.

Only this introduction is a joint effort. Apart from this each author
accepts sole responsibility for his own contribution, though each has benefited from the other's willingness to criticize not only his style and presentation but also his views on particular topics. In the final analysis, however,

each author has been at liberty to accept or reject the criticisms made and the two contributions thus remain highly individualistic in content, form and style with the only significant elements of uniformity emerging out of the style of the cartography (all done in the Economisch Geografisch Instituut in Rotterdam) and from the joint decision to avoid footnotes and specific references and to substitute for them annotated reading lists at the end of each chapter. This was felt to be more appropriate to a book which can do little more than introduce the complexities of the subject and which aims, therefore, to stimulate interest in more comprehensive statements on various aspects of the spatial structures of Latin American economies and societies.

In spite of their individualism, however, there are elements of a common understanding between the authors as to the nature of the discipline within which they work: in particular, in respect of the validity of examining geographical issues within the framework of Latin America. These ideas perhaps need a little attention in order to place the book in its appropriate scientific and regional contexts.

Both of the authors had their training in English schools of geography which were essentially possibilistic in their approach to the interrelationships of man and his environment and which treated regional geography as the 'crowning glory' of the subject, in the sense that what one learned on the systematic side of the discipline was considered to be useful principally in helping with the discovery and analysis of regions on the earth's surface. Each of these elements in their academic backgrounds seems to be highly relevant to their study of Latin America, where the diversity of physical environments and of the many human groups that have been involved with them over hundreds, or even thousands, of years has produced a complex set of regions in the continent. Several books which have emerged from such analysis already exist. (Again, see the reading list at the end of each chapter.) This book, however, is not an alternative to those others, for not only would such a study have been somewhat superfluous but it would also have failed to reflect the authors' more recently evolved central interest in the study of systematic themes in geography as an end in themselves and not merely as an aid to studies in regional geography. Perhaps their exposure to work in other disciplines as part of their studies on Latin America, particularly work in economics, sociology and politics, as well as trends in geography itself in the last two decades, persuaded them that an account of the general aspects of Latin America's spatial structure would be a worthwhile task.

Thus, several years of research experience, coupled with visits to different parts of the continent and their development of parallel teaching programmes, clearly showed the authors that many spatial patterns in Latin American societies had continental-wide manifestations. From country to country and region to region spatial patterns repeated themselves, indicating the basic similarity of the processes at work and the potential validity of an interpretation which sought to isolate, describe and explain them. This perhaps takes the approach of the book some way away from what is normally expected of a geography text concerned with a large world region, but it certainly does not take it anywhere near the new frontiers of the discipline. Some of our colleagues will undoubtedly feel that the search for, and the analysis of, the specific and the unique has still been given too much attention in comparison with the attention to the universal as demanded by modern spatial analysis. However, we hope that these latter critics, as well as the more traditional regional geographers, will, nevertheless, accept our view that we have written a book with a specifically geographical viewpoint and not a book about Latin America's history, politics, sociology and economics etc. which, after being appropriately simplified, are suitable for the tender minds of geographers! It is certainly true that both authors make use of a great amount of information provided within the classificatory systems of these other social sciences and that both make use of the vocabularies, approaches and methods that emerge out of the other social sciences with which each author has some familiarity. In spite of this, the point of view of the authors remains quite firmly geographical as they strive to present a reasoned analysis of the ways in which economic, social and political phenomena are distributed over space and of the processes that have been at work in determining these spatial patterns.

Therefore this book is concerned with the 'why' of where human activities have occurred in Latin America. It is also concerned with the consequences of this on the societies involved, for societies do not just have a spatial component in their political, social and economic structures. Their spatial components have feedback effects on the progress or otherwise of the societies themselves, thus implying that there are important policy considerations which emerge out of spatial structures. This is but a very recently generally-recognized fact of modern 'interventionist' style governments, even amongst the industrialized nations, and it is still something which remains barely recognized at all in the planning of the development of the non-industrialized countries of the world. Even if it is recognized, there is little awareness of what could or should be done about it! Hopefully, therefore, this book may make a modest contribution towards a better understanding of some aspects of the spatial structure of societies in Latin America and it may even have a little effect in persuading the policymakers, and their almost invariably non-geographic advisers, of the significance of the spatial structure of their countries' economies and societies.

The authors wish gratefully to acknowledge all the help they have received in the preparation of this book. For Dr. Preston some of the ideas he presents and the ways in which the material is organized are derived from successive generations of Leeds students who attended, criticized and participated in his Latin American course. His field material has only been collected thanks to the friendliness of Ecuadorian and Bolivian peasants, townfolk and experts. Rosemary helped and encouraged but, of course, the faults remain those of the author. Professor Odell also had the opportunity to evolve his ideas out of discussions with students of Latin American geography at the London School of Economics and particularly with John Kirby, Alan Gilbert, Alan Lavell and David Slater who, in the years between 1966 and 1972, worked for their doctorates on economic geographical problems in Chile, Colombia, Mexico and Peru respectively and through their research efforts greatly extended their supervisor's understanding of the spatial processes in the continent. In Latin America itself Professor Odell has benefited from the advice of academics and regional /urban planners in many countries and in various international organizations and would wish to acknowledge his indebtedness to them. Nearer home, various other people have helped in more mundane but nevertheless essential ways. Preparation of the manuscript was willingly handled by Mevrouw van der Kaag-de Munnik and Mevrouw Van Reijn-Herscheit, Secretaries in the Economisch-Geografisch Instituut and by Mevrouw Van der Heiden-Jenkins. The cartographic work was a major task and was done efficiently and effectively by Dr. J. E. C. Schoevers, the cartographer of the Economic Geography Institute—with help from Dr. M. W.van Beijeren Bergen en Henegouwen. Needless to say, however, any faults which remain in the text or the maps remain the responsibility of the author. Finally, to his wife and children, a very big thank you is more than due. They not only remained at home whilst he was studying in Latin America, but they also gave him sufficient leave of absence from his familial duties to complete the text and the other work associated with it.

Rotterdam/Leeds   P.R.O.
March 1972   D.A.P.

Contents

Contents

List of Maps and Plates

1

Plates (Photographs by David A. Preston)   *Facing page* 54

CHAPTER 1
An Introduction to the Region

It is necessary to say a little about the area with which the book is concerned. In a general way the choice of Latin America does not need justifying. It exists as a well-defined world region and in the post-war period the idea of a Latin America which includes all nations and territories lying to the south of the Río Grande has become widely and formally accepted. Earlier concern about the existence in the continent of non-Spanish/Portuguese-speaking territories has evaporated as one after the other of these territories has secured its independence and then, normally after a few years of indecision, has determined to take political and institutional action to tie itself to the rest of the continent where the 'Latin' countries have, again after some hesitation, decided to accept the newcomers into the Latin American camp. To-day, only the small French Caribbean territories, together with Suriname and the Netherlands Antilles, which form part of the Kingdom of the Netherlands, and British Honduras, plus a few other tiny British 'possessions', lie outside the political hegemony of Latin America. Even these remnants of political colonialism have many common elements in their history of settlement and exploitation which tie them in closely with the rest of the continent except in the narrowly political plane. Thus, writing in terms of Latin America as 'everything south of the Río Grande' is to-day hardly going to offend any susceptibilities providing one remembers the corollary that internal differentiation is nevertheless important: which is all very well provided that one is going to proceed to a country-by-country or a region-by-region survey.

But, as indicated in the Preface, we are not proposing to do this. Instead the presentation will be concerned with spatial phenomena which, by implication even if not explicitly, we claim to have some general relevance within the whole of this world region. The validity of essaying such a claim lies

3

in the substantiative parts of the book; and the reader will have plenty of opportunities to concur with or to challenge the views expressed. In brief, at this point, one can point to such a phenomenon as the universality of Spanish or Portuguese influence. Their earlier domination of the social and economic life of the continent has been translated into a continuing influence which is still of significant proportions, most notably through the impact of long-lasting institutions and forms of development such as city patterns and the urbanist pattern of society, which more than a century of independence has not managed to eradicate. Or one can see the continued, near continental-wide trend towards urbanization and the concentration of political and economic power in the capital city and/or chief port of each country; or the continuing importance of the extractive type, export-orientated activities in the economies of nearly every Latin American nation; or the continued existence of little-populated frontier regions, with still less developed resources, even in countries where other parts of the national territories are becoming crowded and are lacking in opportunities for rapidly growing populations. Such themes have been enormously important in formulating the spatial structure of the Latin American societies and economies and are dealt with at length in the appropriate sections of the book.

The authors are not unmindful of the tremendous physical and human diversity of Latin America. Their own work in different parts of the continent ensures this. Thus, they accept the validity of the traditional geographical books which illustrate this diversity through their presentation of the countless facts that together go to make up the face of the continent. The authors would indeed go further, and be prepared to argue that it is only from such knowledge that reasonable hypotheses which seek to explain spatial patterns are likely to emerge. This is particularly important in a situation in which we are working in alien environments and societies, such that the value judgements implied in the assumptions that must be made before any hypothesis can be tested or any model calibrated are, consciously or not, influenced by inappropriate backgrounds.

The authors are not Latin Americans and consequently they look at the continent as outsiders. Their interpretation may well be different from that of the Latin American as, for example, in the contrasting views of the economic geography of the continent as seen by a Brazilian and a European. The Brazilian sees vast areas of the continent undeveloped not only as a result of a lack of people but also because the colonial powers had little interest in developing agriculture and industry of a sort that would compete with their own domestic industrial interests. The European, on the other hand, sees a half-empty continent with little industry save in a few particularly favoured places, and even there industrial production is seldom so efficient that it can produce goods of a high enough quality to enable them to be exported to the former colonial powers.

It is particularly important to grasp the distinctive characteristics of Latin America's social organization as a prerequisite to understanding the attitudes of Latin Americans not only towards their own problems, but also towards the solutions that others recommend for them. Firstly, Latin American society is much more clearly divided than the society of most European countries. The rich, upper class tends largely to be outward looking. They esteem most highly goods which come from industrialized countries. Their children, perhaps after completing a university course in their own country, naturally travel to Europe or North America. If they are educated, they are often better read in the literature of the Old World than the New. They are accustomed to social inequality on a scale now largely unknown in Europe and think it quite natural that they should profit from it. The middle class, which is nearly always less numerous than in Western Europe or North America, is, on the other hand, strongly nationalistic, believing more than most in contemporary political slogans and convinced of the reality of the economic imperialism of the Great Powers, in particular the U.S.A. It is often an admirer of the freedom which Cuba has gained from the U.S.A., even though it knows little about it and is far from being communist or even socialist in attitude. The working class can be divided into the proletarian urban workers and the peasants of the countryside. Both are primarily concerned with self-protection, the former with securing adequate working conditions and wages through labour unions and the latter with small-scale landownership and with the maintenance of personal freedom to farm it as they wish. The attitudes of both groups to other countries tend to be little more than the parrot-like repetition of the views of their more middle-class leaders to whom such views are often suggested by national political leaders.

Among the articulate Latin Americans it is important to understand that there is great pride in nationhood and suspicion of outside intervention in any form. Although it is about 150 years since most Latin American countries were formally under colonial rule, a series of political and even military interventions in the affairs of Latin America countries, first by Britain in the 19th century and more recently by the U.S.A. during the present century, has convinced many Latin Americans that the major powers wish to treat Latin America, like the rest of the Third World, as a series of dependent states whose external relations can easily be manipulated. In more economic terms, as is pointed out in later chapters of this book, much of Latin American industry belongs to foreign companies and is thus oriented primarily to benefiting their investors rather than the economies of the countries where the industry is located. The nationalization of many foreign concerns in Latin American countries since the nationalization of the Mexican petroleum industry in 1938 reflects these views.

In the light of all this it is unduly ingenuous for Anglo-Americans or Europeans to go to Latin America expecting to be loved. The history of the continent *from the Latin American point of view* has been one of prolonged exploitation by the colonial powers or industrialized nations. And this exploitation is seen by Latin Americans to be continuing. What, after all, they argue, is the logic of Bolivian tin being shipped as ore to Liverpool for smelting when Bolivia has ample resources of hydro-electric power to make the tin locally; or of Colombia or Brazil shipping coffee beans to Europe and the United States when instant coffee could so easily be made exclusively in the coffee-producing countries? Why, too, should Guayana and Suriname ship their bauxite to the U.S.A., Canada and Western Europe to be refined and smelted when they have a vast potential for hydro-electric power development on which locally built plants could operate and at the same time provide job opportunities in countries with too few jobs chasing too many people.

It is best therefore to approach Latin America not with Eurocentric ideas about what Latin American attitudes ought to be, but rather in the knowledge that relationships between Latin America and the outside world have not been equally beneficial to all parties. Both these considerations and other differences between the continent and the industrialized countries of Western Europe are so important that they inevitably make the task of the non-Latin American student more difficult and expose his research to certain dangers. Two examples illustrate this point as far as geographical studies are concerned.

The first arises when a European-born and trained geographer gets involved in the study and analysis of, say, regional differences with Latin American countries, for this puts him out of his geographical depth in respect of at least three sets of characteristics which place his familiar European-based ideas apart from those of Latin America. In the first place he has a fundamental familiarity with a situation in which the existence of unused and/or unpopulated parts of national territories has been the exception rather than the rule for many generations; secondly, his experience is of countries whose geographical size is modest, so that, given their well-developed transport infrastructure, there is little cause for concern about the differential incidence of transport costs in the movement of goods and for the time distance involved in people moving around the country; thirdly, he is a member of a society in which there is a general consensus of opinion in favour of an equitable geographical distribution of incomes and of job opportunities. Useful geographical work by such a person in Latin America thus depends upon his willingness and ability to appreciate and understand the significance of the differences between his own background and the background to the regions he aims to study. This is a process which involves not only learning, but also experience and a 'feel' for the contrasting conditions. Without this, a mechanistic application of, for example, a Christaller-type settlement network analysis as evolved in West European conditions, to the different geographical scale and the contrasting spatial organization of society in Brazil or Argentina seems likely to produce inappropriate results, as does an application of the types of spatial investment policies used to help the depressed areas of western Europe in the political, social and geographical conditions of the large Latin American countries.

The second example is in the case of urban geographical studies in which hypotheses have generally been based on experience with North American cities. Given this experience, the expectation of the scholar investigating any city structure is that he will find a declining central business district surrounded at best by urban slums or at worst by racial ghettoes. Then, according to normative models, these will gradually merge into areas which are in a process of social decline until the suburbs proper are reached. There, a gradual increase in affluence and a gradual decrease in housing and population density will reflect increasing distance from the city centre. This model of reality that the North American (or British) geographer carries with him to Latin America is now found to be at best inadequate, and at worst positively misleading, for the typical Latin American city has a centre in which 'all the action' is concentrated and in which many of the socially most acceptable people still prefer to live, with a residential location on the central plaza being amongst the most desired of all situations. The suburbs, if they exist at all in a North American sense, are limited not only because of lower standards of affluence, but also as a result of different life styles. And finally, instead of the grandest suburbs of all on the outskirts of the city, one finds there the shanty-towns of the 'marginalistas', the recent immigrants to the Latin American cities who find their living space on land that is held unused while awaiting urban expansion. The expansion will inevitably enhance the value of the land, which means that as it is developed so the marginalistas will be driven out to the new periphery.

Appreciation that the 'universal' laws of economic and social geography, like the laws of economies and sociology, have been discovered in the main by North Atlantic orientated theoreticans and 'proved' by testing them in this one major world region, emerges clearly for those who work in a different world region with contrasting values and cultural attributes, many of which, if they can be quantified at all to fit into the normative theories, proceed to upset the traditional wisdom. Because theory and qualification have emerged largely out of experience beyond the confines of Latin America, while the authors have spent most of their time and effort in trying to understand this very 'foreign' continent, this book does not depend very much upon accepted geographical theory and laws: instead it is more problem-orientated as it endeavours to describe and explain some of the phenomena and the processes which have resulted in particular spatial structures of society, some of which at least are worthy of attention because of their greater applicability to other parts of the Third World than the spatial structures that have emerged in North America or Western Europe.

But this should not be taken too far. Latin America has not been reproduced elsewhere in the world (except possibly in small parts of Africa and Asia which also came under Spanish or Portuguese influence) and its problems are only in part shared by the other developing continents. Certainly Latin America's collective reaction to its subservient role in the world economy has had implications elsewhere, not least through the work of the Economic Commission for Latin America, whose first Secretary General, the Argentine economist Dr. Paul Prebisch, has had a tremendous influence on economic thought in the non-industrialized world. His work with E.C.LA provided much of the initial stimulus for new organizations like the United Nations Industrial Development Organization (U.N.I.D.O.) and the U.N. Commission on Trade and Development (U.N.C.T.A.D.) which, for the first time, brought the views and needs of the world's developing nations into effective focus in international economic and financial affairs. In a more specialized sphere of international economic affairs, that of the world petroleum industry, one sees the same kind of spill-over effect of Latin America experience into other parts of the world. This has emerged from the early control exercised by countries like Chile and Mexico over the activities of the major American and British oil companies, now a general phenomenon throughout the Third World, and from the attempts over the last decade by Venezuela, as a major oil exporter, to control the rate of oil production so as to maintain prices: in 1971 the other main oil producers in the Middle East and elsewhere 'got the message' and, in co-operation with Venezuela, have now achieved all-round higher prices for their oil.

In other respects, however, Latin America's experience is no more and no less relevant to the rest of the Third World than that of any other group of nations. Perhaps Latin America's early political independence from the European metropolitan powers left it too exposed to the might of the United States. This political misfortune was compounded by the fact of its location vis à vis the United States which assumed that the tenuous continuity of the land mass called the Western Hemisphere, and its physical separation from the world of Europe, Africa and Asia, somehow gave it the right to dictate, both in general and in detail, what was and what was not allowed throughout the region. Elsewhere in the Third World the continued role of European powers through to a period when much of their own economic and political life had been 'socialized', in one form or another, perhaps made the colonial relationships much less definitive and has perhaps even resulted in a greater degree of 'enlightenment' about the political, social and economic organization of society amongst the local élite who eventually took over responsibility for the well-being of their nations. The continuing interest of European powers in their recent colonies paradoxically gave the latter some protection against the United States' one-eyed view of the world and the way in which society should be organized and, equally important, gave special economic protection and/or other advantages to many of the important activities in the territories concerned through such devices as Commonwealth Preference and the French and Dutch economic unions. Latin America is still trying, now almost in desperation, to get the United States to make similar arrangements in its trading relationships with the developing part of the continent.

But these differences between Latin America and the rest of the Third World compound another set of differences emerging out of the historical and cultural background. As is shown in the next chapter, most of Latin America has a population which is European or quasi-European in origin; the non-European elements are relatively unimportant except in a few nations mainly in the Andes, and even there the European minorities are socially and politically dominant. Thus, the languages are international in significance; the dominant religion is one with its roots and most of its other adherents in Europe; sporting activities are dominated by European-style games and spending patterns and social structures such as the family

2*

are basically recognizable to a European. In all this, and more besides, Latin America may be distinguished from most of the other countries of the Third World in both Africa and Asia where indigenous cultures have either strongly reasserted themselves over the superficial Europeanness of the colonial period or are in the process of doing so. In other words, European styles and European values are no longer dominant and one wonders if the pathway to 'development' spelled out by European pioneers has much relevance, particularly when the contrasts are further sharpened by the immensity of the rural population problem in countries like India, Pakistan and Indonesia.

Throughout Latin America these doubts are much less strong and, in general, the student of the continent's economic and social affairs will feel that development is going to emerge, or indeed, is emerging already, along very familiar lines. Perhaps, in fact, there is some evidence of too much simplistic 'aping' of European and North American-style development forms and processes, but this seldom seems *entirely* inappropriate: merely somewhat out of place and likely to be moulded to fit the style, requirements and characteristics of the continent wherein they are emerging, in many cases very quickly, within a rapid process of development and change. In other words, the economic and social 'problems' of Latin America seem to be solvable within the general framework of methods and techniques that have evolved elsewhere and could, within the time period of the rest of this century, take most of the continent outside the framework of the 'Third World' and into the world of the more developed nations; in terms, at least, of the creation of mass consumption economies. In the meantime, however, there are significant, if not overwhelming, problems that the continent faces in many different ways in the organization of human (and humane) societies.

This book aims to outline the contribution which specifically geographical analysis can make to the understanding of Latin America and its problems. Thus, it is concerned with the following kinds of issues. Firstly, as has been previously pointed out, one of the main features of Latin American countries is that they are generally large and normally have sizeable areas within their national territory that are only partly occupied. The impact of this generalization on national political, social and economic policies is primarily a study in applied geography. In spite of this there are few other books which have approached the study of Latin America with this specifically geographical viewpoint in mind. Secondly, the analysis of the urban patterns in Latin America has, likewise, received only passing notice from historians and historical geographers and little research has been directed towards analysing the socio-geographical organization of Latin American cities or to comparing the processes discovered to be at work with those known to have been important in European and Anglo-American urban centres. Thirdly, and similarly, analysis of the general aspects of the spatial structure of the Latin American economy on a continental scale has not previously been presented. Such analysis is tackled in the second part of this book which, it is hoped, will provide a framework around which many more studies of differences in economic growth between regions within developing countries will be attempted.

To the geographer Latin America is not only a vast world region but one that offers an intellectual challenge: the challenge of seeking to achieve a satisfying level of understanding of the spatial aspects of Latin American economies and societies. The authors hope that this book will aid such an understanding. But Latin America also presents the geographer, like other social scientists, with the challenge of a variety of problems the solution of which will improve the lot of many people. There are no solutions in this book: but, hopefully, some ideas from which solutions could eventually emerge.

Bibliographical Notes

Familiarity with the basic regional differences in Latin America such as can be gained from reading some traditional regional geography texts will be assumed. The following brief selection of books in English will, however, help to meet any deficiency in that respect whilst others will be useful guides to the Latin American scene.

One of the finest regional geography textbooks ever written in the English language is PRESTON JAMES' *Latin America*, 4th edition (Odyssey, New York, 1969), which has inspired countless students to a greater interest in the region. More recently, a text concerned specifically with the northern part of Latin America, ROBERT C. WEST and JOHN P. AUGELLI's *Middle America: its Lands and Peoples* (Prentice Hall, Englewood Cliffs, New Jersey, 1966) has been published and widely acclaimed. Its treatment of historical aspects and settlement evolution is superior to that of James although it is more pedestrian in dealing with aspects of the economic geography. The chapters on Mexico are particularly noteworthy but that on Cuba for some reason pays no attention to developments there since the revolution in 1959.

H. BLAKEMORE and C. T. SMITH (EDS.), *Latin America: Geographical Perspectives* (Methuen, London, 1971) is a book of essays on different parts of the continent by a group of authors with special regional interests. It provides a useful supplement to the above mentioned books as most of the essays are essentially general surveys. However, the essays by ROBINSON, GALLOWAY and CROSSLEY also provide new interpretations of the areas with which they deal. More specifically on matters economic and social is J. P. COLE, *Latin America: an Economic and Social Geography*, 2nd Edition (Butterworths, London, 1970). It gives a survey of the main features of the geography of each country's economy and society and is useful as a reference book for 'chasing up the facts'.

For serious students and for browsers in libraries the large volume edited by CLAUDIO VELIZ, *Latin America and the Caribbean: a Handbook* (A. Blond, London, 1968), is invaluable. It contains a large number of essays about each Latin American country and about a variety of topics of importance. Thus there are articles on the cinema, architecture, football and music as well as about inflation, foreign policies and peasants, inter alia. Books that appeal to the general reader on social and political problems are not easy to come by, but the English translation of JACQUES LAMBERT, *Latin America: Social and Political Institutions* (University of California Press, Berkeley, California, 1967–) is full of insight and intellectually stimulating. There are two small books for quick reading that provide a good jumping-off point for further study. One is STEPHEN CLISSOLD's *Latin America: a Cultural Outline* (Hutchinsons, London, 1965) which tells interestingly about the continent and its people and which, for instance, refers to Latin American literature that aids understanding of the continent. It includes (pp. 153–5) a list of English translations of some of the more important works in Latin American literature. The second is GEORGE PENDLE's *A History of Latin America* (Penguin Books, Harmondsworth, 1966). This gives an evening's reading on the history of the continent in an engaging way.

PART I

Major Themes in the Social Geography of Latin America

by

DAVID A. PRESTON

CHAPTER 2
Human Groups and Their Landscapes

Introduction

Perhaps you once accepted the idea not uncommon amongst North Americans and North-West Europeans that Latin Americans are 'a lot of brown-skinned dagoes.' Certainly, the belief ran, they are renowned for the mañana attitude—always preferring to put off until tomorrow or the next day what could be done today—whilst culturally and artistically they have achieved very little. It is no coincidence that Pelé, the footballer, is the best-known Latin American. It might even be said that Latin Americans are the White Man's Burden of the New World.

This is nonsense. In many parts of southern Latin America the people are indistinguishable from those of much of Anglo-America. Buenos Aires, for example, is one of the largest cities in the world and the women on its main streets are as smart as any in central London or New York and a good deal smarter than those in Staines, Middlesex or South Bend, Indiana.

The noted mañana attitude is largely the invention of impatient foreigners, unable and unwilling to understand that not all the world does business and takes decisions in the same way as themselves. Latin Americans, to their credit, are almost always courteous and often find North Americans and Europeans arrogant, brusque and discourteous in their dealings with foreigners. The underestimation of the cultural achievements of Latin Americans likewise stems largely from ignorance. Few secondary school children in either western Europe or Anglo-America study Spanish language and literature in any depth, if at all. Those who do study Spanish literature seldom read anything written by the most distinguished Spanish Americans. By contrast in Spain itself in the last two decades there has been an increasing realization that the most important novelists and poets currently writing

15

in Spanish are from Chile, Argentina, Peru or Cuba rather than from Spain. Few recent graduates from Spanish universities would not admit the claim to fame and world stature of Neruda, Asturias, García Marquez or Carpentier and among the younger writers Octavio Paz, Carlos Fuentes and Mario Vargas Llosa are by no means inferior to contemporary Spaniards.

In music, the cinema and the theatre the achievements of Latin Americans have been more modest although Villa Lobos, Castelnuovo Tedesco, Torre Nilsson and Rochas can be mentioned as being not without an international reputation. In architecture, however, the contribution of Latin Americans to their own modern urban landscapes has been notable and the work of Lucio Costa and Oscar Neimayer, especially in Brasília, is a monument to architectural vision in Latin America. Most Latin American capital cities have striking modern buildings, frequently built during the 1950s when such imagination was rare in Britain or Anglo-America. Finally it is neither irrelevant nor facetious to contrast European and Latin American performance in the 1970 World Cup soccer competition in Mexico where Europe produced the totally negative Italian team and the inspired mediocrity of the English in contrast with the brilliant and constructive Brazilians whilst even lowly Peru displayed talents that surprised. Notwithstanding the intellectual achievements of Latin Americans, however, the continent—unlike Europe—still contains primitive hunters as well as areas that are virtually unexplored and this alone suggests a great difference between the big cities and the countryside.

Many of the contrasts that exist in the landscapes of Latin America are the result of the different impact that the inhabitants have had on it. Types of housing, differences in land ownership and the street pattern of the towns, such elements of the man-made landscape all result from historical development through time and a complex cultural heritage. In this chapter we shall look at the human ingredients of Latin America, show where different groups predominate and how each ethnic type has its own very special relationship with the land and with other human groups. (Figure 2-1.) It must not be imagined that the population of any part of Latin America is anything other than the result of a fusion of various groups at different times in the past, but if something can be understood about the differences and their relation to ethnic origin and history, then an understanding of the complex contemporary landscape may gradually develop.

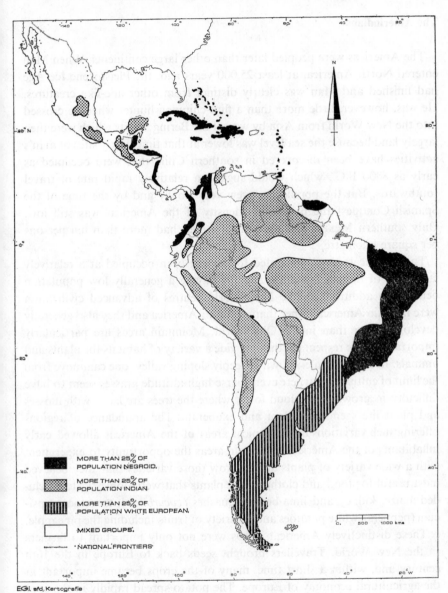

MORE THAN 25% OF
POPULATION NEGROID.

MORE THAN 25% OF
POPULATION INDIAN.

MORE THAN 25% OF
POPULATION WHITE EUROPEAN.

MIXED GROUPS.

NATIONAL FRONTIERS

EGI, afd, Kartografie

Figure 2–1. Distribution of racial groups in Latin America

The Amerindians

The Americas were peopled later than other large continents. When Man entered North America, at least 25,000 years ago, the Pleistocene Ice Age had finished and Man was clearly distinct from other ape-like creatures. He was, however, little more than a flint-chipping hunter when he crossed into the New World from Asia by way of the Bering Straits which were then largely land because the sea level was lower at that time. Early sites of man's activities have been discovered in southern Chile that were occupied as early as 8800 B.C., which would suggest a relatively rapid rate of travel southwards. But the population grew very slowly and by the time of the Spanish Conquest the population density of the Americas was still low. Only southern Mexico and the central Andes had more than ten persons per square kilometre.

The Americas, then, are noted for having been occupied at a relatively late stage of human evolution and for having a generally low population density. In addition, all the New World centres of advanced civilization were in Latin America rather than in Anglo-America and they also generally developed later than in the Old World. Mountain areas are particularly important in this respect for they provide a variety of habitats for plants and animals. In a dozen miles, down a steeply sloping valley, one can move from the limit of cultivation, where even coarse high-altitude grasses seem to have difficulty in growing, to cloud forest where the trees are laced with mosses and plant life seems abundant and exuberant. The abundance of regions offering such variations in the tropical areas of the Americas allowed early inhabitants of the American mountain areas the opportunity to experiment with a wide variety of plants and to grow those varieties that they believed most useful for food and clothing. The plants that were domesticated included maize, kidney and lima beans, squashes *(cucurbitae)*, tomatoes, capsicum (peppers), white potatoes and a variety of fruits including the pineapple.

These distinctively American crops were not only important to farmers in the New World. Travellers brought seeds back to Europe in the 16th century and, within a short time, many of the crops became important in the agricultural economy of Europe. The potato spread rapidly in the cool moist parts of northern Europe and in some places became a staple crop within 200 years. Tobacco and maize were likewise New World imports for which a demand developed that resulted in their being grown in many parts of southern Europe. Maize in particular spread rapidly in the Old World and had reached China by the 1570s.

Besides these achievements in the use of the plant and animal world, the Amerindians in the two main centres of civilization—Central and Southern Mexico and the Central Andes—also developed the arts of astronomy, weaving and modelling to an advanced degree as any visit to the Latin American collection of a major museum will demonstrate.

The most important changes in the pattern of life for the native population of the whole continent resulted from the arrival of the Spanish and later the Portuguese. The most dramatic effect of the Conquest was not a result of the new ways of the lords and masters of the land but rather of the diseases that they brought with them. The native people did not have the resistance to European diseases that the conquerors had acquired as a result of generations of contact with them. Measles, smallpox, influenza and typhus caused large numbers of deaths and the valley of Mexico was ravaged by a smallpox epidemic even as early as 1520 before the conquest of the area was complete. The population also suffered losses through the battles that accompanied the conquest and such events as the civil wars in Peru (1535–1568) cost many indigenous lives. Conditions in the mines developed by the Spaniards in Mexico and Peru were responsible for many deaths. Forced labour used for public works also resulted in a high death rate. It has been estimated that over 85 per cent of the population of Middle America was wiped out in the period 1519–1650. Estimates for population change in the other densely populated area, the Andes, are little more than informed guesses but it does seem likely that the population declined sharply there too and recent estimates suggest that 70 per cent of the population of the Peruvian lowlands may have died off within 50 years of the Conquest.

Despite the sharp decline in the Indian numbers in the main population centres of Latin America during the early colonial period the Indian still remains the predominant human group in large areas. The Indians of the tropical forest lowlands were less affected by the Conquest and many, indeed, scarcely knew of it. The most important changes for the lowland Indians came during the 19th and 20th centuries with the exploitation of the forests for special commodities such as rubber and the colonization of the temperate lowlands of Argentina, Uruguay and Chile by European immigrants.

At the present time the most noticeable Indian segment of the population remains in the highland areas of Latin America. Figure 2-1 indicates in which zones they predominate. A difficulty in delimiting those areas of the continent where Indians are most common lies in defining what makes an Indian. I met and talked with a Chipaya Indian in Bolivia in his home community. He wore a poncho, hat and trousers of traditional Chipaya design. A week later a smartly dressed young man in a blue suit with a white shirt greeted me in the nearby town of Oruro: it was the same man but dressed for a visit to the city. Indian is predominantly a cultural term denoting not a person's ancestry but his current mode of life, his dress and his speech. The areas of Indian settlement are those which are least affected by modern life, where communications are poor and agricultural resources limited: they are often areas that were of little interest to the Spanish. The agriculture that they practise is sometimes purely precolonial but more often using animals and some crops introduced in the 16th century. The plough used throughout highland Latin America is usually similar to a type introduced to the area during the 16th century. Wheat may be an important crop and cattle or sheep the commonest livestock, but the methods by which the wheat is cultivated and the livestock reared have changed little in the last 350 years. In economic terms, areas where the rural people are Indians seldom produce much surplus produce for sale and the value of manufactured goods bought by Indians is very low.

The social place of the Indian is distinctive. In those countries such as Guatemala, Ecuador, Peru and Bolivia where Indians predominate in the rural areas, the term *indio*, or one of its many variants, is pejorative. The rural people are spoken of as being 'only Indians', or 'poor Indians' and children are told not to behave like an Indian. They occupy the lowest place in the social scale. It is customary for people who appear to be of mixed blood, to deny any recent Indian ancestry. To remark that a person, such as a government minister, looks very Indian, is to cast doubt on his virtue, honesty, manhood and respectability.

In a country such as Mexico, where Indians form maybe 60 per cent of the population and where considerable national self-confidence exists, there has developed a pro-Indian feeling which tends to glorify the Indian cultural heritage at the expense of the Spanish. This does not always mean that Indians as a present-day group are necessarily highly esteemed, they may be referred to as being but a pale shadow of the 'noble savages' that existed once upon a time, but the ideal (however unrealistic) of Indian-ness *(indigenismo)* is nonetheless real.

It is possible to portray a very gloomy picture of the role of the Indians in Latin America. They are almost exclusively agricultural people, and thus where onerous land tenure systems exist it is more likely to be Indians who are bought and sold with the land rather than mixed-blooded *(mestizo)* people. But there is an increasing range of opportunities for Indians to leave their traditional environment and find paid employment, particularly in small towns and cities. In some areas, such as near Otavalo in Imbabura Province, Ecuador, the Indians have remained as owner-occupiers of their land, have engaged in small-scale textile manufacturing and sell a proportion of the goods themselves. (Plate I.) They have maintained their traditional dress even though some travel by bus, lorry or even plane as far afield as Rio de Janeiro and Caracas selling scarves and shawls. At least one pop-group in Ecuador is composed of Otavalo Indians! In Bolivia, the Revolution of 1952 together with large-scale agrarian reform has resulted in the virtual abandonment of the term Indian for the rural population and instead it is now referred to as peasant *(campesino)*. In many places this rather dramatic change of nominal status has been accompanied by some degree of social progress.

Negroes

Africans were among those who were first to set foot in the New World in the period after the first voyage of Columbus, for negroes accompanied Balboa when he discovered the Pacific and Cortés when he entered Mexico. Before the Conquest the Spanish and especially the Portuguese had contact with African slaves. The Portuguese had traded along the West African coast since the early 15th century and the first African slaves were brought to Lisbon in the 1440s. Slavery was a human condition to which the Spanish and the Portuguese were accustomed and their attitude towards slaves in the Iberian colonies was more liberal and relaxed than that of the Dutch and British in their possessions in the Caribbean and North America. The Portuguese in particular often allowed their slaves more opportunities to gain their freedom and the interbreeding of Portuguese and Africans proceeded rapidly in Brazil.

Imports of negroes from Africa were made necessary by the decline in native population already referred to, by the general scarcity of native population in the lowlands and by the labour demands of the plantations and mines that became established as the colonies developed. Although there was plentiful Indian labour to be had in the uplands there were difficulties in exploiting it on a very large scale. The Spanish Crown and the Church were concerned with protecting the indigenous population and although their legislation was only partly effective, as witnessed by the evidence of brutal treatment provided by Bartolomé de las Casas, the exploitation of the Indians was controlled.

Few such Christian thoughts extended to Africans. They were used in large numbers on the estates of the Religious Orders, and the Jesuits were probably the owners of the largest numbers of slaves in the Americas.

They had many uses besides those as labourers in mines and plantations. Many were personal servants and bodyguards and others were bought because of their special skills. Some of the Africans were metalworkers more skilled than any that existed in Europe of that period and were purchased to make metalware which was sold. Slaves were expensive; the heavy losses on the voyage from Africa and the low reproduction rate of slaves in the new environment resulted in high prices at all the slave markets. Perhaps curiously, much of the profit from the slave trade went not to the merchants of Seville, Cádiz or Lisbon but to traders from Britain and the Low Countries. During the Colonial Period it is thought that between 5 and 8 million Africans were brought to Latin America. The majority of slaves were brought from West Africa and the Congo and included a wide variety of tribes. The mixing involved during the capture of tribesmen, the transport to the slave market, sale, transport to the New World and their resale at least once more, ensured that slaves from the same tribes were seldom able to keep together and this resulted in a loss of much of their native culture in the course of a single generation. What African traits remained were a mixture of half-forgotten practices and beliefs from a wide range of tribes. Their religions were more resilient and in Brazil witch-doctors practised in many areas where there were slaves; young freedmen were sent from Brazil back to Africa to be trained in the secret arts and to return to the New World as *bona fide* practitioners of witchcraft.

The main areas where intensive lowland agriculture was developed after 1550 in the New World were those to which the largest numbers of Africans were imported; these included N. E. Brazil, the Caribbean and to a lesser extent the Caribbean and Pacific Coasts of Venezuela, Colombia, Ecuador and Peru. The Africans spread inland from these areas and escaped and shipwrecked slaves colonized some of the more remote zones, such as the Pacific coasts of Colombia and the province of Esmeraldas, Ecuador. The Caribbean coast of Central America was colonized sporadically by the British in the 17th and 18th centuries and their African slaves remained, but the present African complexion of the population originates more from British West Indian workers who came to work on banana plantations and those who spread out into neighbouring areas after having worked on the Panama Canal. In the Caribbean, Jamaica, Haiti and the small islands of the Lesser Antilles all have a predominantly negro population as a relic of their colonial past.

Initial settlement in the larger Caribbean islands during the 15th century was exclusively by the Spanish and their interests in the area were associated with the hope of finding precious metals. When what minerals there were had been exhausted by the middle of the 16th century, attention turned to the growing Empire of the American mainland. The shortage of labour that resulted from the virtual disappearance of the native population on the islands as a result of disease had made agriculture there unattractive.

After 1620 the attention of the British, Dutch and French turned to the Caribbean, in particular to the eastern Caribbean islands unoccupied by Spain. By 1640 most of the smaller islands were occupied by one or other of these three European nations. In 1640 large plantations based on the cultivation of sugar were established in Barbados and, based on the import of African slaves, this land-use system spread to many Caribbean islands. By the end of the 18th century Africans outnumbered Europeans by 5 : 1.

In Brazil, early colonial agricultural development on the north-east coast, centred around São Salvador and Recife, was based, as in the Caribbean, on sugar cane plantations and African slave labour. Africans were imported in large numbers for sale in São Salvador after 1538 and in Recife after 1574.

The largest single concentration of negroes in Latin America is in the old heartland of Brazil in the North East. By the 18th century settlement, and with it slaves, had spread south towards Rio and west into Minas Gerais. During the last 75 years, among the large numbers of people moving to the growing urban and industrial centres, there have been many negroes. As a result the areas in Brazil with the heaviest concentration of negroes are in the large cities and on the north-east coast.

Although the negroes were imported as slaves their relations with other inhabitants of the continent are quite distinct from those that have developed in Anglo-America. Escaped negroes impressed the forest Indians by their size, colour and powerful magic. The shipwrecked negroes who settled in the forest region of north-western Ecuador and the Chocó of Colombia lost little time in organizing the local Indians to work for them. On the other hand freedmen were common in all Latin American cities and negroes were able to obtain positions of moderate power in many of the colonies. At the present time, although it is true to say that the colour problem is not as acute in Latin America as elsewhere, it is unrealistic to ignore the fact that racial discrimination exists. Even in Brazil, where a greater degree of racial harmony exists than in many areas, the working class people of the north-east are predominantly black and skin colour lightens with ascending social class.

The contribution of Africans to the Latin American landscape is variable. The plantation as an institution and as a land tenure system was developed by Europeans although based on the use of African labour. The slaves did introduce some African plants that are now used widely, particularly in the Caribbean. These included the congo bean, okra, millet and the mango. Vacant land is widely regarded by Latin American negroes as available for agriculture and squatting is a common form of land occupation in the Caribbean. Some writers believe this to reflect native African attitudes to vacant land.

Following the breakdown of the slave-based society, starting at the end of the 18th century, many negroes left the coastal plantations, took to the hills and established themselves there on unoccupied but poor land as farmers.

In their music and religious beliefs the Africans have profoundly influenced Latin America. Some Latin American dance rhythms, such as the samba, derived from the quizomba of Angola, are in fact of African origin and the use of drums in the music of lowland Latin America is indicative of African influence. The black Caribbean and Brazil are still areas where African-derived religious beliefs flourish. Such beliefs, too, are not confined to the lower classes and many maintain that a former President of Haiti owed the length of his despotic rule to his communion with the gods of Voodoo.

Although the land-use patterns of many of the Caribbean islands bear the imprint of the colonial masters more than of the present, predominantly black, inhabitants, the distinctive cultural tradition of the black Americans has contributed much to the complex civilization that we describe as Latin American.

The Europeans and Others

The influence of the Europeans, and smaller numbers of settlers from the Middle East and Asia, on Latin America has been greatest during the colonial period and then from 1850–1940.

The Spanish conquered Latin America remarkably quickly and with very few men. In a couple of generations most of the continent north of 30°S was explored, albeit cursorily. Even the length of the Amazon was traversed, although by accident. The landscape was transformed as a result partly of the changes in population that resulted, but most of all by the foundation of new towns and by the development of mining. The native population continued their traditional systems of agriculture except where supplies were needed for towns, mines or for export.

The number of colonists was small. Between 1493 and 1519, 5,481 settlers were recorded in the archives in Seville, and a further 13,262 in the period

1520–39. These included administrators, clergy, soldiers and common people seeking their fortune in the new world. Relatively few of these people were bent on founding agricultural settlements. The Portuguese in Brazil were a notable exception to this rule and the settlement of Spaniards in agricultural areas in the Central Plateau of Costa Rica and in Antioquia in Colombia was unusual and gave rise to a land tenure pattern of small, family farms that occurs rarely in those parts of Latin America settled during the colonial period. Cattle and sheep herding as developed particularly in central and northern Mexico caused great changes in the rural landscape as did the concentration of the native population into towns, *reducciones*, which the Spanish Crown ordered for their more efficient control. The Church was instrumental in changing the settlement pattern of large areas. Major examples of this are the northern regions of Mexico and the centre of South America, where the Jesuits had large *reducciones* from Bolivia to Brazil. The old culture of the New World was in many places, particularly on rich agricultural land and near the major towns, supplanted almost totally by new things from Europe.

The orderly grid-pattern towns founded during the 16th and 17th centuries were dominated by graceful churches built with Indian labour and decorated by newly Christianized native artists. (Plate II.) Roads were scarred with the tracks of Spanish carts drawn by mules or oxen introduced from Europe and the upper classes of the local inhabitants even affected Spanish-style dress. The degree of cultural change may be assessed by this description of the Indians of the Chota Valley, Ecuador, written probably in about 1580, some years after the Conquest. 'All the Indians that have plots of coca have horses which they ride like Gentlemen and they come and go to the fields on horseback; and most of them have oxen with which they cultivate their plots and very few of them do not have a pair of oxen; they are great butchers, they like eating meat (beef)...'

At the beginning of the 19th century the continent of Latin America was sparsely settled south of a line from Santiago in Chile to São Paulo in Brazil. In southern Chile the warlike Mapuche (Araucanian) Indians prevented settlement until 1877 and the Indian menace rendered settlement in Argentina south of the humid Pampas, and south of the Mendoza–Buenos Aires highway, hazardous without Indian approval.

During the 19th century though, the pattern of world trade changed with the industrialization of western Europe and the attendant rapid growth of its cities. There were political upheavals too; the abortive 1848 Revolutions, as well as major catastrophes such as the Irish potato famine, which, allied with

3*

a grossly unjust land ownership system, denuded rural Ireland of a sizeable part of its population. On the one hand, industrial and urban development demanded supplies of raw materials and food, and on the other there were powerful forces uprooting people and encouraging them to migrate to new lands. Not all the European emigrants were rural folk; the Pogroms in Russian Poland later in the century sent Jewish people, largely from the towns, to the growing cities of the New World as well as to some of the growing industrial towns of western Europe.

The 19th century, for most countries of mainland Latin America, was the beginning of the Republican period. The yokes of Spain and Portugal were thrown off and new responsibilities were undertaken. One of these was the effective occupation of the newly delimited national territory. The Brazilian Emperor Pedro I, for example, pursued an active immigration policy and as a result of his encouragement some 20,000 Germans came to Brazil in the period 1824–59.

Immigration into Latin America can conveniently be divided into three categories: those who were colonists, attempting to settle in previously only sparsely populated areas; those who came primarily to meet demands for labour in the booming rural areas; and those who came to set up businesses or seek work in the towns. Those attracted under the first category included religious minority groups, such as the Mennonites, who sought isolated areas in which their society could develop unaffected by the stresses induced by close proximity to modern urban developments. The Mennonites settled the western Paraguayan Chaco and part of eastern Bolivia, and the Welsh settled in the Argentinian Patagonia. Others attracted to colonize new areas were German-speaking people and some Italians who pushed back the frontier of settlement in both South Chile and the southern states of Brazil. Many of these settlements only introduced the immigrants to a new set of hardships that replaced those which had originally caused them to leave their homelands. Few people became rich and many fled to the towns for greater security and a better life. The ports of entry, such as Buenos Aires, and growing commercial centres like São Paulo provided a wealth of opportunities and attracted both new arrivals and disillusioned farmers.

Most immigrants who came to Latin America came to work either on existing farms or in the cities. In the Caribbean the gap in the labour force left by the freeing of the slaves was filled by indentured labourers, largely from India and Java. In Peru, Chinese, and later Japanese, were employed in the canefields. In most cases, many of the workers returned home as their contract provided, but a proportion remained, normally leaving agriculture and setting up stores in local towns. Others bought land and developed intensive horticulture quite unlike the existing agricultural systems. The Japanese in the Chancay Valley in coastal Peru, for example, became pig breeders on an extensive scale. In Southern Brazil too, the Japanese immigrants had an important impact on the rural landscape, introducing both new crops and a new, more intensive, agriculture.

In the newly-growing coffee belt of São Paulo and the Pampas of Argentina agricultural expansion was made possible by Italian immigrants who worked as sharecroppers or labourers, but never had the chance to buy land. When fresh areas were opened for expansion many of the labourers moved out to farm new land as colonists, but large numbers congregated in the main cities. Besides the Italians and the Germans, a number of other immigrant groups had an influence out of all proportion to their numbers. The assistance that Britain gave to some of the newly-emerging Republics, partly as a result of the enlightened foreign policy of George Canning, made British immigrants welcome and in Argentina, in particular, British investment was involved in a wide range of activities, including railways, banking, ranching and meat packing. It is no coincidence that two of the smarter parts of Buenos Aires bear the same names as their counterparts in London at that time: Ranelagh and Hurlingham.

Some immigrants specialized in certain occupations. For all their lack of previous experience, Irish immigrants in Argentina found sheep herding a very profitable occupation and the number engaged as shepherds increased from some 4000 in 1852 to 35,000 in 1870 and they were responsible for more than half the Argentinian wool clip. Levantine people are noteworthy in many Latin American capitals and they are frequently involved in the hotel industry, manufacturing and running small general stores. La Paz, Bolivia, for example, has a large cotton mill owned by a Sr. Saïd. There are shops with names such as Galería Beirut and a flourishing Club Libanés on the main street. German-speaking Jewish people are responsible for many jewellery shops, restaurants and money exchanges in Latin American cities.

The contribution of the Europeans to Latin America can be seen at two levels. Firstly, the whole development pattern of the continent was moulded by the Spanish and Portuguese during the colonial period and the towns and cities still bear witness to this. The rural population was reorganized to work on large estates for the benefit of the ruling class. During the 19th century however, new development was achieved much more with the aid of foreign immigrants and foreign capital in Argentina, Uruguay and Southern Brazil and, to a lesser extent, in the cities of the rest of the continent. The development of Caracas, for example, is closely related to the wealth acquired from Venezuelan oil. The new Americans brought special skills, enthusiasm and a determination to start a new and successful life that materially improved the fortunes of both they themselves and the countries whose citizens they had become. Their impact on the landscape was complex for they came from so many countries. No town in Peru is without a Chinese restaurant, and no city in Argentina is without its Italian ice-cream. Traffic in Porto Alegre in Brazil is endangered by the number of bicycles: reminiscent of Germany or Scandinavia.

As a result of the variety of origins of the new settlers, and often because in any one area there were settlers from several countries, there are few areas in Latin America whose rural landscape bears the imprint of people of a single national origin. More often the landscape—pattern of settlement, land use, land tenure and territorial organization—does appear to be influenced by Dutch, French, German or Japanese cultural traits but is still distinctively Latin American with an added ingredient. In Southern Brazil or Southern Chile rural house styles in some places may seem thoroughly Germanic, for many of the first European settlers came from German-speaking parts of Europe, but they grow maize alongside potatoes and they are subject to Brazilian and Chilean law: their children speak Spanish or Portuguese and are similar to other young people in Latin America. A French geographer who studied foreign settlement in southern Brazil was indeed more impressed by the similarities of the settlements and agricultural organization of people with different cultural origins than by their differences. In the islands of the French Caribbean (Martinique and Guadeloupe) the problems that beset the population are essentially those common to most of the Caribbean islands, and the agriculture is broadly similar to other Caribbean islands. The greatest differences are linguistic. The large towns are visibly French influenced. The majority of the vehicles are French. The town houses are unmistakably French, but down on the waterfront and in the vegetable market the scene reverts once more to being distinctively Caribbean rather than French.

The most important feature of the Latin American population is its heterogeneity. In few places in Latin America is the rural landscape other than a complex amalgam of varied influences.

The Mixed Groups

Few women came from Europe with the early colonists. Thus the men took Indian women as their wives and mistresses. The product of these unions, people of mixed blood, known by a variety of terms, added a new racial element to the population. Many of them were brought up in the households of the conquerors, others were forgotten and lived with the native population and were absorbed by them. These people of mixed origins became more numerous as time went on, and it was not surprising that they should have acted in many ways as intermediaries between the Spaniards and Indians. In Brazil there was similar free interbreeding be, tween the masters and the slaves and in the Caribbean too. The charms o- half-caste women were said to be far superior to those of either whitef Indian or negro and the brothels of colonial Brazil seem to have always had women of various colours, to cater for all tastes.

A considerable problem faced a person of mixed parentage. He was accepted by neither Indian nor Spanish groups and his place in society was insecure. Particularly during the Colonial Period, even those who appeared to be of pure white parentage would seldom be favoured for a job if a Spanish-born person could be acquired. Likewise a person with very Indian features would seldom achieve status in his own community since his ances- try was known and not respected.

But the population of Latin America is now predominantly non-Indian and people of mixed race predominate in most countries. In part, the increase of this group has not been the result of continued interbreeding but rather of social status replacing racial origin as a means of categorizing people. It is now possible for Indians to come to Lima or Mexico City, cut their hair, learn to speak Spanish in the locally accepted way, dress differ- ently and thus become non-Indian. The terms used to describe people of this social status are varied and with main regional variations in their precise meaning, but *mestizo*, *cholo*, and, in Yucatan, Guatemala and the rest of Central America east of Mexico, the term *ladino* are the most com- monly used.

In general, people belonging to the mestizo group may be generally identified as speaking Spanish, wearing factory-made clothes and being more conscious of being a member of a nation-state than an Indian whose dress is determined by local tradition and who identifies himself most clearly with his ancestral community.

In areas of predominantly Indian population the geographical distribu- tion of mestizo and Indian population is clear. The Indians predominate in the highland rural areas, the mestizo in the towns of the mountains and throughout the coastlands. This is partly because there were originally few

Indians on the coastlands but more because the lowlanders seem to have suffered even more than the highland people from new diseases. It was to these areas too that different immigrant groups came to work in the fields or trade in the towns. As a result the coastland people are a much more complicated racial mixture than those in the mountains, for Indians, Chinese, Japanese and Europeans predominate in different localities within the same area.

Where people of different racial origin live in the same area, social position seems to be of greater importance than skin colour or racial type. In this sense a colour bar does not operate. On the other hand, there is a variety of evidence to show that the poorer people tend to be black or have dark skins and the richer to be whiter.

By comparison with North America, however, what racial prejudice does operate is of minor importance. The mixed-blooded people therefore have fewer barriers to social mobility than they have, for example, in the Union of South Africa, and this social mobility has also encouraged a greater degree of geographical mobility.

To give some ideas of how the different racial groups can co-exist and to indicate the complexity of the racial pattern in a small area it may be illuminating to describe the settlements of the Chota valley in northern Ecuador (Figure 2-2).

The Chota valley lies at 1,800 m in a deep flat-bottomed valley between the eastern and western ranges of the Andes of northern Ecuador. It is traversed by a shallow braided river course which is liable to some flooding. With the aid of earthlined irrigation channels, water is brought to the sugar cane fields that predominate in the valley bottom. Much of the land is in large estates and the Jesuit fathers imported negroes in the 16th century to work on their estates. In one tributary valley of the Chota is a small village, Ambuqui, inhabited by mestizos who have their own smallholdings but have access to little water for irrigation. They are extremely poor and the majority of their houses are of daub and wattle construction with tall thatched roofs, very similar to the houses in the negro villages (Plate III). Apart from the poor mestizos of Ambuqui, all the land in the valley bottom was until recently farmed by negroes working as virtual serfs on large estates. The main market of the valley is in the small mestizo town of Pimampiro, on a high terrace area 450 m above the valley floor. The land around the town is farmed by mestizo smallholders although three estates also exist. Tomatoes are the most important crop. Some dozen kilometres away from Pimampiro, into the hills, are Indian communities

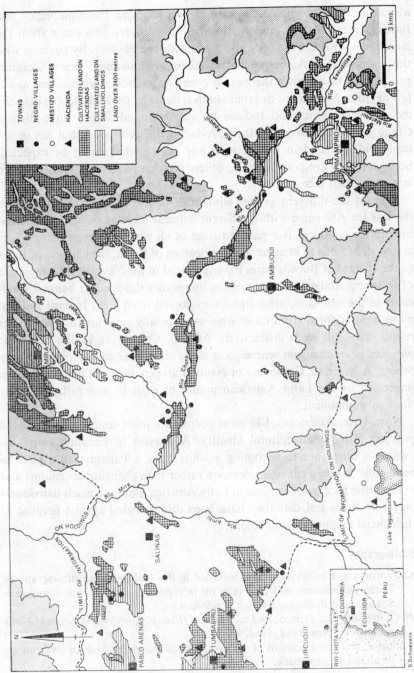

Figure 2–2. The Chota valley region, Ecuador 1961

where maize is grown. At the market negroes come from the valley and Indians from the hills, and both sell to wholesalers who come from the large towns (Plate IV). They also trade with one another. By contrast with the poor folk of Ambuqui, the mestizos of Pimampiro are moderately prosperous. In the town there are a dozen or so Indian families and also a few negroes. No form of discrimination is made by the local people between the mestizo negroes and Indians on racial grounds. Thus three distinct ethnic groups live close together, producing different goods but not necessarily differentiated in accord with any pattern that might be expected. Some mestizos are poor farmers, others are rich merchants. Class is more important than race.

Each of the different groups who came to live in Latin America since the last Ice Age came with a different cultural heritage. What can be seen now in the continent is a partial fusion of all who have gone before. It is always dangerous to imagine that the negroes of Bahía, the Chinese of Lima or the Italians of Buenos Aires have recreated in the New World a facsimile of their ancestral environment. Some things they dropped as being inapplicable in the new land, other items they copied from 1 cal Indians and still more were adopted from those who were socially superior to them. What results may still seem distinctively African, Chinese or Italian but what one sees is an amalgam where some elements appear to predominate over others. A Nigerian, Cantonese or Neapolitan person might indeed be more impressed by the Latin American nature of what he saw rather than its 'foreign' component.

Now, Latin Americans, like most people, are more concerned with social position rather than cultural identity. A peasant in Ecuador aspires to owning a lorry, not to becoming a white man, a Panamanian aspires to being able to buy a car or a television rather than changing his colour, and in this sense race is not an issue in Latin America, however much individuals may sometimes feel that they have been discriminated against because of their facial features or skin colour.

Bibliography

(Only works in English have been included in this and following Bibliographies. These publications will also refer the interested reader to some literature in Spanish and Portuguese which is relevant.)

W. C. BENNETT and J. BIRD, *Andean Cultural History*, American Museum of Natural History, New York, 1964.

A concise, illustrated account of the evolution of the major Andean civilizations. Available in paperback.

E. R. WOLF, *Sons of the Shaking Earth*, University of Chicago Press, Chicago, 1959.
A brilliant, readable account of the social history of Middle America from the arrival of the hunters from Asia to the apogee of the Spanish Empire. Invaluable, stimulating and very relevant to the whole of Latin America. Available in paperback.

J. H. STEWARD and L. C. FARON, *Native Peoples of South America*, McGraw-Hill, New York, 1959.
Useful summary and updating of the monumental *Handbook of South American Indians*. Excellent chapters of contemporary Indian society.

MARK JEFFERSON, *Peopling the Argentine Pampas*, American Geographical Society, New York, Research Series No. 16, 1926.
An account of the settling of Argentina by Europeans: of great interest, value and readability.

OSCAR LEWIS, *Five Families*, John Wiley, New York, 1962; *Children of Sánchez*, Penguin Books Harmondsworth: 1964.
Pioneering accounts of the life of poor Mexicans as told by themselves. Provide a brilliant but savage view of what life can be like in Mexico. *Five Families* is an account of a day in the life of five Mexican families of different social classes and occupations. *Children of Sánchez* is the Sánchez family's account of their life.

GILBERTO FREYRE, *The Masters and the Slaves*, Knopf, New York, 1946.
Verbose, extravagant but brilliant analysis of Brazilian society indicating much of the role of the African in Brazilian life.

JOHN GILLIN, 'Mestizo America' in Ralph Linton (ed.), *Most of the World*, Columbia University Press, New York, 1949.
A useful and informative account of the mixed-blooded people and their varied role in Latin America.

CHAPTER 3

Types of Rural Environment

Major Features of the Latin American Rural Environment

In Europe many of the regional variations of the agrarian landscape are the result of sequent occupance by different peoples over several thousand years. In the New World, by contrast, the landscape has been fashioned predominantly as a result of occupation by immigrants from Europe during one, or at the most five, centuries. Despite this comparatively short period of occupation by relatively recent immigrants, the influence of the indigenous pre-Columbian inhabitants on the contemporary rural landscape is important only in a few areas where population densities are low, for example in parts of the Amazon basin.

In many instances the pattern of cultural change is influenced by the physiography. Relief is an important factor in explaining differences from place to place in the density of the population and in material culture and its associated patterns of settlement and land use. The major physical barriers to communication in Latin America—the Andes, the Mexican Sierra Madre and the eastern margins of the Brazilian Plateau—have hindered free movement of people and thus increased the possibility that local and regional cultural differences can exist. In addition these mountains have often given rise to the existence within a hundred kilometres of several very different physical zones. In an hour one can drive from barren high-altitude vegetation at the limit of cultivation, through temperate mountain basins and then down to arid tropical desert on the coast or to steaming jungle in the continental interior.

There is a very important division in Latin America between traditional and modern forms of social and economic organization and this division can be related to geographical factors. By traditional organization is implied those forms of social organization which place great importance on past practices, where both the family and the community are important units and where respect for the past is an important element of individual attitudes. In traditional communities agriculture has changed little, primitive techniques of cultivation are used, communal land tenure remains in evidence and innovations are treated with suspicion. Traditional economic organization within a community customarily implies a minimum of transactions with outsiders, there being a high degree of self-sufficiency within the community with barter often replacing cash sales and purchases. By contrast, in a more modern rural economy, cash is widely used, a higher proportion of goods is sold and the motives behind many agricultural decisions are commercial. The social organization of a more modern community shows a greater degree of contact with other communities while the norms to which individuals conform are those widely accepted in many different rural areas. The importance of the family as opposed to the community is considerable and, as a result of a greater awareness of changes over a wider area, innovations are less unwelcome.

The division noted between traditional and non-traditional societies is easily recognizable as part of that which differentiates town from country. The same differences can be noted between rural areas and are closely associated with isolation. Physical isolation, distances from markets, or from central urban services, influences the degree to which rural people make use of such services. Rural communities close to a town or city can scarcely not be affected by such proximity. In some cases traditional agriculture, land-use patterns and even land tenure are less susceptible to change because less potential for change exists. Llama herders high in the mountains within ten miles of La Paz can do little else with their land on account of altitude and the low potential for development of the area where they live. Thus both isolation and land capability are associated with the degree to which a community is modern or traditional. This, in turn, is an important influence on the patterns of land tenure and land use as well as the systems of agriculture which are of central interest to geographers studying rural settlement.

It is vital to realize that it is not enough to know that some areas grow maize and others wheat, and that big farms predominate in some areas and smallholdings in others. The understanding of the rural landscape comes from an appreciation of why these areal differences occur and what other related differences there are. While sociologists and anthropologists are centrally concerned with the organization of society and with the nature of interpersonal and intergroup relations, the social geographer is also concerned with society, but most essentially with those elements of society which influence man's use of the land, the form and function of his settlements and his methods of farming. The rural (and urban) landscape can only be adequately explained in these terms through an understanding of some aspects of social organization. A recurrent Latin American problem, to which a solution can be sought in this way, is that of the co-existence of very different types of farming and settlement in a region which is physically homogeneous.

Areas of advanced commercial agriculture may be juxtaposed with communities of subsistence indigenous agriculture and even in a region so agriculturally renowned as the humid Pampas of Argentina, farms rearing prize Hereford cattle on high-quality artificial pasture may be situated next to large estates with scrub pasture and half-breed cattle of poor quality.

One cannot describe adequately the full range of variation that occurs in Latin American rural areas and a more useful approach to an account of the human geography of these areas is through the construction of a simple classification of types of rural environment that can be recognized throughout the continent.

A Typology of the Rural Environment

Classifications of cultural types have been made by those social scientists who are concerned more with differences in social organization than with the relations between man and the land that he both occupies and exploits. In any geographical classification of the rural environment it is necessary to consider not only the social organization, particularly with reference to the organization of labour and the relations between land owners and their workers, but also land tenure, the economic organizations that are associated with farming and the techniques of agricultural exploitation that are employed by different groups of rural people.

From a consideration of these factors, four types of rural environmental organization can be clearly distinguished:

1. Freeholding rural communities
2. Family farms
3. Estates
4. Industrial plantations

We shall use these four types as a means of indicating the main characteristics of rural settlement in Latin America and thus seek to bring some order to the complexity of the rural scene. It must be understood however that this typology is nothing more than a tool, an aid to the understanding and, by its nature, it can only be used to explain a proportion of the variation in Latin American rural landscapes; some cases doubtless exist of areas which do not match any of these types, but this is a danger inherent in the use of any system of classification.

A. Freeholding Rural Communities

A rural community is a group of people inhabiting an area of variable size whose name is that used to identify the human group. Almost all rural people will tell you not only the name of the locality where they live, but also the name of the larger area and group of families: the community to which they belong.

The distinctive feature of this particular type of rural group is that its individual members are owners of much of the land that they cultivate and are thus freeholders. In addition, the community as a corporate body is also a landowner, since common land also exists that can be used by any or all members of the community, to which they have no claim as individuals but only as members of the community. The freeholding community is distinctive by being, together with the estate, the type of rural settlement with which the greatest degree of conservatism is associated. This notwithstanding, freeholding communities have been increasingly subject to change and very great variations can be observed among them.

a. Communal land tenure is rare

Cultivable land is regarded rightly as such a sufficiently valuable commodity that it is almost invariably held by individual families and divided among heirs on the death of the father. Even in those rare instances where cultivated land is owned by the community and divided up and farmed by each person individually and then reverts back to the community after cultivation ceases, there is usually other land that is unquestionably the property of individuals: for example, the houseplot. However, pastureland is more frequently owned by the community as a whole and no-one can claim a right to graze his animals over one area and to exclude the livestock of other people from it. Similarly, water in streams and rivers is often held to be common property, although in practice it seems frequently to be appropriated by a few for their exclusive benefit. Often the exact status of land is difficult to discover if no titles are held either by individuals or by the community. Even if the community does hold documents that define individuals' exclusive rights to land, they do not always help to clarify exactly which land is involved.

Typically the amount of land occupied by each family in the communities is very small and seldom capable of supporting the whole of the family. Some members are thus forced to engage in other activities, such as petty commerce, to supplement their income. This is by no means universally true and in some localities communities have vast areas of relatively poor land, isolated from roads and therefore seldom of interest to the acquisitive individuals who robbed the traditional communities of their lands in so many other areas. In the Central Altiplano of Bolivia, where rainfall scarcely exceeds 200 mm, communities may cover 400 square kilometres and in one community, Escara, it was calculated that an average family would possess 0·46 ha of cultivable land and another 230 ha of scrub where sheep and llamas are grazed. The land here, however, is so poor that even these large areas are barely enough to support a family. Even where land is scarce some individuals may have very much more cultivable land than others.

More recently created tenure forms include the *ejido* communities formed in Mexico after the Revolution of 1910. Of the two types of *ejido* the most common is that where the land is farmed by individuals but where ownership is vested in the community as a whole. Other *ejidos* (only one in twenty) are collective farms in which large fields are maintained where the people work collectively for the benefit of all in common. In socialist Cuba the new land reform has called into existence both state farms, where the State owns the land and employs wage labourers, and collectives, not very unlike the collective *ejido* or the Russian *kolkhoz*.

The systems of land distribution that exist in peasant communities generally tend to ensure that families have parcels of land in areas of different agricultural potential. In Aymara-speaking areas of southern Peru and Bolivia the cultivated areas away from the dwellings are often called *aynokas*. In each of these, every member of the community has several plots of land, some of which will be on good flat alluvial terrain whilst others will be on poorer, sloping, thin-soiled hillsides.

The process of gradual dismemberment of the freeholding communities, which has continued off and on since the colonial period, has resulted in their being now largely confined to areas that are either isolated or of poor soils. Thus in the broad inter-Andean valleys it is not uncommon for the valley bottoms to be occupied by estates and the communities remain clustered on

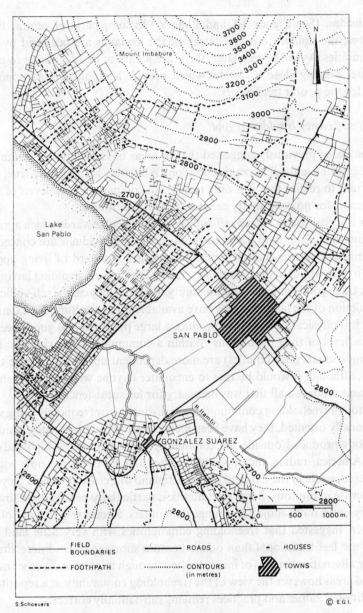

Figure 3–1. Estates and freeholding communities, San Pablo, Ecuador

the hillsides. (See Figure 3-1 and Plate V.) In some parts of central Peru, however, the uplands are in estates, and the lowlands are occupied by free communities. As will be seen later, there are a variety of advantages to communities existing close by estates which provide a supply of work opportunities for the poorer freeholders.

b. Self-sufficiency is seldom a goal

It has been previously suggested that in areas of traditional agriculture a high degree of self-sufficiency is common. While this is frequently true, it is important to realize that it is only realistic to compare relative levels of self-sufficiency, for no community can produce all that it needs.

Nor is it realistic to regard self-sufficiency as a goal towards which agriculture and, therefore, land use is oriented, because individuals are concerned primarily with having enough goods to maintain a standard of living appropriate to their status in the community, rather than merely avoiding having to buy or trade goods outside the community. Whether they can be self-sufficient is a function of the land that they have available for agriculture, the extent to which it is physically possible to produce a large proportion of goods needed and the level of their aspirations. Within a community it is axiomatic that some individuals (and families) are more dependent upon cash income than others, although it would be rare to encounter anyone who had no cash income and produced all that was necessary for his subsistence.

Although freeholding communities are distinctive by frequently being very traditionally oriented, they have been increasingly subject to a rising demand for goods produced outside the community. Throughout the highlands of Latin America, radios, factory-made clothes and footwear are now widely purchased, while in the flat land of the Altiplano of Peru and Bolivia bicycles are likewise ubiquitous. Some communities, particularly near to large towns, are very much more subject to change than others. Recent research in Bolivia has even suggested that freeholding communities with very little land per family are less traditional than others because shortage of land necessitates seeking alternative sources of income, often through migration. In other more isolated areas however the view of the freeholding community as a repository of traditional values and practices remains substantially correct.

c. Traditional agricultural systems prevail yet change exists

The most striking aspect of the systems of agriculture employed is that they have often been subjected to only minor changes over a long period of time. Traditional crops predominate in the field, whether th[...]s, maize and squash as in Central America or potatoes, quinoa an[...]n the Andes. European imports, principally wheat or barley, a[...]f greatest importance in the estates rather than in the communiti[...]

The land-use patterns however are relatively unrevealing if we [...] them to differentiate this type of rural occupance from others. Th[...] agriculture, that is the techniques of cultivation employed, and th[...] of land use in successive years, is what distinguishes this for[...] settlement from others most clearly. In the context of a traditio[...] there is only limited incentive to vary agricultural techniques. [...] wide range of varieties of the principal crops to suit all conditio[...] and potatoes in particular should not be thought of as single crop[...] community may use half-a-dozen varieties of each product regu[...] another half-dozen under special circumstances. For example, ea[...] of potato is known to thrive under a particular set of conditions and[...] thus has a rich variety of alternative crops available to him. The u[...] crops can serve several alternative purposes: to provide for new tas[...] family has developed or to produce a surplus for cash sale or to[...] extra need (e.g. fodder) on the farm. Maximization of production i[...] sought within the cultural norms of the community, alternative practices are held to be risky and, unless there is a surplus of production available, new techniques, crops or methods are unlikely to be employed. Fallowing, for example, is widely practised as a necessity either to avoid soil exhaustion or to conserve moisture or a combination of each. There is evidence which shows that the period of fallowing, which in some parts of the Andes may be as long as 25 years, is also a reflexion of the supply of land. Where there is little available land, fallowing is for a short period and has even disappeared completely; in other areas with plenty of land, fallowing for long periods remains common. But we have already indicated that the view that the freeholding community is the bastion of conservatism is no longer true, particularly in those areas where there is adequate land for experimentation and where contact with the dynamic life of the cities through migration encourages a more modern attitude to farming. Thus freeholding communities can be found which have turned to new forms of agriculture (often growing vegetables) that have made their members the most prosperous farmers of their region.

d. Communities as social organisms

The role of the community in the organization of agriculture is far from negligible. Where communal lands remain, they are administered by the

community or its nominees. Agricultural activities which involve the cultivation of successive fields wherein all families have land, may similarly be
communally organized. Families, groups of families, or even the whole community may nominate individuals to guard crops against thieves, encroaching
livestock or even evil spirits. Where communal cultivated land remains
it may be cultivated with the labour of the whole community. Individuals
are also frequently accustomed to call on relatives and neighbours for labour
for harvesting, housebuilding or other major tasks, in return for which the
obligation to labour similarly in return is recognized. These ancient systems
of working the land may be sometimes supplemented or even replaced by the
non-traditional form of hired labour.

Freeholding communities guard their land jealously. An assault on the
land of a member by someone from another community is often held to be
an attack on the community as a whole and the assaulted family can count
on everyone's support. Disputes within the community may be submitted
to elected community officials for solution before they are presented to
external legal authorities.

Social sub-zones within communities may also be more clearly recognizable than in modern rural societies, and extended families occupying contig-
uous areas, or groupings within the community, such as moieties, may
occupy distinct sections of the community land. In central and southern
Peru, as well as in much of highland Bolivia, rural communities are sub-
divided into *ayllus*, each occupying separate territory. The ayllus have their
own names and even their own subsidiary posts of authority. The farmland
of people of each ayllu is usually separate. They are small sub-villages within
the community, in many ways like the *capulli* into which the larger villages in
central Mexico used to be organized.

A further feature of socio-geographical concern is the mobility of members of these communities. Many writers have viewed traditional peasant or
Indian communities as relatively static and subject to little change. It seems
now however that although many elements of community life change little,
the individuals who make up the community are mobile. In many areas
pressure for land has forced some young men to travel far in search of work;
heads of families, throughout highland Latin America, are accustomed to
travel to lowland areas to work on the sugar or banana plantations to earn
money for ceremonies at home such as marriages, or patron saints' days.
Slack periods of the year have likewise long been used for trading journeys,
often to exchange local produce for goods from a different climatic zone.
More recently urbanward migration has affected many rural areas.

B. Family Farms

The salient characteristic of the foregoing settlement type was the importance of families belonging to a cohesive socio-geographical entity: a community. Family farms however are found in areas where all land is individually owned and where the most important unit of land holding and agricultural exploitation is a farm that is small enough to require normally only the labour of the nuclear family of the operator, that is the farmer, his wife and children. Such a definition does not exclude farm holdings where extra labour is employed at peak periods but its essence is that the use of such extra labour is unusual.

It is also important to realize that differences between farmers are much more adequately expressed by levels of production than by area of land controlled. Thus it is unrealistic to think of a family farm as being of a particular size. In an area of irrigated horticulture one hectare might adequately support a family, while maybe 250 hectares of high-altitude pasture and cultivable land might be necessary to support the same size of family at a similar level of living.

The parts of Latin America where such farms predominate are frequently those that have been effectively colonized within the last hundred years as well as those atypical areas of much older colonization such as the Central Highlands of Costa Rica or the Antioquia area of Colombia. Argentina and Uruguay, as well as the southern states of Brazil, are typically zones much of whose rural population is based on family farms. For example it was estimated that in Argentina in 1960 one-third of all families engaged in agriculture were operators of family farms. Areas of recent colonization are also characteristically formed of largely family-sized farms, in part because colonization is more often carried on by individual families than by corporate groups.

a. Ownership is not the commonest tenure

In Argentina, where family farms are more widespread than elsewhere, as many such farms are operated by non-owners as by the owners themselves. Frequently the pattern of ownership will reflect the excessive concentration of land in the hands of a few families which is common in regions such as the Andes, but this is not necessarily to be seen in the way the land is used. Some landowners prefer to split their large holdings into a number of family farms which are rented, frequently on short leases, to would-be farmers. A considerable variety of forms of leases exist. In some cases the rent is paid in cash, in others in a proportion of the harvest and, in the past, some landlords stipulated the cash crops to be cultivated. Legally tenure is not always secure; occupiers may not have title to the land they farm, or the renters may only have a short lease which discourages investment in improving the land for improved yields in the future.

Family farms are also found in areas where for one or more of a variety of reasons large estates have never developed and where the local population has become less Indian in its cultural attitudes. The areas of family farms in some places may be traced back to grants of land given to common soldiers and other lesser folk during the period following the Spanish Conquest. In the Chancay valley north of Lima, for example, although much good land was broken up into medium-sized estates which were awarded to members of the nobility, who normally chose to reside in Lima, grants of land were made around small towns to people of lesser importance to encourage the development of more middle-class farmers, who would live on the land and farm it themselves.

There is not enough evidence to suggest that this was a widespread occurrence and an alternative course of events to explain this phenomenon could have been the spontaneous settlement of immigrants from the Old World, in the 17th and 18th centuries, and later fusion with the local Indian population creating a rural population of people of mixed blood. In highland Ecuador, the northernmost province of Carchi and the southernmost one of Loja are predominantly inhabited by mestizos occupying small and middle-sized holdings. Both areas are sufficiently far from Colonial centres that there might have been little demand on the part of the nobility for grants of lands in these regions.

b. Production for national markets predominates

A standard comment made by social scientists about freeholding communities is that their surplus production seldom reaches the national market and their economies are not externally orientated. Family farms, on the other hand, most commonly grow crops for sale and expect to purchase a much higher proportion of goods for their own consumption than do workers on traditional estates or people living in freeholding communities. This is partly the result of their different social evolution. Family farmers are more in contact with regional and national centres than are other rural people. They are likely to have relatives in the centres, whilst they themselves belong predominantly to the cultural group that is distinguished by having clothes of factory-made cloth, by wearing shoes and by using a wider variety of manufactured goods in their houses. In order to have the money to buy these goods, which are necessary to maintain their standard of living and status in the community, crops must be grown to be sold for cash. This tendency is further stimulated by the need of those farmers who rent their land to have money or surplus produce with which to pay their rent. Thus both cultural and economic factors combine to encourage the family farmer to produce cash crops.

The concentration on cash crops results in the susceptibility of these farmers to market fluctuations and to exploitation by middlemen. Although small-scale producers in freeholding communities are frequently grossly exploited by merchants and storekeepers, this only affects a small proportion of their livelihood. Family farmers on the other hand may depend for their very existence on the sale of coffee, bananas or vegetables. Family farmers are seldom able to store their harvests and thus all sell their crops to merchants at roughly the same time: the market is oversupplied and prices fall. A sack of coffee that could normally sell for sufficient money for a month's food will then only produce enough for two weeks. The effects of market fluctuations are often exaggerated to rural people by merchants, who exact a high margin of profit by informal artificial price-fixing agreements.

An economic problem which affects family farmers and which is a powerful hindrance to their economic progress is the lack of funds to effect improvements. Often the volume of production from each farm is insufficient fully to warrant even simple devices for improving the quality and thus the value of what they produce. Coffee growers in Colombia, who are typically small-scale producers on family farms, have difficulty in constructing adequate drying floors for the coffee and likewise in the provision of water for washing the berries. Here the lack of community solidarity often makes the logical conclusion, the formation of co-operatives, difficult to achieve. Family farms are sometimes even remarkably similar to traditional freeholding peasant communities in their economic orientation and, in some isolated pioneer areas, such as some of those in Santa Catarina and Rio Grande do Sul states in southern Brazil, family farms exist which, for want of adequate communication with the outside world, are as internally oriented as peasant farms in highland Peru. Here attempts at producing a saleable surplus were frustrated not by the lack of a market but more by lack of means to send the produce to market.

c. Cash cropping by primitive methods

The emphasis on the production of cash crops has already been mentioned but it should not be thought that, because family farms are more market-oriented, they are necessarily modern in other ways. Although in some areas, particularly where vegetables, fruit and flowers are produced for a market, family farms can achieve high levels of productivity and efficiency, these types of holdings are more frequently characterized by low levels of efficiency and the use of archaic forms of production. Fertilizers and improved varieties of seed are adopted only by a deviant minority and reliance for a good harvest is placed more on a suitable combination of weather for growth and ripening than on giving Nature a helping hand.

A feature of cash cropping in many areas of the world where small farmers predominate is an excessive reliance on one crop. This obviously makes the income of farmers even more susceptible to price fluctuations, but even where several crops predominate one is usually the most important throughout the region and fluctuations in the price of this one crop have more effect on farmers than changes in the prices of others. Coffee producers in Colombia are a particularly good example of this dependence on a single crop and on a smaller scale this situation could be duplicated in many other parts of Latin America. Rare indeed is the farmer described in the Lake Patzcuaro area of Mexico who observed what vegetables others in his area planted for cash and then planted different vegetables himself, thus trying to ensure that he would not produce a crop with which the market might be glutted.

d. Family and community

If emphasis was laid, in the description of freeholding communities, on the importance of the community rather than the family, it should not be supposed that the community in areas of family farming is of no importance. Many areas of family farms are associated with small quasi-urban settlements but there is nothing comparable with the agro-town of Mediterranean Europe. There has been a system of regional government in parts of rural Latin America since long before even the Vikings came upon the New World. But the administrative unit which includes family farms is more often identified as a national political division rather than as a cohesive social entity such as the freeholding community. The organization is often looser; some people living in a particular parish or canton may be unaffected by, or uninterested in, belonging to it, but for the majority it is the social and political unit through which they are connected to the provincial and national government. In areas of recent colonization, social organizations are quickly formed and petitions drawn up for the creation of new civil regions.

The looser social cohesion of these areas permits a greater degree of geo-graphical mobility. Family opinion rather than community attitude is likely to affect the decision to migrate. The social environment of a community of family farmers is often conservative and one where innovations are adopted hesitantly and after long periods of preconditioning. Young people in this environment often feel very discontented and constricted and some of those communities which have experienced most emigration are those where family farms predominate.

C. Estates

One of the distinguishing characteristics of Latin American land tenure is the excessive concentration of good farmland in the hands of a small number of families. In countries such as Peru, Chile or Brazil between one-half and three-quarters of the agricultural land is owned by a few aristocratic families. In some regions as much as 90 per cent of the land may be owned by less than one per cent of the population. The estates, variously known in Spanish as *haciendas*, *estancias*, *fundos* etc., are also distinctive by being virtually feudal social enclaves, where all power is in the hands of the landowner and personal liberty is an alien ideal, unpractised and little-known. The corresponding low-land form of tenure, the plantation, was distinguished originally by employing slave labour and by producing cash crops, principally sugar cane, and has evolved in some rural areas into impressive semi-industrial undertakings. By contrast the highland estate has changed little except where agrarian reform legislation has changed existing structures, as in Mexico and Bolivia.

The large estates are characteristic of the highland areas of Latin America: particularly in Central America, and in the Andes from Venezuela to Chile. The Brazilian highlands as far south as Paraná state are also characterized by large estates but social conditions there are somewhat less oppressive than in the Andes. In parts of Argentina, particularly the north-east and, to a lesser extent, in the humid Pampa, large estates occur but they are frequently asso-ciated with less rigid social conditions than those in Brazil.

a. The land does not belong to those who work it

The land in a large estate is owned by a family or an individual and he has a legal title for this land. Despite the apparent simplicity of this form of ownership, some land is rented by the landowner to his labourers in return for a wide variety of services. Only rarely and recently have rural workers been able to have either a formal labour contract or title to the small plots of land leased to them by the landowner for their house and farmland. They thus have no security and no effective rights in law. Exploitation by landowners is therefore widespread and even where laws do exist to protect estate workers (such as in Ecuador) they are virtually unenforceable. This may be compared with the insecurity of tenure resulting from a lack of legal evidence of ownership that afflicts many rural people with smallholdings in different parts of Latin America, and in the Caribbean.

Although the working population on large estates have little security they are nonetheless bound to the land in a variety of ways. The *yanacona* of Peru, the *huasipunguero* of Ecuador and the *inquilino* of Chile are all rural workers who owe services to the landowner in return for which they have the right to the use of a small parcel of land. However, in Peru, for example, the exact definition of *yanaconaje* varies from province to province and even from one property to another. But while the majority of workers on the estates occupy a lowly position and receive a small plot of land in exchange for as much as six days labour a week on the estate, others have different tasks, such as shepherd or carpenter, in return for which they may receive payment in kind, or the right to plots of land. Some estates even rent large sections of land to others who want to farm but this means only a change of master as far as the workers are concerned. In other cases, land may be share-cropped by an enterprising worker, or by someone from a nearby settlement. As a result of this variety of arrangements, the apparent simplicity of a land tenure pattern comprising large estates and few landowners is illusory and a single property may have people cultivating different areas under a wide variety of tenurial systems.

b. The economic goal is normal production with minimal investment

The main advantage of ownership of a large estate for many people is the social prestige and economic security that it brings. Capital invested in land tends to increase in value and, where currencies lose value quickly and devaluation is a routine occurrence, as in most countries of Latin America, a safe haven for investment is highly regarded. Socially, investment in industry is less prestigious than investment in land and in many Latin American countries, politicians and prominent public figures tend to buy land rather than stocks and shares.

Although those investing in land are frequently powerful and respected persons, they seldom wish to invest in making the land already acquired more productive, so that little money is available to carry out improvements and better farming systems. Moreover, the rate of return from land ownership is not expected to be high and little incentive exists for increasing output. Many estate owners are concerned more with maintaining output at its present level rather than increasing output or productivity. Labour is seldom in short supply and need be paid virtually nothing. The workers are frequently required to produce small payments such as eggs and to transport the landowner's share of the harvests to the owner's town house. In Bolivia some owners maintained shops in the town stocked with produce, delivered regularly from their estates at no cost to themselves. With advantages such as this high rate of return for little effort, it is not hard to imagine the lack of incentive to increase production further.

An important feature of the production from estates is that it is predominantly geared to a local or national market. Relatively rarely, as in the coffee estates of Central America, Brazil and some parts of Colombia, is production destined for export. The less archaic estates in eastern Bolivia and the River Plate lands frequently employ paid labour in contrast to the semi-feudal obligations that restrict the Andean estate worker. The conditions of work and the rates of pay are however still very different from those experienced on modern coastal plantations.

c. Traditional agricultural systems are common

Although dairy farms in Ecuador and parts of Chile near to the major cities may employ a limited degree of modern technology, a sizeable proportion of the total agricultural production from estates is the result of the application of old-fashioned, even pre-Conquest methods. Yields of crops grown on estates are very much less than on properties of a similar size in comparable areas of Europe. Ecologically the estates are situated on the best land. Mention has already been made of the characteristic landholding pattern in Ecuador where large estates occupy valley bottoms and Indian communities crowd the inferior land on hillsides. But despite these natural advantages the land use is frequently geared to minimum investment and traditional agriculture. (See Figure 3-1 and Plate V.) Pastureland is commonly on high-quality alluvial soils even though grain or vegetables sown on the same land would yield higher returns. Even where the landowner has adopted improved methods, for example perhaps high-quality wheat is sown with fertilizers, the workers still cultivate their own plots with hand tools to grow traditional indigenous crops such as maize, potatoes and beans.

In parts of Bolivia the system of agriculture before the agrarian reform of 1953 involved the peasant cultivating the whole arable area of the estate using traditional methods and the produce from the landlord's land, which maybe amounted to one-third of the total area, was delivered to him: but all decisions regarding cultivation were taken by the workers. One problem that estate owners face is the proliferation of their workers: each mature worker's son may petition the landowner for a plot of land in return for work duties. In several instances in Ecuador, Peru and Bolivia so much of the land was taken up in workers' plots that the landowner found the area of land cultivated for his benefit diminishing each year. The alternative to this is expelling workers and their families. In one area of Bolivia where an estate owner decided to give up arable farming and change to sheep rearing, he evicted dozens of families from the land, leaving them without any means of support.

d. The landowner as a father figure

Apologists for the estate owners describe the workers as children who depend on the landowner to such an extent that if he were to leave they wouldn't know to whom to turn. There is little doubt that the closeness of the bond between worker and master is an important feature of this landholding system. At baptisms, weddings, births and deaths the master (landowner) is called upon to be an honoured guest. He is the godfather (and father too in some cases) of the children of the estate and is the person who may order the police to release any of his men put in jail for being drunk on market day. The coin has another face though, for it is he too who calls the army to quell any sign of mutiny and to shoot squatters if they refuse to move. The landowner has the ear of the police, the lawyers, judges, priests and politicians and little can effectively be done to counter his will.

The master–worker (*patrón–peón* in Spanish) relationship is the main characteristic of this system. Seldom does any social class exist besides that of rulers and subjects. The overseers in some areas are intermediaries, in the Andes often being socially superior *mestizos*, but in other places the overseers are elected regularly by the workers themselves. Although the estate labour force is part of the estate as a social entity, within it many of the traditional social habits remain. Traditional agricultural ceremonies are held and traditional posts of authority exist within the group. This is particularly true in those parts of the Andes where estates were created during the last hundred years out of freeholding communities. Freedom is a scarce commodity. Although workers may be ejected summarily, equally their labour may be valued and escaping workers caught by the police and returned to be punished, often brutally. The landowner acts both as a cushion and a barrier against the outside world, for he introduces no modern methods, often discourages education and punishes those who seek to leave his land.

D. Industrial Plantations

The rural settlement type most typical of the colonial empires of European powers in the lowland tropics is the plantation. The Dutch, French, British, Spanish and Portuguese established similar systems of farming tropical lands geared to the supply of goods for export. Major industries in western Europe of the 17th and 18th centuries were supported by supplies of sugar, indigo, cotton or tobacco, while the slave trade that provided the labour for this farming system likewise made the fortune of many a European merchant.

In Latin America the plantation became established throughout the Caribbean, on the shores of Central America, on the north-east coast of Brazil and in the irrigated valleys of the Peruvian coast. It was a feature of colonization and during the late 19th century it was replaced in some areas by more modern, efficient, almost industrial undertakings. During the last 70 years this process of modernization has continued and there are now clearly two separate types of plantation. The colonial plantation is becoming progressively less important and for this reason, and because it is extremely well described in many books and articles, the main emphasis here will be on modern plantations, of the sort that are known as *usinas* in Spanish America (or *usinha* in Brazil) as opposed to the old *ingenio*. The traditional plantation was commonly family-owned and employed numbers of slaves, later indentured or hired labourers, to cultivate the land and to work what machinery was needed. A strong link often developed between the plantation owner and the workers even though the one exploited the other. As demand for tropical produce gave rise to increased production in many areas of the world, plantation owners found it increasingly difficult to sell their goods at a competitive price and they either sold their land or amalgamated it with other estates and introduced more mechanization. Foreign companies became interested in tropical produce, especially bananas and sugar, and invested money to open up newl and for plantations and in buying up old plantations to form larger units. They were concerned with productivity and tried to establish factory-type relations with workers, paying them well but not allowing them land to cultivate. Mechanization was accelerated to reduce the labour force and skilled technicians were employed to supervise the processes of production. As a result, in many areas plantations of a traditional type were succeeded by larger, more efficient, more highly-mechanized holdings employing labour on a much more impersonal footing. A more recent modification of the plantation is the transformation into state farms, as has happened in Cuba, as a result of which the direction of the plantation and the profits from its operation are appropriated by the State which manages it on behalf of the workers.

The plantation is distinct from the estate, although also a colonial form of institution and land tenure, by being predominantly located in tropical lowland areas and by being a land-use system geared to the production of large quantities of one commodity for export. The modern forms of plantations are distinctive in being the principal way in which business corporations invest in Latin American agriculture. In a continent where massive investment in agriculture is unusual this alone makes the modern plantation a noteworthy phenomenon.

a. Corporate ownership predominates

Whereas in the other types of rural holdings that have been described a variety of forms of tenure can be encountered, the plantation is characteristically owned by a family or corporation and its land is not leased. The workers on highland estates produce much of their own food and part of the rationale of the system is that it is unnecessary to pay them much in the way of wages. In order for maximum use to be made of the land and also to avoid accepting a permanent labour force, workers on modern plantations are provided with housing, usually of a relatively primitive nature, and are paid either a daily wage or a wage varying according to the amount of work they do. By contrast, the traditional plantation was accustomed to give rural plots of land to the workers and in this way was superficially similar to the estate. The slave-worked plantations frequently had quite large areas farmed by the slaves who were sometimes allowed to sell produce from their plots on payment of a percentage of their takings to their master.

Major landowners in the Caribbean are the leading banana companies, the largest of which by far is the United Fruit Company. They have been accustomed to cultivate only a part of the land that they own, particularly in Central America. In part this has been the result of changing fortunes in the banana trade but at least until recently large reserves of land were kept unused, allegedly for future expansion. In many areas this unused land has been invaded by squatters who maintain small family farms untroubled by their precarious legal position. By 1971 however, the United Fruit Company had disposed of much of its unused land in Central America.

b. An externally-oriented economy

The aims of plantation owners were primarily to produce a surplus of one particular crop for sale overseas or to a major national market. The methods of agriculture demanded a lot of workers and frequently some small degree of mechanization as, for example, for crushing the cane in the case of sugar.

In areas such as the Guianas the volume and value of production was such that landowners where possible built their own roads or else used river transport.

The continuing demand for crops like cotton and sugar into the 19th century ensured the continued existence of the plantations, but cotton came into competition with that produced in Anglo-America, and increased competition made it more difficult for the smaller units to survive. In sugar areas, small estates often contracted to supply cane to the large mills in place of the small crushing mills powered by donkeys or by hand that were relics of the pre-industrial past. In other cases large mills bought up surrounding plantations to ensure for themselves an adequate supply of cane of the correct quality.

The new plantation crop of the present century was the banana and it became associated with large-scale operations with a highly complex and integrated supply and marketing operation. The United Fruit Company, in addition to its huge banana plantations, also owns railways, telegraph services and a modern and efficient shipping line. In only two areas in fact are large quantities of bananas produced for export in medium-sized estates and family farms: in the Turbo area of northern Colombia, which developed during the middle 1960s and in lowland Ecuador, the world's major banana-exporting region.

The tendency towards the predominance of major producers, already noted for sugar, has been repeated for example in the establishment of near-monopolies in the production of bananas and tobacco. Here major companies seek to maintain their position in the market by preventing the growth of minor competitors and refusing to buy the production of peasant farmers who have no alternative outlet for their produce. This has been one of the most serious charges levelled against the large companies of the capitalist industrialized countries although there are signs that in the newly-developing areas the companies are concentrating on marketing and on taking measures to ensure a high-quality crop rather than engaging in agriculture themselves. In the Turbo area of Colombia, the United Fruit Company has associated itself with the newly-developing area of banana cultivation on the Caribbean coast, not by establishing large estates but rather by helping farmers in return for guaranteed deliveries of bananas to the U.F.C. for shipment. In Ecuador the same company handles part of the packing and shipment of bananas and has little direct contact with growers. As labour becomes progressively more expensive and labour unions become more active it is reasonable to expect an increase in mechanization and in productivity. The greatest improvements in Latin American agriculture in the last 25 years have come not from the underprivileged peasant sector but more from the highly-capitalized and already productive plantations.

c. 20th-century agriculture

Because production is geared to the provision of a single cash crop a great deal is invested in the land; drainage is carried out or irrigation water provided and fungicidal spraying from the air is commonplace. Investment in experimentation may even be carried out and new varieties of crop or fertilizers tried out. Emphasis may likewise be on ease of harvesting as much as productivity.

The resulting land-use pattern shows a high degree of uniformity. Rotation may not be carried out and vast areas of cotton, cacao, sugar or bananas are the result. Housing is confined to areas of limited use for agriculture and often there is a central complex with offices, workers' housing, machine sheds and the warehouses for packaging or treating the produce of the area.

For access to markets, ease of communication is important and the central settlement complexes of plantations are frequently sited on the coast where there is a harbour, on a navigable waterway or on major rail or roadways. Particularly in banana-producing areas efficient port services have grown up which have developed and are now used for a wide range of trade quite apart from that associated with the plantation.

d. Personal relations diminish in importance

As the methods for treating the crops become more efficient and streamlined, so too does the treatment of the labour force. The labourers are paid according to piece rates, they buy most of what they eat from local stores and may even know little about agriculture other than what is related to the particular task in which they engage. Alternatively the labourers may be migrants from the mountains who work for a season cutting cane, picking cacao pods or coffee beans. The traditional paternalism that marks the old plantations as much as the highlands estates has been replaced by a more industrial relationship between foreman and labourer. The migrant workers often seek to establish the customary relationship with the managers, perhaps by asking a foreman to be a godfather to a child, but a paternalistic concern for workers is not typical of social relations in plantations.

Large numbers of labourers are required and a degree of specialization of jobs occurs, thus allowing differentiation between the workers on the grounds

PLATE I. Indian family selling spun wool, Otavalo market, Ecuador. Many of the Indian communities in the province of Imbabura in Ecuador make at least part of their living from selling woollen textiles. A high degree of specialization often occurs whereby a family may only partly process the wool before selling it. In addition, all weave their own clothes. The two women and the little girl in the illustrations are wearing traditional costume, but the old woman on the right is from a different community and can be distinguished by her headgear. The raggedly dressed Indian (upper left) is a poor, maybe landless, peasant earning money by acting as a porter in the predominantly Indian textile market.

[Facing page 54]

PLATE II. Facade of the church of la Compañía, Quito, Ecuador. A feature of colonial towns is the attention lavished on churches, many of which were built within a century of the foundation of the town by the Spanish. Quito has at least three other churches of similar architectural merit and 57 churches in all. The Society of Jesus (the Compañía) was rich in both wealth and artistic talent and its churches are often among the most magnificent in Latin American towns.

PLATE III. Negro house, Tumbabiro, Ecuador. Few house styles are truly typical of particular ethnic groups but many houses in negro communities in the inter-Andean valleys appear distinctive. Here the roofing material is sugar cane leaves on a lattice of poles (as seen on the left-hand house), the walls are of packed earth on a pole frame as can be seen from the right-end wall of the near house, set, in this case, on a stone base for solidity. The interior consists of one room but there is an outside 'veranda' covered by the roof where people sit to do minor jobs or just talk. A wooden barrier at the doorway keeps itinerant pigs out of the home. Rather unusually there is an outside oven at the end of the veranda.

PLATE IV. Pimampiro market, Ecuador. The characteristically mestizo town of Pimampiro is situated near to areas inhabited by negroes, mestizos and Indians and its market is a meeting ground. In the middle foreground is one of a number of open air eating places operated by Otavalo Indian women whose husbands are butchers and pig dealers. Beyond, seated on the ground, are negroes from the Chota valley selling tropical fruit and beyond them, to the left, are stalls selling clothes and hardware owned by mestizo merchants from Pimampiro and from other larger towns in the vicinity. The lorry visible is from an estate and is selling potatoes produced there.

PLATE V. Estates and freeholding communities, San Pablo, Ecuador. This illustration relates to the map Figure 3.1 and is a view towards Mt. Imbabura looking across the eastern end of the San Pablo depression. The lake is just off the photograph to the left centre; the town of San Pablo is barely visible amid the eucalyptus trees on the right centre. Large estates occupy the well-watered bottom land where dairy cattle graze large fields. Beyond and on the slopes of the mountain (an extinct volcano) on poorer land are the Indian *parcialidades* (freeholding communities).

PLATE VI. Rosapata, an ayllu of Orinoca, Bolivia. Freeholding communities in the Central Altiplano are situated in an area of exceptional poverty. The view is across the salt flats of Lake Poopó looking towards the eastern Cordillera 100 km away over which cumulus clouds are developing. Largely communal pasture land borders the salt flats; the villages themselves, near the hillfoot, are on sandy but fertile land where good crops can be grown only when there is adequate rainfall. Here some land is sub-divided amongst community members each year for cultivation. Most cropland is on the stony hillsides where fallowing for as long as 15–20 years is practised.

PLATE VII. Hacienda Carpuela, Northern Ecuador. In the bottom of the Chota valley, in N. Ecuador, irrigation makes cultivation possible. Much of the land is owned by large estates such as Hda. Carpuela. Sugar cane for the estate is being grown in the foreground to the left of the Pan American Highway. Further away are the small fields of the estate workers, the *huasipungueros*, where avocado pears (hence the many trees), sweet cucumbers, tomatoes and aniseed are grown. The village of the negro *huasipungueros* is uphill from the main irrigation channel on barren land. The dusty hillsides are grazed by wandering herds of goats and donkeys. To the left of the village, across the road, is the estate house.

PLATE VIII. Escara, western Central Altiplano, Bolivia. The town, also shown on Figure 4.1, lies at the foot of a rocky hill of volcanic origin. The church and associated chapels date from the sixteenth century. The town contains a mixture of poor peasant thatched cottages and improved tin-roofed houses but each stands in a plot large enough to allow some crops to be grown. Shops are visually indistinguishable but civic pride has led to the main square being embellished by a bandstand, a flag pole and concrete benches. Beyond the town is dry dusty land used for growing quinoa (a native grain) and beyond that is poor scrub pasture on which sheep and llamas graze.

PLATE IX. A colonial street, Colombia. House fronts in colonial towns are often bare of ornament save for window grilles and middle-class homes have no imposing doorway. Life is oriented towards the central patio.

PLATE X. La Paz, Bolivia. The capital of Bolivia nestles in a basin below the Altiplano. The Central Business District lies in the valley bottom and the major commercial establishments along longitudinal highways. Shanty towns cover the hillsides above the city but the vacant land there is owned by the municipality through whom the migrants can buy it. The smart suburbs are lower in the valley —the north American colony, for example, is in the transverse valley in the centre of the far right of the photograph.

PLATE XI. Mera, Ecuador. Towns within zones of colonization spring up quickly and have neither many conveniences nor much visual merit. Timber is cheap therefore houses are of wood and they line the only street. The forest begins at the end of the back garden. Plentiful bars for weary colonists give the town a 'Wild West' look. A military camp lies to right of the road in the picture.

PLATE XII. Newly cleared land, near Puyo, Ecuador. Some trees are left standing, often for shade. In this site bananas and coffee are being grown amid burnt tree stumps. The colonist at first has only time to build himself a simple home.

PLATE XIII. Areas of spontaneous and planned colonization near Caranavi, Bolivia. Although limited areas of good land can be cultivated near to the River Coroico it will be appreciated that the majority of the land is sloping and some on slopes approaching 15°. Much of the land is planted to bananas and also cacao, coffee and citrus fruit.

of status and skill. Migrant workers who return regularly often become semi-skilled at one particular job, earn more money and may even decide to stay. Workers on the modern plantation are free in ways which workers on highlands estates are not. They are seldom tied to their work by debt or other obligations and often they move to buy land in areas not far from where they have worked on plantations. But this freedom is both beneficial and detrimental to the interests of the workers. While he is free to leave, so also his employer is free to dismiss him and where the employer is a large company occupying a wide area, there may be few other chances for employment, particularly if the worker is dismissed for political reasons and blacklisted. A major characteristic of plantation labour however is that there are only brief periods when a lot of manpower is needed and, particularly in areas of sugar cane growing, for much of the year labour needs are slight. Thus in major sugar-producing areas, such as in Cuba before the Revolution, rural workers may be employed for only a few months each year during the sugar harvest and have to spend the remaining part of the year in penury, or in a completely different form of employment. It is partly for this reason that temporary migration from the highlands in the Indian parts of Latin America is regarded as a particularly satisfactory way of supplementing the income of highland peasant farmers and providing short-term labour at harvest periods.

A General Conclusion

It is misleading to hope that the stereotypes that have been described offer any more than a panoramic view of the reality of rural Latin America. Some areas surely fall into none of the broad categories that have been described. Above all it must be realized that most areas of the continent are changing, some very rapidly. Two such aspects of change, relating to the establishment of new land tenure systems with agrarian reform programmes and the increase in colonization of new lands, are dealt with in a succeeding chapter. Change however is a universal process. An important element of change can be described by the elephantine term *embourgeoisement* that French social scientists have used. This describes the gradual assimilation of urban 'middle class' capitalist values by rural people. This process affects rural workers who live nearest to major urban centres and who are in areas where commercially-oriented agriculture predominates, and this includes a substantial proportion of Latin American farmers away from the Amazon basin. Even in highly traditional social areas such as highland Latin America, young men in rural areas are increasingly aware of urban values and modern methods of business even if their fathers resist many changes. Thus, while it is unrealistic to suggest that a majority of agricultural holdings in Latin America are, in a Western European sense, modern, there is nonetheless a much stronger trend towards change than was discernible a generation ago.

Bibliography

WAGLEY, C. and M. HARRIS, 'A typology of Latin American subcultures.' In D. B. Heath and R. N. Adams (Eds.), *Contemporary Cultures and Societies of Latin America*, Random House, New York, 1965, pp. 125–147. The original article under the same title appears in *American Anthropologist*, **57**, 42–69 (1955).
A valuable and, in its day, pioneering attempt to describe the features of Latin American society according to a classificatory system. Of considerable relevance to geographers and particularly relevant to the understanding of rural society.

BARRACLOUGH, S. and A. DOMIKE, 'Agrarian structure in seven Latin American countries', *Land Economics*, **42**, 391–442 (1966).
An analysis of seven major studies of the land tenure and associated problems in Chile, Brazil, Argentina, Colombia, Ecuador, Peru and Guatemala. Of considerable importance although strongly slanted towards economic considerations.

PRESTON, D. A., *A survey of land tenure and land use in peasant communities in the Central Altiplano of Bolivia*, Washington, Research Papers on Land Tenure and Land Reform No. 6, Pan American Union and Inter-American Committee for Agricultural Development, 1968.
A study of an extremely arid region where agriculture is primitive and where freeholding rural communities predominate.

CARTER, W. C., *Aymara communities and the Bolivian agrarian reform*, University of Florida Press, Gainesville, 1965.
Based on research in several former estates and freeholding communities near to La Paz.

ICAZA, J., *Huasipungo*, Dennis Dobson, London, 1962.
A novel written in 1934 by an Ecuadorian deeply concerned with communicating the conditions under which the Indian population live on large estates. Well written, shocking and informative.

KELLER, F. L., Finca Ingavi—a medieval survival on the Bolivian Altiplano, *Economic Geography*, **27**, 37–50 (1950).
A useful account of the organization of a Bolivian estate before land reform.

PAN AMERICAN UNION, *Plantation systems in the New World*, Washington, Social Science Monographs No. VII, Pan American Union, 1959.
A collection of essays by leading students of the plantation in different parts of the New World.

HUTCHINSON, H. H., The transformation of Brazilian plantation society, *Journal of Inter-American Studies*, **3**, 201–212 (1961).
Excellent, well written account of the old and new socio-economic forms of the plantation as they have evolved in N. E. Brazil.

DESSAINT, A. 'Y., 'Effects of the hacienda and plantation systems on Guatemala's Indians', *América Indígena*, **22**, 323–54 (1962).

A. DAVID HILL, *The Changing Landscape of a Mexican municipio: Villa Las Rosas, Chiapas*, University of Chicago, Chicago, Research Paper in Geography No. 91, 1964.

CHAPTER 4

Characteristics of the Urban Environment

The large metropolitan cities of Latin America are like other cities of similar size in Europe or Anglo-America; towns on the other hand are quite unlike towns elsewhere, even in Spain and Portugal. The impact of Spanish culture on the New World was often greater in the towns than in the country. Social pride and personal preference led many of the early settlers to stay in urban centres, no matter how small they were, and the results of commercial activity were often to be seen most clearly in the town buildings. The once-rich mining town of Potosí had 30 churches, reputedly one for each new mineral find made.

Chronicles of the travels of the Spanish invaders in the mainland America often read like a list of towns *(villas)* founded, each after a few days march and a battle with the local Indians. Some of the towns were on new sites that proved to be unsuitable and were moved once or even several times until by trial and error a good site was chosen. Other settlements though were on the site of old Indian towns or forts; Mexico City on the site of Tenochtitlán is the most notable of these. Urban living was not widespread prior to the coming of the Spanish and many centres were of predominantly ceremonial significance. The majority of the population lived outside the town. Industry and mining before the 16th century were generally on too small a scale to have been associated with the building of sizeable towns. The towns that the Spanish founded were planned in an orderly fashion, with a rectangular street pattern quite different from that of towns in Spain. A Royal Ordinance of 1523 went so far as to lay down the steps to be followed when a new town was laid out and this to some extent accounts for the similarity in the pattern of colonial towns. Many of these towns remain today as monuments to their architects and builders and even those that have expanded well beyond the limits of the colonial settlement have kept the major public buildings of the central plaza intact.

The towns built during the colonial period show the greatest socio-geographical difference from those in the Anglo-Saxon world by being oriented not to a central main street but to a square *(plaza)* in the geometric centre of an orderly grid of streets. The centre of many an English town is the High Street, and in the U.S.A, Main Street, but this is seldom true of Latin American towns. To be sure, North American towns often have central squares, where the courthouse and other public buildings are located, but commercial and social activity centres primarily on those roads where most of the shops are located. In Latin American towns, where the colonial street pattern remains, commercial activity is more dispersed; some administrative centres are located on the plaza as are cafés, bookshops etc. Revolutions frequently start in a crowded meeting in the main plaza, and the evening social gathering, particularly in small towns, is uniquely focused there. It is there that people gather for firework displays, parades and a wide range of activities.

Urban centres vary not only with the origins and aims of their past and present inhabitants but in relation to their economic role in the urban system of the region and nation of which they are part. Urban geographers are accustomed to speak of an urban hierarchy: something analogous to the 'pecking order' that has been observed in social groups of animals. At the top of the urban hierarchy is the metropolitan centre, the primate city, which performs a wider range of functions than any other city and which is more populous than any other urban centre. According to the criteria used, a number of levels in the hierarchy can be observed. Using cultural or social criteria, a similar structure could be created where urban centres were differentiated by the form, complexity and territorial organization of social groupings.

It is most instructive, however, in Latin American circumstances, not to take any one system of urban classification but instead to distinguish three clearly different urban settlement types: the rural market centre, the colonial town and the metropolitan centre, since each represents situations that occur in Latin America in many different forms. Once again it is emphasized that many towns may have some of the characteristics of more than one of the types; for example the centre of Lima has some of the characteristics of the colonial town, concentration of administrative offices and ceremonial centres around the main square, a uniform grid pattern of the streets; but perhaps 80 per cent of its inhabitants live away from the old centre of the town and the business centre of the city is in the newer, rather than the older, section of the city.

RURAL MARKET CENTRES

Small towns varying in size from maybe 300–1000 inhabitants are an important element of the urban system. They are socially distinctive because their inhabitants are clearly superior to the rural population of the surrounding areas but, on the other hand, their inhabitants feel inferior to people in the large regional and national urban centres whose inhabitants include a much greater variety of social classes than do small towns.

The inhabitants of the small towns are seldom predominantly farmers, rather they make their living from providing services to the rural people, particularly by buying and selling goods. Some families may own land but seldom does all their income come from farming. Typically, for example, the husband and his sons might farm but his wife would maintain a shop that could provide much of the family's cash income.

Rural market towns are thus distinguished from smaller urban nuclei, hamlets or villages, by their clearly urban nature and the acknowledged difference between the townsfolk and the rural population. These towns can be differentiated from the larger centres by their size, lack of urban-located industry, the limited range of services that they offer and the fact that they serve a restricted geographical area. Such small towns are often isolated and relatively inaccessible by comparison with larger and more important centres.

A. Town and Country

The social distinction between rural and urban people is very sharp. It is clearly mainly people of a lower social position who work on the land. The towns are inhabited, so townsfolk would say, by people of substance, merchants, small landowners and shopkeepers. The representatives of authority, the police and local political representatives, live in the town and certainly never in the countryside.

The countryman, for his part, whether he likes it or not, has to go to the town to buy paraffin for his lamp, matches to light it and beer for his daughter's christening. The people who are most likely to buy his crops or to lend him money to buy a pure-bred ram or bull are from the town. If a farmer is disliked by people in the town they can refuse to sell him anything and refuse likewise to buy anything that he wishes to sell. It seems in short that although there is a symbiotic relationship between town and country, each needing the other, it is the townsman who derives greatest benefit from this and the countryman is very much at his mercy. The exploitation that takes place is amply indicated by the frequency with which peasant revolts are directed against neighbouring small towns. In the period following the 1952 Revolution in Bolivia, the peasants in part of north-east Potosí, both those living in freeholding communities as well as those on estates, besieged the nearby town of San Pedro de Buenavista, where the townsfolk had thoughtfully armed themselves with automatic rifles. The peasants accused the townsfolk of trying to encroach on their land, and of charging unnecessarily high prices for goods in their shops. A bloody battle ensued at the end of which the surviving peasants were forced to retreat.

If the people of small towns are powerful in their own areas, they are still in part subservient to the regional centres, in particular provincial capitals. In most Latin American countries positions of authority from Prefect (of a province) down to local postmaster and holders of rights to sell alcohol (frequently a government monopoly) are held by people in favour with the national political regime. Thus townsfolk who aspire to a position of importance need to be allied with the correct political group and with those who make the minor appointments. Therefore the people in the larger regional centres look to their friends and relatives in the capital to help their nomination, while people in the small towns look to friends in the regional capital who, they hope, will gain important positions and who will then nominate *them* to positions available in the smaller towns. What happens effectively is that a social hierarchy of towns is established where people in each town depend upon others in higher-order towns for their patronage. The small towns, therefore, dominate the countryside but are themselves subject to the larger towns.

The population of the small towns is far from homogeneous although the majority of the people belong to the lower and middle sectors of society. A proportion of the inhabitants are labourers with no land of their own, or servants of those families rich enough to have servants. Some work as apprentices or workers in the minor local cottage industries such as shoemakers, tailors or hatmakers. The most distinctive social element in the small towns, however, is the middle class: shopkeepers, small landowners and merchants, for they are seldom found in the countryside. All this group are distinguished socio-geographically by being much less tied to their home areas than the rural farmers and they are much more likely to have contacts in the larger towns and cities and to make journeys there regularly themselves. They are thus far more integrated into national, political and economic life than the farmers.

B. Physical Aspect of the Towns

Many of the small towns are of relatively ancient origin and were founded during the colonial period. Thus their form and the buildings they contain reflect many of the conditions under which the town was first founded. A rectangular street pattern is common with the centre of the town defined clearly by a square on the edge of which is found the church, often built during the colonial period, and other public buildings such as the offices of the mayor, the local traffic inspector and maybe the policeman, as well as a school. Figure 4-1 and Plate VIII show the plan of a small town of 400 inhabitants in an arid area of the Bolivian Altiplano.

Few houses are of two storeys except around the main square and along the principal road. In very poor towns there may even be no houses with more then one storey. Roofing materials are also an indication of the social aspirations of the inhabitants. Thatch predominates throughout the poorest towns, and in the houses of the poor around the edge of any town. Depending on the availability of materials tile is common as well as slate or stone in mountain areas. A recent innovation carrying with it increased prestige is the use of corrugated iron as roofing material. Walls are built of mud and straw pressed together in a wooden frame; more recently mud bricks have become widely used. Increasingly houses are painted, and where white predominated, now pastel colours appear. In the rural towns in Bolivia that have been spontaneously developed by the local workers, it is very noticeable that pinks and blues occur together with the more traditional white. In the smallest towns it is common to have garden plots where crops can be cultivated, as can be observed on the plan of Escara (Figure 4-1). Small market centres in recently developed colonization areas in tropical lowland areas and in places such as the three southernmost states of Brazil are very different. Settlement in general is initially concentrated along the roads and only at a very much later stage does it spread away from the highway. As a consequence service facilities tend to be scattered along the highway and only slowly does a market centre become identifiable. This process has been described in detail as part of the colonization process in the inner areas of Santa Catarina and Rio Grande do Sul in Brazil as well as in Bolivia and Ecuador. Under such conditions the development of clearly identifiable rural market centres is confined to locations where highways meet or at bridging points of rivers, where produce is gathered by merchants before being sent to the major urban centres.

Amenities not found in the country make any town distinctive and it is

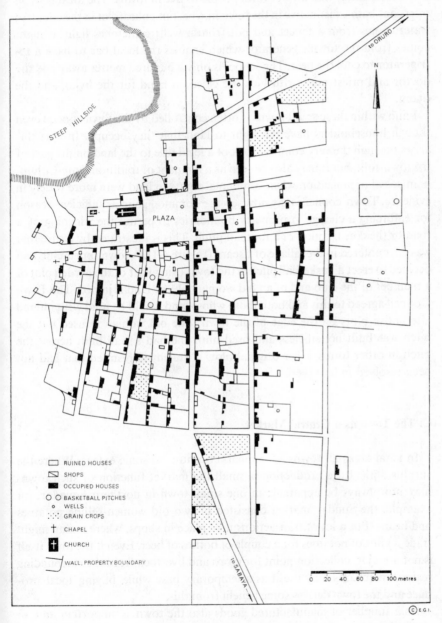

STEEP HILLSIDE

PLAZA

- ⬜ RUINED HOUSES
- ⬛ SHOPS
- ■ OCCUPIED HOUSES
- ○ O BASKETBALL PITCHES
- ○ WELLS
- GRAIN CROPS
- † CHAPEL
- ✠ CHURCH
- WALL, PROPERTY BOUNDARY

0 20 40 60 80 100 metres

© E.G.I.

Figure 4–1. Escara, Bolivia

often such things that attract rural people to live in towns. The local *pensión* offers hot baths, distinctive in the town maybe, but unheard of in the country; water comes from a faucet and not from a well; sometimes light at night comes from the town's generator which enables the local bar to have a refrigerator to cool the beer. The school is only a hundred metres away and the doctor and priest may, with luck, be close on hand for the living and the dying.

Land within these small towns is often controlled by the town council even though householders have the right to land that they occupy. In part this arises through the very common lack of a legal title to the land on the part of the townsfolk, but it may also be seen as a remnant of traditional pre-Columbian social organization when communal rights to land were more widely in evidence. Town councils may now see the common good as sufficient reason for enforcing a change in property boundaries to permit the widening of a road or the construction of a football pitch. This is illustrated by a case that was encountered in the village of Escara (Figure 4-1). A town sports club had decided to erect a basketball pitch in the town using part of the garden plot of a member of the club and of an old woman whose land adjoined. The Town Council agreed to this and both those whose land would be used were offered alternative plots on the edge of the town. The old woman refused but the pitch was built nonetheless and used until she had a wall built across the pitch in order to mark her original plot. A stalemate resulted that had not been resolved in late 1966.

C. The Town as a Central Market

In rural areas all towns act as market centres to some extent. Where the surplus agriculture production is small the market function of such towns may not always be apparent; in one small town in northern Ecuador, for example, the Sunday market consisted of two old women selling potatoes and beans. But a lot of transactions take place in shops, where a man might trade 3 kilos of potatoes for a couple of bottles of beer. Even if the town itself is not a major collection point for crops and livestock from the surrounding region, merchants may use it as a temporary base while buying local produce and the town derives some benefit from this.

As a supplier of manufactured goods also the town is important and, in particular, items of everyday use, such as flour, salt or matches are in constant demand no matter how poor the surrounding rural area may be. The profit margins on goods sold in town stores vary in relation to the availability of other sources of similar goods. Thus in isolated areas of Brazil goods may cost double their price in São Paulo, a difference which is not wholly accounted for in the extra cost of transportation. On the other hand, in northern Bolivia knitted goods smuggled from Peru are cheaper in the small towns near the frontier than in La Paz. The cost of smuggled goods to the merchant increases with every customs post that has to be passed, where either a bribe is necessary or some goods are confiscated. Thus the cost of goods rises rapidly with increasing distance from the frontier according to the number of customs posts. Smuggled Argentinian champagne in Bolivia costs 40 p in Cochabamba but 60 p in La Paz over 500 km further from the frontier. The competition for the sale of coca leaves (for chewing) however is sufficiently great that no major differences in price occur between the city of La Paz and the small towns 80 kilometres away.

Rural people can avoid using their local town for buying and selling by travelling further to another centre. This takes time and may lead to relatively little cash benefit. The small towns are a crucial stage in the flow of agricultural goods from the areas of production to the centres of consumption and are likewise the principal agents through which manufactured goods and basic necessities are sold to the rural population.

The rural centres should be seen as numerically important small towns that link the rural population with the urban life of each country. They occupy one of the lower positions in any urban hierarchy and they are very numerous. By reason of the great contrasts between urban and rural living the towns are archaic in their social structure, undemocratic in their use of power and monopolistic in the abuse of their role as market centres. Despite this, to the rural population they are trendsetters and farmers often aspire to becoming town dwellers. In short, the rural towns are the main link in Latin America between the backward rural areas and the more progressive and dynamic urban sector.

COLONIAL TOWNS

Many of the towns founded by the Spanish and Portuguese during the colonial period still exist at the present time and have changed relatively little during the past three centuries. Other towns founded during this period became important centres, developed industries and have grown in size and character to such an extent that they are physically indistinguishable from other cities of similar size of more recent foundation. The towns of the colonial period that have survived with little change, particularly in their central areas, are sufficiently distinctive, both physically and geographically in terms of their internal arrangement, to merit special attention. In addition some elements of the social problems of colonial towns still influence the social geography of both small rural towns and large metropolitan centres.

Physically the colonial-type towns are larger versions of the small rural centres. Built on a rectangular street pattern, centred on a large and often well-kept plaza with other squares in the outskirts of the town, and with the principal buildings in the centre, the colonial-style town seldom appears modern to the visitor. Such changes as do occur usually take place behind the old facades of the buildings and the palatial structures around the central square may pass from being a personal palace to becoming the offices of the regional development corporation. The Governor's palace may become the centre of the regional bureaucracy while the archbishop's residence may be turned into a museum. Houses remain small, seldom exceeding three storeys around the central square and diminishing in size to a single floor within 200 metres of the town centre.

Houses were characteristically built around an interior patio and the street entrance of larger homes was often an archway wide enough to permit a carriage to enter. The side of the house facing the street is usually unadorned and if windows open on to the street, they are protected by elaborate wrought-ironwork. (Plate IX.) The houses of the nobility frequently had ornate balconies overlooking the main square where the family could watch the demonstrations and displays that have traditionally taken place there. Most towns had, and continue to have, market buildings, usually away from the centre, in order that the sale of goods can be controlled and taxed for the financial benefit of the municipality. Streets are frequently surfaced with cobblestones although perhaps the square and main thoroughfares will be given a modern smooth surface. High pavements of stone are sometimes reminders of the period when the streets were awash in the wet season and pedestrians were high above the splashes made by passing vehicles.

Colonial towns, such as Popayán in Colombia (77,000 inhabitants), serve people from rural districts and other smaller towns from a large area. Its amenities make it very distinct from the small market centres to the visiting rural worker. It is here that important political figures live, and where there are firework displays on national holidays. To buy a major item like a mechanical cultivator, or even a bicycle with three gears, it may be necessary to come to the big town. Even the poor who live in these towns have access to a greater variety of amenities. There is drinking water within 100 metres, a school offering more years of education than any in the countryside, a medical dispensary and a priest or even a bishop ready to hand for those in need.

A. Top People Live in the Town Centre

A widespread principle of social organization in space is that the upper classes tend to live in certain zones of the periphery of towns while the labouring groups live in or adjacent to the centre of the town. Although this generalization is most true of British and Anglo-American cities it is also true in many other countries. However, a most distinctive feature of the social geography of

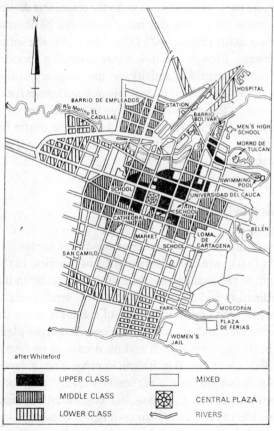

Figure 4–2. Popayán, Colombia: a colonial town

the colonial towns is that the arrangement of people of different social status in the town does not conform to the social patterns of modern towns. Various urban ecologists have described the ideas underlying this feature in detail. In the towns founded during the Spanish colonization it was customary, when the town was first laid out, for the leading citizens to be allocated plots around the main square, around which would be the church and the principal public buildings. Lesser citizens built their houses on the available land further from the centre. In newly-developing urban nuclei in colonization areas a similar pattern can be noted and without doubt this type of social zoning is common in newly established towns: only at a later stage in development do the social élite move outwards. In Spanish America the socially privileged were seldom so numerous that they could not all be accommodated in and around the main square; moreover there was seldom any of the rapid industrialization that might render parts of the town close to the centre less desirable to live in. As a result, even to the present day many towns can be observed where this type of zonation exists (Figure 4-2.) Often, naturally, the social pattern has begun to be eroded. Rich people now aspire to owning a modern house and living away from the centre of activity, on the periphery of the town, along shaded avenues and where land is available to build houses for their children. The old mansions in the centre are too large to be occupied by a single modern family and in any case the value of land in the centre has often now become so high that only business concerns or the regional government organizations can afford to buy or rent it.

B. Barrios and Neighbourhoods

Social areas within towns or cities known as neighbourhoods in the U.S.A. or *quartiers* in France are called *barrios* in Latin America. In the old colonial town the origin of the distinctive nature of the barrio lay in the colonial period when ordinances laid down where people of certain social origin, in particular Indians, should live. The creation of sub-units in the colonial period has often contributed to the barrios being ingrained in the plan of the town: each barrio having its own church and on occasions its own central plaza. The famous *diablada* of Oruro in Bolivia (a procession of dancing groups) is composed of groups each from a particular workers' guild or barrio within the town. Such segments of the towns, like neighbourhoods in Anglo-America, retain their identity and have their own name. Today in a large town they may even have their own football teams.

C. Colonial Towns in a Modern World

Although colonial towns were in part arbitrarily founded by the conquerors, those that have survived as viable urban centres in the present century are those that fulfil important economic roles as regional centres. The extent to which changes have taken place in a particular town may thus be said to be as much a function of the change in the region which the town serves as within the town itself. The coastal areas of Latin America are more prosperous and modern than the highlands and the colonial centres of the coast. Towns such as Trujillo in Peru or Panama City have been transformed by spreading residential areas, expanding slums and developing industries. By contrast, in the mountains agriculture has changed relatively little and the volume of business in the urban centres has grown only slowly and Popayán (Colombia), Cuenca (Ecuador), or Salta (Argentina) remain colonial towns in atmosphere and appearance, even though they have outgrown their colonial boundaries.

Change in the towns of this category comes more on their periphery than in the centre. New suburbs grow but they are grafted onto the old urban plan without necessarily transforming the old pattern. Gradually, however, the new suburbs include homes for the old upper class who formerly lived in the town centre, as has been indicated above, but this is only a stage in the slow process of urban evolution which has come belatedly to these towns.

As economic centres these towns collect goods from surrounding rural areas and from the small towns that have a lower rank in the urban hierarchy. These goods support some industries, such as flour milling, but much of what they collect is passed on directly to the major markets—the metropolitan centres. These transactions provide employment for a part of the middle-class, white-collar group in the town. The town also is a centre for the distribution of manufactured goods, received from the major industrial or commercial centres, for consumption in the town and for sale to the rural people who come to town to trade. Because of these commercial functions the town contains not only an aristocracy whose chief source of wealth and power is the ownership of land and the manipulation of sources of political patronage, but also a solid group of citizens who live from retail and wholesale trade, from the management of small industrial establishments and through employment in government offices. In the small towns, by contrast, there are few people who can aspire to being well within the middle class and certainly only a handful who could be classed as white-collar workers.

The colonial city then is an historical anomaly, a town that has not grown or changed sufficiently to have thrown off its past. It is located more often in backward highland areas than amid the hustle and bustle of the coastlands, but it nonetheless offers a quality of living and a range of opportunities, both social and economic, which are the envy of villager and peasant.

METROPOLITAN CENTRES

The colonial town is a distinctively Latin American phenomenon, the metropolitan centres of Latin America are basically similar to such areas in other highly urbanized parts of the world. Four urban agglomerations: Buenos Aires (7 million), Mexico City (6 million), São Paulo (5 million) and Rio de Janeiro (4 million) are among the two dozen largest urban centres in the world, and another six urban areas have a population in excess of 1 million*.

Perhaps one-third of the population of Latin America lives in towns and cities with over 20,000 inhabitants, and of these one-third live in the four largest metropolitan areas mentioned above (see Figure 4-3). In Argentina, Cuba, Chile and Venezuela over half the population live in towns. The proportion of the population living in urban areas is perhaps less important than their role in the economic and social life of each of the countries. People living in cities, particularly large metropolitan areas, are better educated, earn more and are more involved with national political life than people from the small towns and the countryside. It is in the cities that major decisions are taken which affect the lives of everyone in the nation. As a result, in the past and to some extent at the moment, people outside the big cities are jealous of the fortune of the city folk. This is of course not peculiar to Latin America but these feelings are particularly bitter in countries where there are few very large cities. They are also of great importance in encouraging people to migrate to the cities. In Colombia, where there are four cities with over half-a-million inhabitants, Baranquilla, Cali and Medellín rival Bogotá for the jealousy of the non-urban population. A considerable amount of inter-city rivalry occurs too but this frequently consists of the smaller urban centres complaining of the growth of the capital or primate cities.

The concentration of a sizeable proportion of the population in cities is by no means a recent phenomenon. Even during the early colonial period there

* Santiago (2·2 million), Bogotá (1·7 million), Caracas (1·7 million), Havana (1·7 million), Lima (1·4 million) and Montevideo (1·2 million.) In each case the population refers to the total urban area and not just to the adminstrative unit of the city itself.

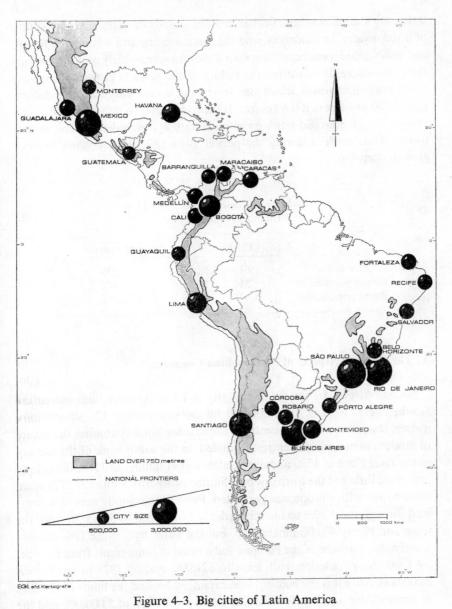

Figure 4–3. Big cities of Latin America

were only a small number of urban centres, usually the administrative centre of a viceroyalty, or Audencia, and the more wealthy and aristocratic Spaniards maintained residences there even if they travelled widely or if they owned lands elsewhere. It was often the failure of the Spanish crown to establish other important towns which has led to the concentration of population, power and prestige in a few centres. It seems however to be a principle of city growth that the largest cities grow most rapidly, excluding of course new towns. Thus in Peru during the period 1940–1960 the following rates of growth occurred.

Population increase in Peru 1940-1960
(numbers in thousands)

	1940	1960	per cent increase
Greater Lima	614	2,079	239
Urban population	512	1,340	162
Rural population	5,905	6,955	18

A. The Physical Aspects of Metropolitan Centres

Buenos Aires is by far the largest city in Latin America, and indeed the Southern Hemisphere. Its 7,000,000 inhabitants occupy 120 square kilometres. It was not a colonial centre of importance but it epitomizes the nature of modern metropolitan centres. Founded on the south bank of the estuary of the river Plate in 1536 and again, after initial failure, in 1580, the colony prospered little and the town saw only limited prosperity until after 1778 when trade by sea with Europe was permitted. Prior to this goods were sent overland through the Andes to Lima in order to be shipped to Spain. By 1800 the town had barely 40,000 inhabitants, but the latter half of the 19th century saw the development of the Pampas and a flood of immigrants from Europe. By 1900 the population had leapt to 821,000 and by 1925 to more than 2,000,000. After this the built-up area expanded beyond the limits of the City of Buenos Aires until in 1960 the City had a population of 3,000,000 and the whole metropolis contained over 7,000,000 people. A result of this growth has been the spread to embrace townships on its margins (see Figure 4-4), the development of a new port over 50 kilometres downriver and the increasing congestion of traffic in the centre of the old city. Radial boulevards were built

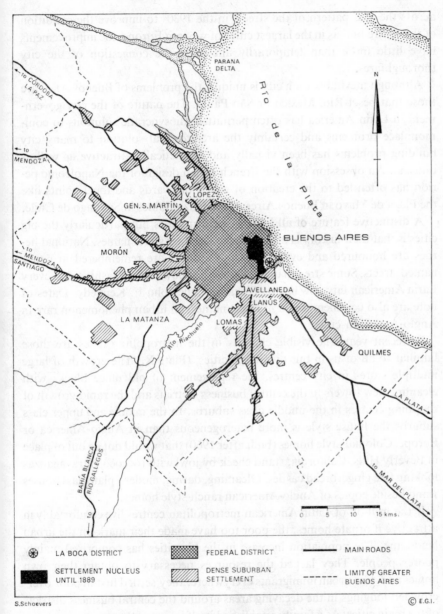

Figure 4–4. Buenos Aires: its metropolitan region

6*

across the grid pattern of the streets in the 1930s to improve the condition of the centre but, as in the largest cities of western Europe, the improvements have little more than temporarily alleviated the congestion of the city thoroughfares.

Although inevitably each city is unique, the problems of Buenos Aires are those that beset Rio, Mexico or São Paulo. The nature of the city government in Latin America has often permitted idiosyncratic solutions to commonplace problems and certainly the architectural solution to many city building problems has been visually and aesthetically attractive as well as unusual. An obsession with the French urban design of the Napoleonic period has often led to the creation of wide boulevards and focal points like the Plaza de Mayo in Buenos Aires or the Plaza Bulnes in Santiago de Chile.

A distinctive feature of all Latin American cities but particularly the big cities is that their history is often reflected in their street names. National heroes are honoured and even poets and authors are remembered in newly named streets. Some street names change to follow current fashion and every Latin American city now has its Plaza or Calle John F. Kennedy. Dates of note are also commemorated in street names, an urban phenomenon rare in Anglo-American cities.

In recent years the visible changes in the metropolitan cities are those familiar to all of us in our own large cities. (Plate X.) The growth of large multiple stores in city centres, the replacement of old office blocks with gleaming new towers in the central business districts and the rapid growth of shopping centres in the middle class suburbs. In the middle and upper class suburbs the house style is more heterogeneous than in Anglo-America or Europe. Colonial-style homes (built after 1960) that would not be out of place in Beverly Hills, California, stand cheek by jowl with roccoco extravaganzas looking like gingerbread castles. Gleaming, daring, modern plateglass houses stand beside copies of Anglo-American ranch-style homes.

If the well-off of Latin American metropolitan centres live comfortably in attractive if ornate homes, the poor too have made their mark on the urban landscape. The population increase in the big cities has comprised mainly poorer people. They lacked the resources necessary to obtain their own homes and, like urban immigrants everywhere, they settled first in poor overcrowded lodgings in the decaying areas around the central business districts of the main cities. As a family established itself in one of these reception areas its members found some sort of employment and learnt more about city life, then they usually moved out to occupy their own piece of land in one of the rapidly developing squatter settlements on poor unused land on the edge of the city. A sea of poor shanties occurs on some parts of the edge of most large cities in Latin America. In Rio they are called *favelas*, in Lima *barriadas*, in Medellín *tugurios* but, whatever their name, they are the predominant housing for the urban poor and especially for recent immigrants. All cities are attempting to help the newcomers. Some cities help them to negotiate titles for the land they have illegally occupied, all make some effort to provide teachers for the new schools, main sewage, water and electric power, but few manage to re-accommodate more than a small proportion of the worst housed. But to the rural-born migrants, even those living in a shack with cardboard walls and a tin roof, being able to earn enough money to live is preferable to being a poor peasant, owning no land and with little prospect of being able to earn money. By rural Latin American peasant standards, the workers of the big cities are well-off and that is why more migrants arrive each day to the cities. The shanty towns are located on the least desirable land, often on steep hillsides as in Rio, or in Santiago, along rail tracks, and although initially the houses are flimsy, insanitary and inadequate they are improved over time and paper walls are replaced by mud bricks and whitewashed two-storey structures are by no means unknown in long-established squatter settlements.

B. Ecological Patterns in the Big City

The zonation both into physical areas and by social groups is very different from that in the rural market centres. There the central plaza marked the geographical centre of the town and where those with highest social status lived. Those with a lower social position lived further away from the centre. This is clearly quite contrary to the prevailing theories of urban social ecology. In Anglo-American cities the centres are non-residential business districts, and people of highest social status live far out on or beyond the city limits. In reality the big city and the small town are such completely different places to live in that it is hardly surprising if the social geography of each is distinct. Smaller cities such as Mérida in Yucatán have begun to change from the small town pattern towards that of the big city: many of the upper class, both the new rich and the aristocracy, have moved to smaller but more modern homes on the edge of town and offices and shops have taken over the mansions of the rich. The rural immigrants likewise cannot always find somewhere to live in the city and thus live in newly urbanized areas on the edge. The development of neighbourhoods *(barrios)* has been a logical result of the segregation of new housing of different people of differing social status on the edge of the city. In the large cities industry has needed more space to grow and this has further increased the complexity of the urban pattern. As the arrangement of land use in the growing cities has changed so, by and large, has it come to resemble more closely the urban patterns of large metropolitan centres in the northern hemisphere.

Latin American towns and cities are the most rapidly changing part of the continent and thus it is as important to understand the patterns of social class and land use in the old and the new towns and the directions in which change is taking place as it is to be able to describe in detail the urban pattern of any one urban centre.

Conclusion

Although the types of urban settlement where the majority of the Latin American urban population live have been analysed there has been no mention of several highly distinctive types of urban settlement which are of significance in certain parts of Latin America.

In other chapters some indication is given of the role that extractive industries play in the Latin American economy. Associated with extractive industry, distinctive urban settlements have developed; on the one hand mining settlements of the colonial period, some of which seem to have avoided many of the rules that colonial period urbanists were supposed to follow, and, on the other hand, more recent 'company towns' located on oilfields, mining areas, or near to large sugar, cotton and banana plantations.

The colonial mining towns were located, naturally, close to major mines, even if no suitable site for the development of a town existed. Some, like Zacatecas in Mexico, are huddled in narrow mountain valleys, others, like Potosí in Bolivia, are at exceptionally high altitudes (4,000 m), but they have in common the fact that relatively few such towns retained their importance over the centuries. Ouro Preto in Brazil is typical of many old mining centres in that it remains a city with narrow streets, old churches and other fine colonial period buildings but it has ceased to be an important regional centre, having been long since outstripped by Belo Horizonte.

More modern mining centres are frequently associated with the ownership of the mine, or mines, by one company and the associated company towns thus have a degree of homogeneity that might otherwise be lacking in their visual appearance. Such towns as Chuquicamata in Chile, or Toquepala in southern Peru, have all the characteristics of a company town but in addition they are like the colonial mining towns in that they are located away from major routeways and often, as in the case of Chuquicamata, far from densely populated agricultural zones. Major oil centres also spawn a host of small company towns, such as El Tigre, San Tomé and Anaco in N.E. Venezuela, but also, when associated industries are located there, more diversified industrial complexes often locate around existing minor regional centres. Maracaibo in Venezuela, despite its old centre, owes much of its rapid growth to its position on one of the continent's most developed oil-fields and its character is more that of an oil centre than a regional capital; Tampico on the Gulf coast of Mexico has likewise developed from being a minor regional centre to being a major industrial town with services and housing of a better quality than might have otherwise have been expected. San Pedro Sula in northern Honduras is a similar type of town whose growth is closely linked with its proximity to the main headquarters in Honduras of the United Fruit Company. Its traditional though prosperous central area contrasts with the smart houses, gardens and paved roads of the white-collared workers and the company town of La Lima, 11 kms to the east—the actual HQ of the United Fruit Company—might not be out of place in Florida, so smart and clean does it seem. Above all, this type of town and those previously mentioned are enclaves of development in an underdeveloped region and there is a prosperity unexpected in such an area which contrasts sharply with the poverty of the surrounding rural areas.

Apart from the influence of foreign companies on the urban scene in Latin America, a modern development of note is the establishment of wholly planned new cities in sites where no settlement previously existed. The most visually impressive of these is Brasília but the rapidly developing centre of the industrial complex at the junction of the Orinoco and Caroní rivers in S.E. Venezuela—Ciudad Guayana—is planned to become the largest new city in Latin America. Older planned new cities founded earlier this century include Belo Horizonte, a major industrial city in Minas Gerais in Brazil, and Londrina in the state of Paraná, founded in an area of expanding agriculture in the 1930s and now the centre of the new coffee zone with important agricultural processing industries.

The importance of the development of such new cities is that it reflects a willingness of planners and governments in Latin America to realize that the development of new areas is necessarily linked with the development of new urban centres to serve them. The problems posed to planners by both Ciudad Guayana and Brasília are complex and stimulating and Brasília represents a new development in capital city planning. If a unity of plan were a major characteristic of the towns founded during the colonial period, so a search for new ideas and forms may characterize the new cities of Latin America.

Bibliography

SCHURZ, W. L., *This New World*, Dutton paperback, New York, 1964.
An extremely useful and interesting account of a wide variety of features of Latin American landscapes in both town and country with a wealth of bibliographic references.

SCHNORE, L. F., 'On the spatial structure of cities in the two Americas', in P. M. Hauser and L. F. Schnore (Eds.), *The Study of Urbanization*, Wiley, New York, 1965, pp. 347–99.
A valuable analytical study of city structure in Latin America compared with widely used models of urban spatial organization. An extensive bibliography.

HOUSTON, J. M., 'The foundation of colonial towns in Hispanic America' in R. P. Beckinsale and J. M. Houston (Eds.), *Essays in Honour of E. W. Gilbert: Urbanization and its problems*, Blackwell, Oxford, 1968, pp. 352–390.
An important analysis of the problems faced by city founders in the early colonial period in the New World.

SCOBIE, J., *Argentina: A city and a nation*, Oxford University Press, New York, 1971.
In the context of Argentinian historical development selected chapters include an account of the development of Buenos Aires up to the middle of the present century.

HAUSER, P. M. (ed.), *Urbanization in Latin America*, UNESCO, Paris, 1961.
A collection of studies of the problems and possible solutions that face urban centres throughout Latin America. Most articles refer to specific cities. Information on Lima and Rio de Janeiro is particularly useful.

LEWIS, O., *Children of Sánchez*, Penguin Books, Harmondsworth, 1964.
Life in Mexico City for the poor as told by the members of one family to a North American anthropologist. Enthralling, impressive and exhaustive.

WHITEFORD, A. H., *Two Cities of Latin America (Queretaro and Popayán)*, Doubleday paperback, New York, 1964.
An account of the class structure and associated characteristics of the inhabitants of two cities, one of which retains many of the characteristics of colonial towns.

CHAPTER 5

Land Reform, Colonization and Urban-ward Migration: the Changing Face of Latin America

A major reason for discontent in Latin America is the wide gap between the income and way of life of the rich and the poor. Every country, not least the U.S.A. or the United Kingdom, has people who are extremely poor and whose poverty is in part a result of the failure of society to provide for them. In the countries of Latin America (and indeed throughout the Third World) the proportion of the population who are poor according to any one of a variety of criteria is very much greater than in the advanced industrialized countries and in some regions, such as rural Haiti, maybe as many as half of the inhabitants are poverty-stricken. The reasons for this poverty are various but include the monopoly of political power, wealth and ownership of land by a very small segment of the population. Where extreme poverty exists alongside obvious exploitation of many by a few then discontent exists which may erupt into revolution.

The aspect of this problem which is of concern to geographers is the uneven distribution of land and resources and the systems of farming the land which are associated with this maldistribution. Of particular note to social geographers is the pattern of conditions that gives rise to attempts to change the exploitive system. The lack of opportunities for rural people either to maintain or improve their living standards gives rise, on the one hand, to the demand for measures to re-allocate land more equitably and, on the other, to a movement by rural people away from their birthplaces to newly-developing colonization zones, often in tropical lowlands, and to the rapidly-developing urban centres.

In this chapter these movements will be examined in order to understand something of the new settlement patterns that are emerging. Even land reform in densely populated areas results in changes in both agricultural systems and the spatial organizations of settlements as well as in the legal ownership of land. Settlement in new lands is an ancient process but it has become more rapid and widespread in the past twenty years. Latin America is fortunate in having so much land available for future settlement, even if the agricultural potential of much of it remains to be investigated and proved. In addition, in some desert areas, particularly in Mexico and Peru, new irrigation schemes are bringing fresh land under cultivation and making an even greater contribution to the national economies than do the colonization projects in humid tropical lands. Finally, the movement of rural people to big cities, although a worldwide phenomenon, is particularly striking in Latin America and this results in particular forms of urban settlement that merit examination.

LAND REFORM IN PROGRESS

One purpose of land reform may be assumed to be to effect a modification of the relations between man and the land he uses and thereby to solve some of the grave problems that affect life in rural areas. It is unrealistic to criticize the results of some land reforms by referring to such abstract matters as a balance of payments crisis that seems incomprehensible to rural workers, whose concern is a lack of title to land that they and their forefathers have cultivated, as well as the excessive demands that the landowner makes upon their time without any form of payment. Indeed, it may be said that the most far-reaching Latin American land reform programmes that have been carried out, those in Mexico, Bolivia and Cuba, were directed more at achieving a wider measure of social justice for rural people than at increasing the value of agricultural output. Because of this, in this chapter, we shall be concerned with the ways in which man–land relationships have been altered: the new forms of land holding that have emerged, the changes in land utilization, the pattern of cropping or grazing that has resulted and the degree to which the quality of rural living has been changed by increased income from various sources.

Land reforms can be divided into two categories according to the land holdings that result. On the one hand there are those reform programmes that are *redistributive*, where estates or vacant land is sub-divided and allocated to individual families, and on the other there are those that are *collectivist*, where the ownership of the land is retained in the hands of a corporate body such as the community or even ultimately the state. A sub-division is also desirable between collectivist reforms where ownership is in the hands of the community, however that may be defined, and those where ownership rests with the state. This is an essential difference for example between the Mexican collective *ejido* and the Cuban State Farm or *granja del pueblo* (which in turn are roughly parallel to the *sovkhoz* and *kolkhoz* in the U.S.S.R.).

There are a number of theoretical advantages to collectivist reforms. They retain large land ownership units and are thus in a better position to engage in large-scale farming and to avoid the sub-division of the land as a result of inheritance. A degree of stability in the land-holding pattern is also assured since illegal sale of the land is virtually impossible when ownership is vested in a community rather than an individual. In practice, collective ownership often means a splitting-up of the land into small parcels of land farmed on an individual basis and decisions about farming methods and crops rest with individuals. Often, indeed, the only collective action in which individuals may engage is litigation whilst collective purchases of equipment, seeds or fertilizer and sales of produce are as difficult to stimulate as in rural free-holding communities. The main disadvantages of reforms that permit this sub-division of land are largely economic. Individualization of productive units, even though in collective ownership, often leads to traditional methods of peasant farming continuing to predominate and overall productivity remaining static. Furthermore, the process of individualization erodes any will that community members may have to co-operate, rendering later development of collective organization much more difficult.

State farms operate in a completely different organizational framework and with distinct man–land relations. The rural workers in this system are paid employees of the State and are paid by the State in proportion to their work contribution. The management of the farm is in the hands of an individual appointed by the State, not by the workers, and although workers may have opportunities for criticizing the management, the production goals are set by a central planning agency. The advantages of this system are obvious. Cropping systems can be precisely determined in the light of national and regional needs, economies of scale can be gained, especially where expensive machinery can be used and where a single crop can be grown over a wide area. The labour force need be no larger and no smaller than is necessary and theoretically the barriers to a high degree of efficiency are minimized. The disadvantages are various but chief among them in Latin America is the unwillingness of rural workers in many areas to accept a wage-labourer status without any land of their own. Thus the development of state farms in the Andean highlands is impossible to achieve because, despite the degree to which they are grossly exploited, rural families have the use of small plots of land which in practice, in the short term at least, are theirs to do what they like with and their prime goal is to obtain security of tenure for their house and land. But if state farms are as unthinkable in highland Peru as they are in highland Guatemala, on the coastlands the situation is different, for labourers are accustomed to working for wages without having the use of any land. It is this sort of situation in which state farms are a possible alternative form of tenure.

Whatever form of revision of land tenure institutions takes place, or is proposed, there is a large body of intellectual opinion in favour of some sort of land reform. Frequently agencies whose business is land reform are remarkable for the high degree of dedication and personal commitment that their personnel display. Why then are land reforms so few in Latin America?

Firstly it should be recognized that on paper most Latin American countries have at some time passed a Land Reform Law, but that such laws have seldom had any effect, notwithstanding the heady enthusiasm: 'the land will become for the man who works it' shown by Latin American governments in the 1961 Declaration of Punta del Este. The reasons why land reforms have not been carried out lie primarily in the simple fact that most Latin American countries are controlled by a small sector of society which, in addition to having political power, also owns much of the best farmland. It is unrealistic to expect thoroughgoing reforms from the very people who stand to lose most by them. In addition, those who would gain most from agrarian reform, the rural workers, are often ill-organized and without adequate political representation. In many countries only the literate may vote and if 80 per cent of the rural population is illiterate, as is common, then a sizeable sector of the adult population is thus disenfranchised.

To Marxists the simple answer to this problem is that an agrarian reform can only come about through a broadly-based revolution and an impressively large number of non-Marxist students of Latin American affairs believe this to be the most effective way of bringing about reform. It is hardly surprising that Anglo-Americans, not least the U.S. Government, have developed an alternative view. This is that *integral reform* is to be achieved by the establishment of family-sized farms supported by a comprehensive programme which includes agricultural extension work, supervised credit and organized marketing. This is, as one very experienced observer said, 'a partial and very narrow projection of Anglo-American institutions' and presupposes the redistribution of land.

Few Latin American countries have either the manpower, in the form of trained rural extension agents, or the money to invest in an expensive social reform whose economic results are hard to forecast and in many cases include a period of static levels of production. Thus the actual experiences in effective land reform in Latin America have been restricted either to countries whose governments, at least for a time, felt a deep political and ideological commitment to help the rural people, or to those who had the money to engage in a type of reform which would help the toiling masses without causing too much inconvenience to the rich and powerful landowners. Other reforms have been scarcely worthy of the name, employing large numbers of bureaucrats and generally carrying out land redistribution in one small area to which foreign visitors can be taken in order to be impressed with what has been achieved.

LAND REFORM IN ACTION

Three countries will be looked at in greater detail: Bolivia because the 1953 agrarian reform was singularly effective and essentially redistributive; Cuba as the sole example of socialist-inspired agrarian reform in the Continent and lastly Colombia as an example of ineffective non-reform.

Bolivia

The high plateau, the Altiplano, at 3,800 m above sea level is one of the most desolate and barren highland areas in the New World but almost all of the most fertile areas were part of large estates. In 1950, 70 per cent of farm units were smaller than 10 hectares but occupied only 0·4 per cent of the farmland, while 8 per cent of the farm holdings, over 500 hectares in size, occupied 95 per cent of farmland. These data refer to the whole country and it is possible that an even greater proportion of large estates existed in the northern Altiplano and the fertile valleys in the vicinity of Cochabamba. Apart from the concentration of agricultural land in the large estates, pressure for land reform resulted even more from the semi-feudal conditions under which the estates were farmed. The workers, who seldom received any wages, were obliged to work between two and six days a week for the estate and in addition to provide labour, services or goods for other tasks. In return they received a houseplot and adjacent land (usually known as a *sayaña*), additional crop-land further away as well as grazing rights for a limited number of livestock.

Although large estates were common in most parts of Bolivia, except for the northern forestlands and the desert central and southern Altiplano, where

rainfall was generally less than 200 mm, it was in the highlands of Cochabamba and La Paz departments where the servile ties of the workers to the
estates were most onerous. It was in these regions that the agrarian reform
of 1953 had the greatest social impact. The great domains of the Suárez
family in the humid tropical north-east were broken up, as were other
estates in the Santa Cruz region, but in general it was the result of political
pressure directed against individuals rather than the normal process of
reform which brought changes here.

The agrarian reform decree established three categories of holding. Properties were declared *latifundios*, which were subject to total expropriation,
where the workers had been abused, the landowner had seldom resided and
where the forms of agriculture practised by the landowner were archaic.
Medianas propriedades (medium-sized properties) were declared where the
landowner had resided and had used some more modern farming methods.
These holdings were subject to expropriation in part only if their size exceeded the maximum laid down for its ecological zone (varying, for example,
from 6 ha in the irrigated vineyard valleys of Tarija to 350 ha in the cold
desert of the southern Altiplano). Small properties *(pequeñas propriedades)*
were inalienable so long as they did not exceed the local maximum (3 ha in
the vineyard valleys to 35 ha in the southern Altiplano) and those few
estates employing modern methods, the agricultural enterprises *(empresas
agrícolas)*, were subject to the maximum appropriation of half their land
and were permitted to retain 80 ha in the vineyard valleys and 800 ha in the
southern Altiplano. The procedure for expropriation was complex, tedious
and expensive. But whether or not individuals and communities received
titles is irrelevant, for within two years of the reform most of the peasants
had of their own accord taken over the estate and sub-divided the land
amongst themselves. The work of the agrarian reform service was thus
primarily one of legalizing existing situations, arbitrating disputes, surveying
properties and issuing titles. Up to the end of 1969 they had distributed
titles to 266,066 families covering 11·7 million hectares of land. Probably
only 40 per cent of those who should benefit from the reform have so
far received titles. The effect of the land reform was often more far reaching
than was initially intended, and although the freeholding communities of
peasants were not directly affected by the legislation, many of them had
lost land to neighbouring estates. So long as they had lost land later than
1 January 1900 they could sue for repossession. They were thus able to
demarcate at least a part of the boundary of the community which was
previously ill-defined and, in some cases, to obtain more land. Peasant free-

holding communities were also affected by the changes that were taking place in the nearby former estates. Many formed their own peasant unions and others adopted some of the changes in way of life or agriculture that some former estate workers were engaging in. From 1969 onwards freehold-ing communities have increasingly benefited from agrarian reform procedu-res and not only have their boundaries been surveyed and legally determined but in some cases, increasingly in 1970 and 1971, individual holdings have been demarcated and individual as well as communal titles have been awarded.

The most noticeable change in the spatial organization of rural commu-nities that has resulted from the land reform is the development, in several areas, of new nucleated settlements, often in association with new weekly markets. In the area between Oruro, La Paz and Lake Titicaca (see Figure 5-1), as well as in several places in the Yungas of La Paz, rural people have built new towns around a square, often on a highway, thus forming a tiny new village that in time grows to become a small town with 150–250 houses. The houses are two-storey structures, with windows and a corrugated iron roof quite unlike the traditional houses of the countryside. Many remain empty because their owners prefer to live in the countryside, near to their flocks and fields. On market day the square becomes thronged with people and the previously empty houses are full of life. These new towns result from the desire of many rural people to have some sort of urban centre with a wider range of services than they previously had available; from the encour-agement given by the peasant union organization to the formation of such towns to stimulate progress; from the need of some members of the com-munity to have a central site where shops can be established and where minor businesses (such as tailoring) can thrive; and finally because the development of new periodic markets following the 1952 Revolution itself encouraged urban growth associated with the market place.

The new markets established since 1952 are a result of the need for a proc-ess of exchange to link the peasants as the sole rural producers with the ur-ban centres as markets for their produce. Goods which previously the land-lord had sold were now disposed of by the peasants. Many lacked adequate means of bringing produce to cities like Oruro or La Paz and so the urban-based merchants came out to buy the produce.

The changes in agriculture that have resulted from the land reform are variable: while in several regions there has been a transformation of agricul-ture, in others there has been relatively little change that can be directly attributed to the reform. The income of many farm families has risen since

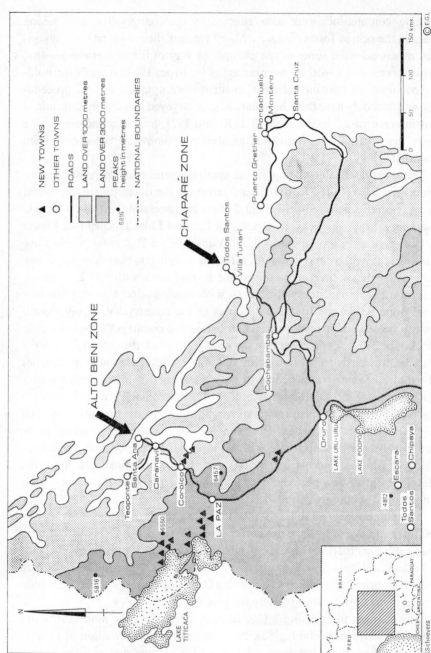

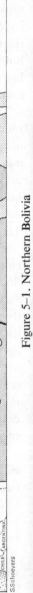

Figure 5–1. Northern Bolivia

sizeable areas of cultivated land which were previously producing goods for the landowner now produce at least the same volume of goods for the rural workers. Although remarkable changes in the land-use system are uncommon, it must be noted that the potential for change is low. Over much of the Altiplano and the mountain areas rainfall is deficient and frosts common. Where water is available accumulations of soluble salts may make crop growing virtually impossible. Changes in land use that have occurred may be divided into (1) increasing the area of cropland by clearing scrub or ploughing up pasture and (2) intensifying agriculture by planting vegetables or fruit and engaging in what is virtual market gardening. The former changes can be observed in many areas of the Altiplano and in places in the Yungas of La Paz. In one estate on the edge of Lake Titicaca, the pasture next to the estate house, which was in an area of good soil with water readily available, was sub-divided amongst the workers in 1966. It was planted to barley by most people in the following year, and yields were more than double what they were normally. The most spectacular increases in production have been noted in the irrigated lower valley of Cochabamba, in parts of the Yungas of La Paz and in the irrigated valley below the city of La Paz. In each of these areas the intensification of agriculture has been associated with the cultivation of vegetables (in the La Paz valley and the lower valley of Cochabamba), flowers and fruit (La Paz valley) and the cultivation of coffee and extension of the area of coca planting (part of the Yungas). It has been estimated that the value of agricultural production in the lower valley of Cochabamba has increased *tenfold* as a result of these changes in land use. Thus, although in many areas there have been comparatively few changes that are attributable to the land reform, in some areas, each with a relatively high population density, there have been changes and in some of these very remarkable increases in production have occurred. However, the long-term effect of the reform on Bolivian agricultural production as a whole has been negligible. The most important increases in production are those resulting from the extension and intensification of farming in the tropical lowlands, particularly in the Santa Cruz zone, rather than from changes in the highlands.

Cuba

The pre-revolutionary situation in Cuba was quite distinct from that in almost any other Latin American country. The rural labour force was far from being an impoverished peasantry; the income per head in Cuba was higher than in most Latin American countries and Cuba was one of the more literate nations in Latin America. Nor was the concentration of large estates so remarkable as in Bolivia. In 1946 57 per cent of the farm area was owned by 3 per cent of the farmers. A more hurried and incomplete census in 1961 suggested that among the estates to be affected by reform 73 per cent of the land was owned by 9 per cent of the farmers.

The need for land reform in Cuba arose less from the concentration of valuable land in large holdings than from the fact that the national economy was dominated by the role of sugar, which was produced in a large part by North American companies. Immediately prior to the Revolution in 1959, 22 of the most important sugar companies occupied 1·8 million hectares of land and 13 of them, all North American, accounted for 1·2 million hectares and had an average size of 90 thousand hectares. In addition to this domination by foreign companies of production of the most important crop, the rhythm of work associated with sugar production was highly irregular. The Cuba Agricultural Census for 1946 revealed that 400,000 people were temporary, paid workers and comprised one-half of the employed agricultural labour force; more than half of them had worked for only four months or less in the year and only 6 per cent of them had been employed for nine months or longer. Data from 1956–57 suggest that the unemployed seldom comprised less than 9 per cent of the labour force but that during the slack season from May to November unemployment could rise to include over 20 per cent of the labour force. Thus seasonal unemployment and attendant poverty were common despite the high levels of *average* income that Cuba enjoyed compared with, for example, Haiti.

A firm commitment to effect a land reform, as part of a revolutionary programme, was made by Fidel Castro in his famous 'History will Absolve Me' speech at his trial in 1953 and a provisional agrarian reform law was prepared three months before the overthrow of the Batista regime. When this law was put into effect in May 1959 all estates larger than 402 hectares were to be expropriated with compensation; tenancy was abolished (tenants were to become owners); 27 hectares of land was to be distributed to each small tenant farmer, including squatters, free of charge but on condition that it was not mortgaged, sold or sub-divided on inheritance; properties owned by foreigners and land companies were expropriated and co-operatives were to be formed to farm this land. Later, the maximum permitted size of estates was reduced to 67 hectares. The whole process of reform and much control of agricultural production was guided by the National Institute of Agrarian Reform (I.N.R.A.) which was a land reform organization and Ministry of Agriculture rolled into one.

The most important aspect of the reform has naturally been the reorganization of the sugar estates. At first the large estates were run either as State farms *(granjas del pueblo)* or as co-operatives (that is collective farms), and the latter predominated in the sugar cane areas. In 1962 the collectives were abolished and became state farms. In the words of the head of I.N.R.A. they had become 'dead organisms with hundreds and hundreds of members who wanted to have nothing to do with them.' While workers in state farms were paid a guaranteed wage and had a variety of benefits such as new houses and schools, the collective workers were less well treated by the State and conditions of life for them were greatly inferior to those on state farms, even though many collective farmers were able to get good prices for some of their goods on the black market. The remaining small farmers, farming a total of 3·5 million hectares (in 1961) are incorporated into State planning insofar as they are supposed to sell their produce to the official buying agencies at a fixed price. The majority (94 per cent) own plots of land smaller than 67 hectares. In recent years the small farmers near to large towns have been subject to pressure to either sell or rent their land to the State in order that larger land-use units could be created which would be more suitable for mechanization. Their role in agriculture seems not to have been important and the small farmers have not benefited from the revolution as much as have workers on state farms.

The spatial organization of agriculture has been transformed by central planning but the size of the farm units that have been created has been often so large (some as big as 130,000 hectares) that efficiency has not been achieved. Increased regionalization of agriculture is forecast for the early 1970s with some areas least suited to sugar being turned over to other crops. Attempts are being made to make each province self-sufficient in foodstuffs to decrease crop specialization. This is in part to improve the use of the labour force and should avoid the necessity of moving large numbers of people from one province to another, which consumes valuable transport facilities and necessitates the provision of expensive accommodation for temporary workers. In 1968 the province of Havana for the first time imported less food than it exported.

The main crop under the reorganized agriculture is still sugar cane. Sugar production remains variable and hurricanes have seriously damaged canefields but production in the early 1970s may approach the 10 million ton target set long ago by Fidel Castro. Mechanization proceeds slowly and the rural labour force is frequently insufficient to obtain the fullest possible harvests. Diversification, after a disastrous period in which a large number of experiments at developing new crops failed, has been moderately successful. Tobacco production has climbed steadily, reaching 100,000 tons in 1968,

Livstock

citrus fruit have greatly increased in importance, production having doubled 1962–69 and a quadrupling of production is expected, based on new plantations, by 1975. An improvement in cattle herds is under way, including improvement of stock, use of artificial insemination and an increase in the number of livestock. Politically disinterested observers are impressed by the emphasis not only on improved rural social conditions, among which the expansion of education is the most striking, but also the amount of investment in research into new crops and livestock.

The Cuban land reform is directed within an ideological framework even though the ideology is sometimes subject to drastic revisions. But it is not based on individual land ownership. Fidel Castro observed in a speech in August 1962 that no further land redistribution would take place because 'after one piece of land the peasant would want another.' In the particular case of Cuba there is little doubt that this was practical as well as based upon sound socialist doctrine.

For the Cubans, as for the Bolivians, their land reform has been a social success and carried out at a grass roots level. Most Latin American land reforms are little more than hesitant steps in the wrong direction made by people lacking either conviction of the feasibility of the procedure or the will to act. Colombia's land reform is such as this.

Colombia

In common with a number of Latin American countries Colombia had a land reform law on the statute book long before the present law came into being. In 1936 a land reform law was passed which attempted to regularize the question of squatters' rights and which also contained the provision that land left uncultivated for ten years could be expropriated. By 1946 however the government of the time was disinclined to enforce a clause that would alienate precisely that sector of the population from which it drew its support: the large landowners.

Although Colombia's main export crop, coffee, is grown on small and medium-sized holdings, the best land in the most populated areas is held in large estates. Recent data suggest that almost one-quarter of farm families own no land, while another 47 per cent live on holdings too small to support a family: 70·2 per cent of farm families thus have inadequate land resources. The 1960 Census showed that in the Departments of Colombia (roughly the effectively occupied parts of the country) half the holdings were less than 3 hectares in size and in Antioquia and Boyacá over 60 per cent of the cultivated land was in farms larger than 500 hectares and 20 per cent larger than 2,500 hectares. The case for agrarian reform is undeniable. On economic grounds even the World Bank has criticized a land tenure system whereby cattle graze on the rich plains on big estates, while smallholders over-exploit the surrounding steep hillsides. But the political situation in Colombia has made a thorough-going reform impossible. Traditional hostility between the two major political parties flared into a civil war from 1948–58, known as *la Violencia*, and minor guerilla skirmishes continue in several parts of the country. La Violencia caused disruption in rural areas, and encouraged many to flee to the wilderness of new colonization zones; this resulted in a number of estates being abandoned and subsequently taken over by land-hungry squatters. In 1948 a pact was established between the Liberals and Conservatives which has result-ed in the country being ruled for alternate periods by each party for twenty years.

In 1961, in the wake of the Punta del Este Agreement whereby Latin Amer-ican countries pledged themselves to tackle, among other things, land reform, Colombia passed her Social Agrarian Reform Law. This established a piece-meal approach to reform coupled with adequate compensation for land ex-propriated. There were no flamboyant phrases to proclaim the universal rights of all to land and the main task of the land reform institute that was founded (I.N.C.O.R.A.) was to promote the settlement of independent culti-vators on family farms. The land necessary for this was to come, in order of priority, from public lands, lands farmed by tenants or sharecroppers and only lastly lands deemed to be inadequately cultivated by their owner. Com-pensation varied from long-term bonds carrying a low interest rate for uncul-tivated lands, to short-term, high-interest bonds and a proportion of the value in cash for the more highly valued land: that is, land adequately cultivated by the owner, sharecroppers or tenants.

Work of I.N.C.O.R.A. has been concentrated on giving titles to squatters, as was the aim of the 1936 law, on expropriating unused land and on irriga-tion projects aimed at settling large numbers of people in situations where highly productive agriculture would be possible. Projects were started in all departments but local opposition from large landowners was fierce and organ-ized. In 1963 in Valle department, for example, a plan to develop a large irri-gation project covering 30,000 hectares, only 8,000 hectares of which would be expropriated to be allocated to new settlers, was blocked by local estate own-ers who planned instead to build a sugar mill which would use sugar from the whole 30,000 hectares. Relatively little has been achieved by way of solution to the problem of the 50 per cent of farm families living on holdings too small for their needs; for example, up to early 1960 I.N.C.O.R.A. had distributed 2·8 million hectares to 100,000 families but much of this land was in previously unoccupied areas and little had been done to shake the power of the big landowners in the fertile but overcrowded valleys. By mid 1969 I.N.C.O.R.A. had redistributed ont of the land expropriated only 1,194 parcels of land covering 13,600 hectares.

Conclusion

It has not been possible to describe and analyse the experience of Mexico, whose land reform is the oldest in Latin America. Here a revolutionary land reform has been carried out over a period of fifty or more years. Now much of the land that can be expropriated has been distributed but many landless peasants remain. Large ranches in arid land, where intensive agriculture is impractical, have remained and an important sector of middle-sized properties has grown up. It is on these that the most dramatic rise in productivity has occurred.

It is impossible and unnecessary to survey the faltering steps towards reforming land tenure that other Latin American countries have taken. Venezuela has made a valiant effort at colonizing and effectively developing land on the northern edge of the Llanos and has preferred resettlement to expropriation, which is politically expedient if socially dubious. Chile, under the Christian Democrat President Frei, embarked on a serious effort at restructuring land tenure in the Central Valley and a number of important new ideas in institutionalized, as opposed to revolutionary, agrarian reform have been tried out, chief among which is the establishment of collective farms. However, the area so far affected is only a small proportion of the total in large estates, but newly-elected President Allende has promised a more thorough-going agrarian reform. In the summer of 1969, the Peruvian military government announced a fundamental revolutionary-style land reform which could well transform land tenure in the richest agricultural areas of Peru. First reports suggest that the reforms are being implemented both in the coastal sugar and cotton plantations and in the highlands but that local landowners are managing to dilute many of the measures.

The most frequent criticism of land reform programmes is that they lead to a decline in agricultural production. There is plentiful evidence of changes in production patterns following agrarian reform but these may, as in the case of

Mexico, be associated with civil strife. The principal aim of any land reform is, however, social rather than economic and it is unfair and largely irrelevant to judge a socially motivated change by its economic results. Land reform does usually bring important improvements to rural areas—schools, roads and expanding towns—and the rural population is thus drawn more effectively into the life of the country. Rural people become consumers even if only in a small way and the market for goods is increased, thus providing more impetus for the growth of industries. Those who suffer most from agrarian reform are the landowners whose estates were so badly tended that they were entirely expropriated. Many had substantial alternative means of financial support; a few had nothing and now live in penury. This seems a small price to pay for an improvement in education, living standards and social progress in rural areas.

A more serious criticism of distributive land reforms is that they create a multiplicity of small plots which can be divided upon inheritance, and thereby the problem of large estates is solved only by the creation of small uneconomic holdings. Collectivist reforms avoid this pitfall and, more often, as was seen in the case of Cuba, have problems resulting from holdings that are too large to be easily managed. One move to combat the growth of small holdings *(minifundia)* has been legislation to prevent the splitting-up of holdings awarded by agrarian reform, but where this runs contrary to the established practice of inheritance it is likely to be ignored. In areas where large estates were absent *minifundismo* is a frequent problem. Many land reform programmes in Mediterranean Europe for example have been aimed more at consolidating small holdings into family farms than dividing up land on large estates. As yet relatively little has been done in Latin America to combat this problem.

COLONIZATION

Land reform is concerned with solving some of the problems of rural areas where there are too many people and too little land available for them. An obvious solution to land shortage is to encourage people to move to other areas where land is available for farming. Latin America has more land potentially available for settlement than many other continents, for the population is highly concentrated in a small number of areas. Almost every Latin American country has extensive areas that are virtually uninhabited and only El Salvador and Uruguay have nowhere for new colonization to take place.

If we seek to identify a common pattern in those areas where high population densities occur and where there is an acute shortage of land, it will emerge that each has been settled a long time, has a good system of communications and often a sufficient degree of physical homogeneity to make it markedly different from surrounding areas. Thus, for example, in Costa Rica settlement is concentrated in the central valley between 500–1000 metres in elevation and nowhere else in the country has a comparable density of population. The area moreover is hemmed in by mountains on two sides and the most accessible areas, towards the Caribbean and the Pacific, have different climates and vegetation and thus present very different agricultural problems from the central valley.

Shortage of land is of course only relative. An area which is unable to provide a living for its inhabitants can be transformed by sowing crops which produce more or which ripen sufficiently fast to permit two crops a year. The provision of water for irrigation can increase productivity enormously. Thus for shortage of land to be linked with a demand for new areas for colonization, there must also be only limited possibilities for improvements in existing farming systems or the soil must be sufficiently exhausted for its fertility to be seriously impaired. The rate of agricultural change in many of the areas with land shortage is so slow that a livelihood can only be provided for all if some people migrate elsewhere. Colonists however are by no means all would-be farmers from the overcrowded rural areas. Investigations in various parts of Latin America have shown that a sizeable proportion of colonists, even a majority in places, are townsfolk, frustrated by the social straitjacket of small-town life, who seek their fortune as farmers even if they have scarcely handled a machete before.

The zones of Latin America that are potentially suitable for settlement include parts of the Amazon basin, in particular the lower foothills of the Andes; the margins of the Llanos of Venezuela and the Gran Chaco; parts of the Pacific and Caribbean coastal slopes of southern Mexico and Central America; and the western parts of Goias and of the southern states of Brazil. Irrigation is a possibility in many arid zones. The recently uplifted mountains of the western side of the continent have been deeply incised by streams whose gorges offer many sites for storage reservoirs or hydro-electric power installations. The long stretch of coastal desert in western South America from Peru to Chile has a number of areas whose highly productive agriculture is based on irrigation. Further areas are expected to be irrigated in the future and the barrier to the extension of irrigation is largely the financial one of the high cost of bringing water to new areas and of the subsequent administration of settlement.

Although considerable differences occur in the problems and needs of colonists in different areas it is possible and useful at this stage to outline some important prerequisites for successful colonization.

1. *Roads*. Without adequate means of communication colonists cannot easily enter a colonization zone nor can they send out their produce to be sold. Railways are inflexible because travellers have to rely on a single entity (the railway company) for transport and only one means of transport, trains, can be used; rivers are apt to flood, to be rendered dangerous by rapids and, only too often in South America, flow in the opposite direction to that in which people want to go. The development of new roads in coastal Ecuador heralded a boom in land, new farms were established and poor farmers who lived in isolated parts of the forests found a road on their doorstep by which their produce could be transported to the main seaport, Guayaquil, in a few hours. Similarly a valuable study in Central Peru has shown how the fortunes of small isolated settlements in the mountains have fluctuated with changes in accessibility. A recipe for simple colonization is really: 'Build a Road' or for the cynical: 'Plan to Build a Road'.

2. *Adequate soils*. A heartbreaking characteristic of many tropical soils is that their fertility is easily impaired and high-crop yields of the first years after clearing the forest give way rapidly to poor yields as the soil fertility declines and erosion progresses. In some areas currently colonized in Bolivia competent soil studies have suggested that the land cannot sustain cropping for more than 5–10 years and that it would best be suited to properly managed afforestation. Methods of clearing forests and the nature of rainfall should be studied in relation to soil fertility in order that not only should the soil be maintained in as good a state as possible but also that systems of agriculture should be established that have the best possibility of long-term benefit to both farmer and land. To achieve this an efficient extension service is needed.

3. *Education*. People coming to colonization areas seldom have much agricultural experience that is relevant to the new area. They often are not even accustomed to living in tropical lowland areas and are unaware of the dangers and advantages of different ways of living. Working during the midday period when the sun is most powerful is commonplace in the mountains but exhausting and even dangerous in humid tropical lowlands. Personal hygiene assumes a greater importance in a humid lowland environment where bacteria multiply rapidly. The means of telling people about the ways in which the old-established inhabitants overcome these problems is by education.

Schools can not only educate the young but people of all ages and thus enable them to make the most of their opportunities. Schools can also inculcate principles of good farming and so help farmers produce more with the greatest benefit to themselves.

The above issues imply a need for previous planning and exploration which is often slow and costly. Governments, subject to political pressures, want quick results. A plan initiated by President X is of little value to him if it comes to fruition during the term of office of President Y, who will naturally claim as much credit as possible for himself. The aims of colonization in many parts of Latin America have been to settle a limited number of families as quickly as possible and to be able to show some positive results within say five years. International agencies, such as the United Nations, the World Bank or the United States Agency for International Development, have a similar need to show results quickly, which often conflicts with a scientifically formulated policy designed to give optimum social and economic benefits. The colonist who is fortunate enough to obtain a plot of decent land not far from a road is still faced with a host of problems which suggests a third important prerequisite for colonization.

Planned and Spontaneous Colonization

A large part of what has been written about colonization has been concerned with areas where colonization has been centrally planned and closely supervised from start to finish. Thus, for example, we know more in Ecuador about the Santo Domingo de los Colorados colonization project which involved only a small number of people than we do about colonization elsewhere in the Guayas lowlands, the Esmeraldas region and the east Andean foothills.

Planned colonization implies the organized movement of selected individuals and families to areas of new settlement where supervision of agriculture and marketing is maintained and even controlled. In some schemes houses are built for the new settlers and feeder roads link their lands to the national markets. Such colonization is expensive: it may cost between U.S. $ 1200–4000 to settle a single family, but only those most likely to be successful are chosen, they receive advice on what to grow and are helped in a variety of ways to establish themselves. Despite this by no means all planned colonization schemes are successful.

Spontaneous colonization is the result of small groups of pioneers travelling on foot to isolated areas where land is unused and there establishing themselves. As their production of surplus goods increases then they send them on muleback or by canoe to the nearest road. In many cases spontaneous settlement is associated with the building of a new road and new colonists settle beside or within easy reach of the highway. Thus they are able to retain contact with the rest of the country and with the market for their saleable surplus. The essence of spontaneous colonization is that there is no selection of colonists, that nothing is provided for individual settlers save the opportunity to establish individual title to a piece of land, and the main investment that national governments make is the provision of highways. Clearly in some cases there is not even a highway and in others a wide range of services are available: feeder roads, schools, agricultural extension agents and machinery pools to help clear the land for cultivation.

There are manifold advantages to planned colonization. If all goes well your selected colonists are eager, industrious and ready to accept new ideas. Social workers and teachers ensure that people get over initial difficulties, adapt to a new life in a changed environment and are able to devote all their energies to farming. Economists like planned colonization too. Cost accounting enables a flow of data on how much everything is costing the government. Farmers can be directed to plant crops for which there is a ready market and which give them a satisfactory return. Co-operatives can more easily be established since people are ready and even eager to take advice and thus, notwithstanding the high cost per family established, great benefits can accrue both to the settlers and to the national economy. These advantages have a habit of evaporating when actual cases are studied. Pre-colonization surveys of land suitability are not always accurate; successful colonists are not easily identified from among the scores of would-be migrants; trained extension workers are scarce and often unwilling to forsake a civilized city for the steamy jungle; costs of every stage of the project escalate as a result of poor planning, corruption and unforeseen difficulties; the crops selected by experts do not always grow as well as expected away from the experimental station, they may require elaborate processing or the selected progressive colonist may prefer to grow bananas for which he knows there is a market rather than cacao which he believes to be harder to grow and whose price he knows nothing about. Every colonization project has tales of ghastly mistakes and costly errors although success is invariably more common than failure for individual settlers. But the overriding consideration in comparing the success of planned and spontaneous colonization is cost. Even where a large proportion of settlers on a planned colonization scheme have made a success of their farms the unit cost of this to the government is high and the number of people who have benefited is low.

There are a multitude of disadvantages to spontaneous colonization. It is difficult to prevent colonists settling in areas where agriculture is likely to give rise to rapid soil erosion on steep slopes. The crops that the new colonist plants are often those already widely available and overproduction may lead to a fall in price which is crippling to the small producer. Colonists establish themselves at different times and there is seldom any organized nuclear settlement. The later establishment of central services, such as electric power, school, infirmary, municipal buildings, is thereby rendered more difficult. Despite these disadvantages there is no lack of potential settlers. Some work first as labourers for others and gain thereby a knowledge of the zone before obtaining land. Colonists grow a variety of crops although there is a tendency to rely on one major cash crop. Although some colonists become discouraged and abandon their land there is always another person ready to take it over. Difficulties do arise when a plot is abandoned and someone wanting to take over the site cannot discover the original owner in order to take over his land legally. A major advantage of spontaneous colonization is that, in spite of the lack of formal urban centres, settlers do organize themselves into coherent social groups and they elect committees to plan improvements and to petition the national government for new schools, or for a bulldozer to clear an area for a small settlement nucleus or for the establishment of an experimental farm. On planned colonization settlements many facilities are provided and thus the settlers tend to complain about the inadequacy of what they have rather than about what they lack.

There is clearly no solution to the dispute over the merits of planned and spontaneous colonization since they are not easy to compare and both have very different advantages. It is most useful to look at several well-tried projects in different areas to see what sorts of changes have been effected and the extent to which the colonists have adopted modern farming systems.

1. The Fuerte Valley, Mexico: Irrigation, Modernization and Land Reform

The Sonora Desert on the N.W. coast of Mexico renders agriculture impossible except in places where there is irrigation. The area was little settled during the colonial period and it was not until the 19th century that irrigation was extended sufficiently for a few estates to be established whose chief activities were cattle raising and sugar cane growing. The Fuerte valley was the site of a brief attempt to establish an advanced socialist colony when it was hoped that an east–west transcontinental railway would be built to terminate at Topolobampo, a fine port site. A new sugar mill built at Los Mochis domi-

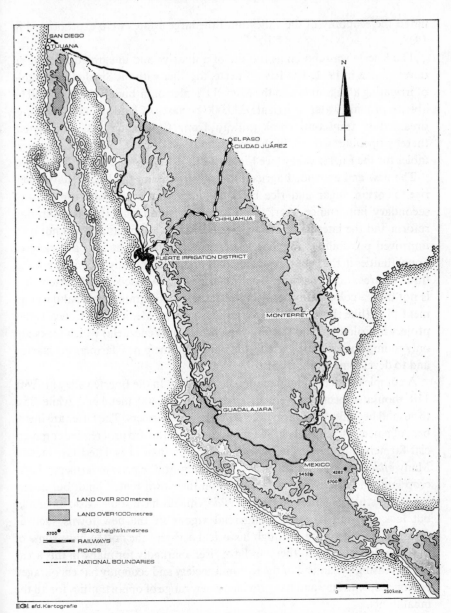

SAN DIEGO
TIJUANA

EL PASO
CIUDAD JUÁREZ

N

CHIHUAHUA

FUERTE IRRIGATION DISTRICT

MONTERREY

GUADALAJARA

MEXICO
5452   4282
5700

LAND OVER 200 metres

LAND OVER 1000 metres

5700   PEAKS, height in metres
RAILWAYS
ROADS
NATIONAL BOUNDARIES

0   250 kms.

EGI afd. Kartografie

Figure 5–2. Mexico: Fuerte Valley irrigation area

nated the economy of the valley until the large estates were expropriated in 1938.

The Fuerte was chosen as the site of a massive and integrated river basin development in 1951. The River Fuerte, together with the Sinaloa, is capable of irrigating a huge area and the Miguel Hidalgo dam built in 1952–56 will be able to provide water to irrigate 230,000 hectares of land. In 1961 the long-dreamed-of transcontinental railway from Chihuahua was completed, thereby opening markets in the centre and east of the U.S.A. to early vege-tables for the Fuerte valley (see Figure 5-2).

The new and expanded agricultural possibilities in the Fuerte have given rise to cotton, sugar and rice becoming important crops, with tomatoes of secondary importance. Agricultural reorganization following the agrarian reform and the later increase in area under cultivation has allowed not only improved possibilities for the existing rural workers but also a variety of opportunities in the newly irrigated lands and in the rapidly growing regional trade centres for immigrants from other parts of Mexico. The Fuerte valley is not only a colonization project but rather an integrated regional develop-ment plan (like those of Papaloapan in Southern Mexico, the Cauca valley project in Colombia and the Guayana project in Venezuela) which seeks not only to improve existing agriculture, but also to help new farmers get started and to develop new urban centres.

A complex system of land tenure has resulted. In the Fuerte valley in 1960, 110 thousand hectares were in *ejidos* (with 13,800 members) while 75·3 thousand hectares were farmed by 2,700 private farmers. The latter are mem-bers of a new, increasingly affluent middle class who are progressive commer-cial farmers and live in the new towns rather than in isolated farmsteads. Many *ejidatarios* rent out their land (illegally) to the private farmers, share-crop land and even work as labourers on their own rented land, but others are successful farmers. The central *ejido* villages have some basic amenities but lack the activity and commercial vigour of the new towns such as Guasave. Furthermore, through historical accident they often have some of the least desirable land. Incomes have risen markedly for many in this area; the increasing dynamism of the regional society and economy has encouraged young people to stay and has provided a new range of opportunities for all the inhabitants.

2. The Puyo Area, Ecuador: Haphazard Roadside Colonization

Colonization in Ecuador has traditionally been left to would-be colonists rather than organized by the national government. The only major highway into the eastern lowlands in the early 1960s was that from Baños to Shell Mera and Puyo, and colonization was concentrated in this area. (Plates XI and XII). More recently the Loja–Zamora-Gualaquiza road has stimulated colonization in the foothills of the southern Andes (see Figure 5-3).

In Ecuador unused land belongs to the state and can be obtained by petitioners who pay a price varying between 10 p and 50 p a hectare according to the desirability and accessibility of the land. The plots are surveyed for the title to be registered and the purchaser has full ownership of the land only when he has paid the price in full. In addition he is required to clear at least one-quarter of the land within five years. People who in 1962 had settled along the newest part of the road, north from Puyo towards Tena, were predominantly folk from the small sierra towns, people such as small shopkeepers and market stallholders. It was they who had some spare money and the necessary individual enterprise to hack out a clearing in the jungle for their own farm. Puyo, which was reached by road in 1947, was the centre of the colonization zone and had something of the air of a frontier town in the American West. Colonists were growing crops predominantly for sale rather than for subsistence and they had money enough to stimulate retail trade in Puyo and to encourage shops to spring up along the new road north. The schoolhouses built every 6 or so kilometres sometimes became new settlement nuclei and hamlets, such as Fátima, 7 kilometres from Puyo, which had 22 houses in 1962 and a number of shops. Many colonists had two houses, one on their land, which was often away from the road, and the other at points such as Fátima where social centres developed. Although sugar cane, from whose juice cane brandy *(aguardiente)* was distilled, was the most important crop, a new commercial crop was the *naranjilla* (a yellow, sweet, tomato-like fruit) the juice of which is highly esteemed throughout Ecuador. Smallholdings do not predominate in the new agricultural zone and a number of small estates have been created, with absentee owners, run by a manager and employing labourers who earn several times the equivalent daily wage of the *sierra*.

The Puyo area has many of the characteristics typical of a zone of spontaneous settlement. The highway has been the prime motivator of settlement and the majority of new farms are within 5–10 kilometres of the road. All the new farmers are producing cash crops although only a limited range. The majority of services are provided largely by the colonists themselves and Puyo and smaller centres such as Fátima are no less successful for being spontaneously developed rather than carefully planned.

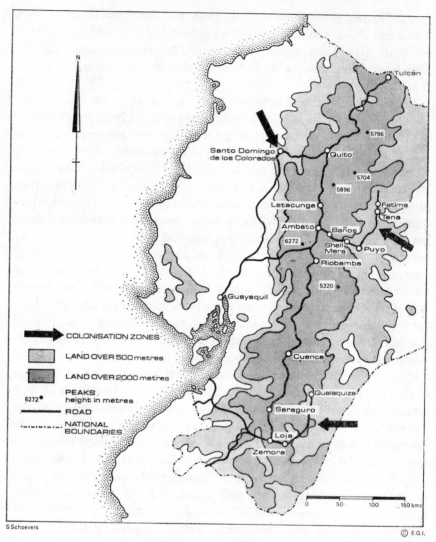

Figure 5–3. Ecuador: colonization zones

3. *The Alto Beni, Bolivia: Planned Colonization on the Cheap*

Settlement in the lowland valleys east of La Paz has continued for several centuries but only recently has it penetrated well into the forest beyond the foothills of the Andes. (Plate XIII.) Much of this settlement has been spontaneous along well-used trails that later became roads. The completion of the highway from La Paz to Caranavi in 1958 encouraged further migration to this zone even though only limited areas along the highway south of Caranavi were cultivable. Part of this zone, beyond Caranavi on the right bank of the Beni river, was selected as one of Bolivia's largest projects for directed colonization since the 1952 Revolution (Figure 5-1). In Bolivia however, the control over the direction of colonization is less all-embracing than in, say, Peru. Little selection of colonists takes place with the result that as many as half find themselves ill-suited to the environment and abandon their holdings. By the end of 1968 a total of 1,464 colonists had settled on land through the agency of the Alto Beni project. Many others had settled spontaneously and in association with other projects in the same region. An interesting indication of the different attitudes of spontaneous and planned colonists is that while the former have repaid 92 per cent of loans made to them by the Agrarian Bank the latter have barely repaid 20 per cent.

Situated 500 metres above sea level, the area is estimated to have some 8–9,000 hectares of good soils where few limitations on cropping practices are necessary. The area is particularly well suited to cacao production and the cultivation of citrus fruit is also particularly profitable. A major difficulty facing many colonists is getting their goods to the nearest highway. The main highway to La Paz is itself often blocked by rockfalls during the wet season and there are relatively few feeder roads. Cost of transportation is high and a complex and generally inefficient marketing system causes maize, for example, to be sold in La Paz for three times its price in the Alto Beni.

Many of the problems that face the settlers in the Alto Beni project are related to the inadequate infrastructure of roads, services and living conditions that they have to depend on. Poor local communications make the work of the few social and agricultural extension workers exceedingly difficult and this further discourages the faint-hearted and may be a contributory factor to the high drop-out rate of colonists. The increasing use of co-operatives, in particular an agricultural co-operative geared to selling cacao established as a result of British technical assistance, is beneficial because not only does it enable colonists to get good prices for their produce but also because it encourages local solidarity and provides an organization within which social bonds can be formed.

The low cost of the Alto Beni scheme, only about U.S. $1,350 per family, is a result of providing little more than roads, land and technical assistance with agriculture. Other agencies provide haphazard assistance and advice relating to sanitation, education and housing. It may be a result of the limited provision of services that many colonists leave, but even if a colonist quits his land other later colonists can make use of what has initially been achieved.

Each of these three areas represents some of the difficulties faced by colonists in Latin America and different approaches to the successful settlement of farmers who, it is hoped, will produce more goods for national and international markets. Successful colonization depends as much on the nature of the individual colonist as it does on the methods by which he is settled or the problems that his new environment poses him. It is in no way true to imagine that the main problem facing settlers from the mountains is the fearsome gloom of the forest and the unhealthy conditions. Many colonists overcome these problems but many more fail for a multitude of other reasons, a number of which are more associated with the personality of the colonist than environmental or administrative difficulties.

MIGRATION TO BIG CITIES

In all countries of the world an increasing proportion of the population is living in towns and cities. Except for newly established towns, it is the big cities that are growing most rapidly. Nowhere is this more true than in Latin America, where we have already seen that an unusually high proportion of the urban population in almost all countries is concentrated in one or two cities. A large proportion of the population of these big cities was not born there, in Lima almost half the population was born elsewhere than in the city, and immigration has played an important part in their physical expansion. In this section we shall examine the particular nature of urbanward migration in Latin America, and particularly the impact of the high rate of immigration on the city centre reception areas and the peripheral squatter settlements.

The study of migration in a wide variety of situations has led to the formulation of theories that attempt to explain a large proportion of migratory movements. It is necessary to review these theories in order that urbanward migration in Latin America may be seen in the context of migration in general. The most widely established theory indicates that migration decreases directly proportional to distance. Thus most migratory movements are short and very few are over long distances. Classic work in Sweden illustrates this very well. However it is immediately apparent that an important number of migrants move far beyond the orbit of the area in which they have grown up, and it is necessary to explain this. One such attempt is Samuel Stouffer's theory of 'intervening opportunities and competing migrants' which suggests that migration between two localities is in part a function of the number of intervening opportunities for migrants and the number of other migrants coming into the same area. In many ways this is an unsatisfactory concept partly because of the varying and often inadequate definitions of the two crucial terms 'opportunity' and 'competing migrants'. At a very simple level however it can readily be appreciated that the number of opportunities for migrants, which directly relates to population size, is greatest in the few large cities of Latin America and this may in a large measure explain this urbanward migration. One hypothesis, which has been inadequately discussed and evaluated, but which is especially relevant to urbanward migration in Latin America, holds that immigration to a location is in part a function of the number of migrants already there.

Who are the Migrants and Where are They From?

A stereotyped view of migrants to big cities is that they are all poor rural people but hard facts do not always bear this out. It may be true to say that the majority of migrants to big cities are from smaller towns and that many rural migrants go to the newer and rapidly expanding towns such as Chimbote in Peru or Volta Redonda in Brazil. In squatter settlements in Buenos Aires it was found that half the migrants came from large towns and in Santiago, Chile, 65 per cent of migrants to the city came from towns with more than 5,000 inhabitants. In Lima however, while some people have suggested that many of the migrants do come from rural areas, a recent investigation showed that 61 per cent of Lima migrants had had some secondary education which suggests that they came from towns rather than the countryside. Some support for the theory that migrants prefer to travel short distances comes from a study of the origins of migrants to the Lima area which showed that the provinces bordering on Lima supplied the majority of migrants.

Where, on the other hand, migration is the result of a natural calamity, large numbers of predominantly rural people move en masse to the nearest cities. The most dramatic example of this is the migration of hunger-driven people *(flagelados)* from the arid north-eastern interior of Brazil when one of the periodic droughts occurs. Dozens of lorries come into the interior to transport people directly, and often for extortionate prices, to the large cities such as São Salvador or Rio de Janeiro in order to find a job and money to live from. Although many return as soon as there is news that the rains

8*

have come, others remain behind and the North East is as renowned for its export of migrants as is Scotland. Although this phenomenon on such a scale is uncommon in Latin America it does account for some periodic migration at irregular intervals and the drought that hit the Central Andes in the late 1960s also caused an increase in the flow of migrants to nearby cities.

Many migrants moving to a city are following the earlier movement of a relative or friend with whom they stay while they establish themselves. This follows closely in the pattern of international migrants; for example Commonwealth migrants coming to British cities and Puerto Ricans coming to New York customarily find accommodation with relatives in a district already crowded with people from the same area.

The cities which migrants select are generally the largest, most prosperous or the most rapidly expanding centres. Centres such as Mexico City, or Mexicali in Mexico, Cali, or Medellín in Colombia and Caracas or Maracaibo in Venezuela. Transport to these centres seldom presents a problem since the importance of the cities is such that buses and lorries travel to them with great frequency and charge relatively low fares.

There is often a predominance of women among migrants and most migrants are aged between 19 and 35. They are frequently frustrated by the limited range of opportunities available for permanent or casual employment at home. Many highlanders obtain money for special occasions by going away to work in the city or in the lowland sugar or cotton estates for a period of several months and this transitory experience gives them a view of the different opportunities available elsewhere. For young men, military service is a further opportunity to get to know other parts of the country and thus learn of the advantages of life in a new area.

Migrants in the Big City

In many Latin American cities migrants collect in distinct areas of the city and at a later stage move out of the initial reception zone into other areas. When migrants first arrive they have only limited money to invest in a home and to start a business or to continue their education. They thus live in the poorest conditions alongside others in a similar predicament. Many are single men or women, whose families have not yet joined them, and thus they rent a room or live in cheap lodging houses where an average of three or four people may occupy each room. Areas where migrants first arrive may properly be termed slums since their population is transient and there is a high incidence of extreme poverty, crime and other indications of social disorganization. Many of the families correspond to the picture of the slum dwellers of

Rio de Janeiro, San Juan, Puerto Rico and Mexico City portrayed in recent documentary books. Gradations exist naturally between the cardboard shacks on the edge of railway lines or rivers and the concrete rabbit-warrens of the city centre peripheries.

Socially then, the internal slums are characterized by a highly mobile and unstable population, by high densities of population and often by containing a large proportion of people who have moved in to the city from outside. The location of such areas follows a clearly recognizable pattern (Figure 5-4). Areas of arrival: docks, rail terminals, bus stations and wholesale marketing centres (where long-distance lorries arrive) are all favoured sites where immigrant quarters develop, although clearly it is improbable that in every city each one of these locations will provide a site for an area inhabited by migrants. In some areas the urban plan of square city blocks may allow an empty area in the centre of each one where rooms can be cheaply built around the courtyard, which thus shrinks to become an alleyway, giving rise in one instance in Lima to 158 people living in 30 rooms in an area the size of a North American city houseplot. There is a striking similarity between these conditions and those in the courtyard slums built by property developers in industrial cities in Northern England during the early 19th century.

If the migrants cluster first in the crowded conditions of the slum areas that frequently surround the centres of large cities, many seek to improve their conditions as quickly as possible and move to a more salubrious area. Municipal and national housing authorities in Latin America seldom have the money necessary to provide either land or houses for the rapidly expanding urban population. Migrants and others have therefore to take matters into their own hands to obtain housing outside the city centre slums. Throughout Latin America squatter settlements have developed on the periphery of the large cities and none can claim to be quite free of squatter settlements or their equivalent. In Lima maybe 500,000 people, or 20 per cent of the population, live in squatter settlements; in Mexico City as many as 2 million people live in peripheral squatter settlements; in Venezuela half the inhabitants of Maracaibo and one-third of those in Caracas live in such settlements. In La Paz, Bolivia, the agrarian reform of 1953 resulted in the ownership of the barren hillside surrounding the city being passed to the municipality and the people who have built homes on the slopes have been given title to the land that they occupy upon completion of a minimum of formalities; they are thus not squatters in law although their settlements are not physically or socially dissimilar.

The squatter settlements are almost invariably on the edge of the town and

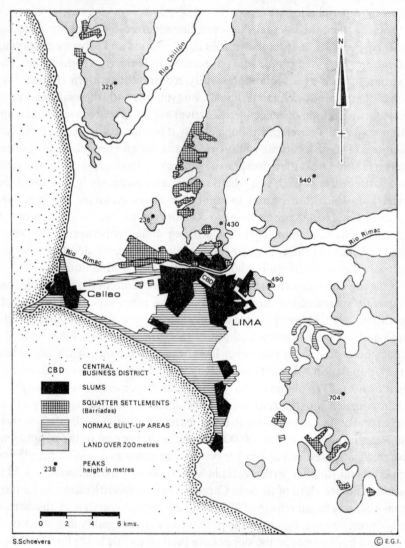

S.Schoevers   © E.G.I.

Figure 5–4. Lima: slums and squatter settlements

where land is unused. Thus in Lima the steep hillsides above the level of the surrounding irrigated areas, previously completely unused, are the most commonly occupied squatter zones. In Caracas vacant land sometimes several miles from the city centre is used; in Rio steep land, held to be unsuitable for the provision of water and sewage facilities, was left free from commercial development and consequently invaded by the poor seeking land on which to build a home. Squatting requires organization since overnight an area must be settled by large numbers of people (over 1000 families in many cases in Lima) who must occupy clearly defined plots and establish dwellings at once, no matter how flimsy. Eviction becomes thus more difficult. The organization necessary for this action results in a high degree of social responsibility which augurs well for the future social action which is necessary to establish schools and other social services. Where sites are sufficiently large, streets are marked out and each family allocated a plot. Vacant plots are left for schools, markets, infirmaries etc. and for municipal buildings around a central square. House styles change with time as cardboard, matting or tin shacks are replaced by houses with mud-brick walls and glass windows. Later, houses are plastered and the exterior painted and maybe an extra storey built to accommodate a growing family.

The squatter settlements develop an urban economic pattern of their own as markets grow and shops develop. Central areas become identified where the larger general stores are and where the central community services are located. Beyond these central areas are smaller nuclei where groups of two or three shops occur on a street intersection and where maybe a bus service starts. On the periphery of the squatter settlement are the newest houses where recent arrivals may be establishing themselves beyond where the original settlement was laid out. Communications with the distant city centre improve to permit a rapid if uncomfortable journey to work.

A socio-geographical phenomenon which is frequently found in both slums and peripheral settlements is the regional association. This is an organization that embraces migrants who have come from the same area. Thus in La Paz, Bolivia, there is an Association of Huarinos, people who all come from Huarina, a small town two hours drive from La Paz. Such associations seek to promote the interests of their home community in the city; they send back money and other gifts to help improvement projects at home, and they petition the government to initiate such projects. They also have a thriving social life, develop sports clubs with football, volleyball or baseball teams and aim to help people from the area to get to know each other, and to settle down in the new environment. In this way many migrants develop a set of friendships in the city with people from the same home area and thus many squatter settlements are composed of people from one particular part of the country, or a series of groups from different parts of the same area.

Because of the degree of organization that is associated with the newer settlements of the migrants they contain few of the elements of social disorganization and deviance which characterize the central city slums. Thus migrants, whose numbers have been rapidly increasing during the last forty years, have occupied distinct parts of cities and the urban sprawl associated with a rapid increase in city size has not merely resulted in the suburbanization that is familiar in western Europe or north-eastern Anglo-America but also in the creation of large areas of new squatter settlements on the edge of the cities.

The Deserted Villages

A writer describing a rural community in southern Peru described it as 'the orphan of its illustrious children'. It was a village many of whose younger people had left and gone to work in the cities. The reasons for this movement are largely self-evident. The rural community affords limited opportunities for employment, social or economic advancement or for contact with the main currents of national life. Those who migrate are thus those who, for a variety of personal reasons, feel this limitation of opportunity most severely.

The effect of migration to the reception areas—the cities—is widely known and outlined in the previous section but the effects of migration on the rural areas from which the migrants come is less often studied. It seems reasonable to suppose that some of the problems such as shortage of land that give rise to emigration are in part affected by this migration. If land is in short supply, when people move away this should automatically mean that there is more land available for those who remain. In fact migrants seldom relinquish their land and prefer to leave it to be sharecropped by a relative. Each year at harvest time many people return from the cities to their native community to help with the harvest and to claim their share. Thus although there is more land available to the stay-at-homes the amount is a good deal less than might be expected and, since they only sharecrop it, they have less freedom of action.

A vital aspect of the rural emigration is that it is as much a 'brain drain' as the movement of British or Latin American scientists to Anglo-America. Many of those who leave the rural communities are among the most dynamic and progressive members. Moreover, they are predominantly young and their loss means that older people become numerically more important in the community and, broadly speaking, resistance to change increases with age. Thus by losing its brighter young people a community is seriously handicapped and its resistance to change may increase. Possibly this will not be true in some cases because the migrants maintain contact with their home community, return regularly and may bring back new ideas which can stimulate change and thus allow rural living standards to improve. In fact this happens only rarely. Migrants going to a big city learn little that relates to farming in their home area: even those going to lowland banana or sugar plantations to work learn only about crops which cannot be grown in the mountains. Their influence is more noticeable in the changing patterns of consumption and living in the villages. Sons and daughters may send money home to their parents, on visits they bring factory-made cloth and transistor radios or a kerosene pressure lamp, and the regional organizations in the cities may send money or materials for a new school or a new roof for the church.

One important result of emigration is that it in turn stimulates further migration. A large proportion of migrants stay with relatives or with friends from the same community when they go to the city and thus a community from which many have migrated has a lot of links with cities which can be used by new migrants. Thus while some communities lose few people as migrants, others may lose over half of the adult population. The geographical pattern of such migration shows that it is generally those communities which have easiest access to cities which lose most people, although periodic physical hazards, such as drought, floods, earthquakes, can cause considerable migration from the affected area. With the increase in number of migrants, what was previously a problem of underemployment, too few jobs and too many people wanting work, has been replaced by a shortage of labour. Women have to do a man's work in the fields and estates have to pay more to attract day labourers.

Clearly migration could have a better effect in rural areas if more aid could be given to rural communities to help them intensify their agriculture. It is ridiculous to imagine that rural emigration to cities is a 'bad' thing and therefore something to be discouraged. If more and better opportunities existed or were created in rural areas fewer people would leave. Even if the squatter settlements of Bogotá or Buenos Aires seem appalling to European eyes it is important to realize that their conditions represent a marked improvement in living for their inhabitants. The aim of this chapter has been to show how the countryside and the city have been changing. Emigration, colonization and the giving of titles to the landless all result not only in movements of individuals but also in a new man–land relationship, the development of a new ecological niche and a new pattern of living. Each of these changes reflects a desire of individuals to improve their lot. The nature of these changed man–environment relations is central to the concern of geographers and the future changes in these spheres will continue to occupy their attention.

Bibliography

Land Reform

UNITED NATIONS, *Progress in Land Reform, Fourth Report*, United Nations, New York, 1967.
A highly informative account of the current state of land reform in a wide range of countries with useful comparative tables.

WARRINER, D., *Land Reform in Principle and in Practice*, Oxford University Press, London, 1969.
A stimulating, informative, critical and intelligent analysis of the meanings and purposes of land reforms in different situations by a scholar with a huge breadth of experience of land reform. Studies of land reform in Latin American countries are included.

SEERS, D. (Ed.) *Cuba: the Economic and Social Revolution*, University of North Carolina Press, Chapel Hill, 1964.
A valuable and well-documented study of aspects of post-Castro Cuba by a group of economists.

PATCH, R. W., 'Bolivia: U.S. assistance in a revolutionary setting', in Council on Foreign Relations, *Social Change in Latin America Today*, Vintage Books paperback, New York, 1960, pp. 108–176.
An excellent general account of the events associated with the 1952 Revolution and associated land reform in Bolivia.

PRESTON, D. A., 'The revolutionary landscape of highland Bolivia', *Geographical Journal*, **155**, 1–16, (1969.)
An account of the changes in land use, settlement pattern and land tenure in highland Bolivia.

Colonization

DREWES, W. U., *Economic Development of the Western Montaña of Peru*, Peruvian Times, Lima, 1958.
An important contribution to knowledge about the importance of communications in the effective settlement and development of remote areas.

DOZIER, C. L., *Land Development and Colonization in Latin America: Case Studies of Peru, Bolivia and Mexico*, Praeger, New York, 1969.
Useful although superficial studies of colonization schemes in the three named countries.

DOZIER, C. L., 'Mexico's transformed north-west: the Yaqui, Mayo and Puerte examples', *Geographical Review*, **53**, 548–571, (1963).
An interesting and revealing comparative analysis of three different colonization areas in western Mexico.

CASAGRANDE, J. B. and others, 'Colonization as a research frontier: the Ecuadorean case', in R. A. Manners (Ed.), *Process and Pattern in Culture*, Aldine Press, Chicago, 1964, pp. 281–325.
An account of social phenomena associated with settlement in the Puyo-Tena zone of Ecuador of considerable interest to those concerned with how the colonists subsist.

Rural–urban migration

PRESTON, D. A., 'Rural emigration in Andean America', *Human Organization*, **28**, 279–86, (1969).
Statement of the range of problems that arise in rural communities as a result of the tide of migration of people heading for the cities.

PATCH, R. W., 'Life in a *callejón*', *American Universities Fields Staff Report*, **8**, No. 6, (1961).
Absorbing semi-fictional account of what happens to rural folk who arrive in the big city, in this case Lima.

DE JESUS, C. M., *Beyond All Pity*, Four Square Paperbacks, London, 1965.
The account of her life by a decidedly bitchy Rio slum dweller. Great literary success in Brazil and useful as an account of how people get by in the slums.

TURNER, J. C., 'Dwelling resources in Latin America', *Architectural Design*, **33**, 360–393 (1963).
Stimulating article on the housing problems of shanty town dwellers largely based on the author's experience as a consulting architect to the Peruvian Government in Lima. The same issue contains many photographs as well as other articles of interest.

MANGIN, W., 'Latin America's squatter settlements', *Latin American Research Review*, **2**, 65–98 (1957).
An important summary statement of present knowledge about squatter settlements in Latin American countries. Contains a valuable bibliography.

MANGIN, W., 'The role of regional associations in the adaptation of the rural population of Peru', *Sociologus*, **9**, 21–36 (1959).
An account of the work of the regional organizations in a rapidly growing city.

Major Themes in Latin America's Economic Geography

by

PETER R. ODELL

Part II

Major Themes in Latin America's Economic Geography

Peter R. Odell

CHAPTER 6

Antecedents to the Contemporary Geography of Economic Activity

The geographical patterns of any contemporary economy are only in part a function of the economic, social, political and other forces currently at work in shaping decisions on the location of new economic activities. A major constraint on any locational decision, whether taken by an individual, an entrepreneur, a corporation or a government, is the pre-existing situation. The way in which this constraint operates can be seen, for example, in decision making on the location of new steel-making capacity. Any contemporary evaluation of a maximum profit location for such capacity, taking into account transport charges on raw materials and finished products and land and labour costs in different locations, would usually produce a recommendation for a coastal site with access to deep water and with plenty of flat land on which to build a modern, well-designed plant. But such recommendations are often negated when the alternative of providing the new capacity by extending an existing plant is considered. Though the existing location may mean higher cost in terms of transport, land and labour, the unfavourable effects of these on the location decision can be more than offset by the savings possible through the economies of scale and other economies (in administration, energy consumption etc.) inherent to a decision to expand *in situ*. In other words, past decisions on location affect the new decision.

In the long term, all societies build up a set of traits which become entrenched in national geographical thinking and which thus influence every new locational decision. In the United Kingdom, for example, the 'north' is traditionally considered to be the 'industrial part' of the country. Though it has, in fact, lost many of the 18th and 19th century advantages it had for industrial development, the impact of this traditional view is powerful enough to persuade governments that they should pursue policies designed to have

117

industry located there, rather than in its areas of preference further south. Thus, any consideration of the location of what is, or even of what will be, can only be interpreted in the light of what has gone before. This applies universally but one can argue that it applies particularly strongly in Latin America where most societies are so well-structured and so conservative that they lack the dynamism of more open societies such as those of the U.S. and Western Europe. Such societal structures in Latin America are mirrored in the geographical inertia which inhibits change in the use of the land and in the reshaping of the geographical patterns of activities.

Pre-Columbian America

Present spatial patterns of economic activity can even be correlated to some degree with the 'economic geography' of the continent in the pre-Columbian period. It has been shown by Steward and Faron (see Bibliography) that in the period before the Conquest there were significant spatial variations in the relative intensity of the use of the land. These arose not only out of contrasts in the physical environmental conditions of different areas but also from the existence of contrasting groups of people variously equipped to make use of the development opportunities offered. These contrasts produced an uneven distribution of the population. For South America alone, estimates of the population at the time of the Conquest range from 8·4 to 75 million but latest scholarship indicates that it was much nearer to the lower estimate and a figure of just over 10 million now appears to be generally accepted. Of this total some 60 % were concentrated into Andean valleys where densities were far above the continental average. Figure 6-1 is based on estimates made by Steward and Faron of the distribution of population in South America at the time of the Spanish Conquest.

Several reasons have been suggested for this heavy concentration of population in the Andean region. First, the existence there of a wide range of altitudes and climates which offered favourable conditions for a broadly based pattern of food production. Second, the existence of soils less subject to destructive leaching than those of the tropical rain forest. Third, the availability of adequate water and of organizational expertise and ability to make irrigation possible. Fourth, the possibility of access to the offshore guano deposits (used for fertilizers) which were imperially controlled by the Incas, whose empire at the time of the Conquest included all this region.

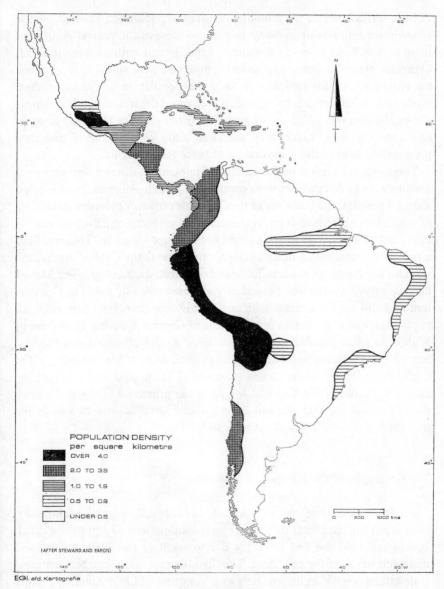

POPULATION DENSITY
per square kilometre

OVER 4.0

2.0 TO 3.9

1.0 TO 1.9

0.5 TO 0.9

UNDER 0.5

(AFTER STEWARD AND FARON)

0   500   1000 kms

EGI. afd. Kartografie

Figure 6–1.   South and Central America: population densities at the time of the
Conquest

A little farther north, the middling-densities of population marked the use of environments similar in many respects to those of the central Andes but in an area without access to the guano deposits and with societies less well organized than the Incas. The societies, however, were still able to produce an economic surplus sufficient to keep the population above subsistence levels and, therefore, able to expand. Throughout the rest of South America, the population was made up of scattered tribal groups. These survived in environments over which they exercised little or no control and they produced little or nothing beyond subsistence requirements.

These general aspects of the pattern of population distribution and contrasting economic activities were repeated in Middle America. In this region the total population at the time of the Conquest probably exceeded 20 million, of which more than half, it has been estimated (see Simpson), lived in what is now Central Mexico under the control of the Aztec kingdom. This area had a density of population somewhat higher than that in the Central Andes and was also dependent on a successful system of irrigated agriculture. The Mayan civilization of Yucatan was numerically and economically much less important and still smaller societies with post-subsistence economies formed small population nuclei in certain upland areas of Central America. Elsewhere in Middle America population was in scattered groups of subsistence peoples. Some were sedentary and relatively numerous, as with the Arawaks of the Caribbean islands; whilst others practised shifting cultivation at best, or nomadic hunting, collecting and fishing at the other end of the scale. They thinly peopled the arid areas to the north of central Mexico as well as the tropical fringes of the Middle American land area.

The Geography of the European Colonization

All this would be of interest primarily to historical geographers, however, were it not for the effects that this geographical pattern of population distribution and land use had upon the development of the Spanish Conquest and occupation of the continent. The Spanish expansion into the continent is described somewhat inaccurately as a 'conquest of Latin America': rather more accurately it can be described as a conquest of the *peoples* of Latin America. The distinction has implications for the determination of the main areas of Spanish interest within the continent. Initial Spanish interests lay in the Caribbean, but the relative lack there both of an indigenous population and of precious metals, made it mainly an area of short-lived interest only; except in terms of the need for bases within the region through which trade between Spain and the more important colonies could pass.

It was the two pre-existing civilizations of the Aztecs and the Incas that so enthused the Conquistadores and their successors. In Central Mexico and the Central Andes respectively, these two civilizations offered not only the labour that the Spanish wanted in large quantities to exploit the areas within which they settled, but also wealth in the form of precious metals and workable and worked land. Their knowledge of both mining and agriculture was to enable the Spanish to build up their level of economic activities in their newly won colonies very quickly. Decimation of the Indian population in the process was of concern to the new civilization mainly because it threatened to denude the continent of the labour essential to the success of the Spanish colonial enterprise. However, in the main areas in which the Spanish took an interest, sufficient of the Indians survived to enable the economic system to work effectively for a considerable period. This availability of Indians as a labour force became almost a *sine qua non* for the development of different parts of the continent.

Thus, under Spanish colonial rule, the spatial pattern of economic development depended by and large upon the pre-existing situation, with use being made of only a few other parts of the vast extent of the continent nominally under Spanish control. The centres of government of the Spanish Viceroyalties were established at Mexico City and Lima and were essentially successor capitals to those of the Aztec and Inca civilizations respectively. Mexico City was built on exactly the same site as the Aztec capital which it replaced, whilst Lima was established on the coastal plain to the west of the Central Andes where the Rimac river and its valley provided a water supply, a harbour and a means of access to the mountain region in which the Inca capital had been built. Moreover, in this new location Spanish experience with low-altitude irrigation agriculture could be put to good use and from it the offshore guano deposits were even more accessible. Elsewhere, Spanish towns were established where Indians were thickest on the ground and where, in many cases, there was already some pre-existing form of urban settlement. Bogóta, Guatemala City, Quito are good examples of this type of development. Around such cities the Spanish settlers, administrators and military personnel participated in or supervised the development of agriculture and the continued search for precious and semi-precious metals.

The Spanish systems of government, of land tenure and of control over the Indians were basically functions of the economic motivations for their settlements, the development of which represented the major feature of the geography of Spanish economic activities in the continent. This had its corollary,

of course, in the virtual absence of any significant early Spanish development in areas of less important or non-existent Indian activities. The most
outstanding example of an area of very little early Spanish influence was that
of the whole of the southern part of South America where, as we saw earlier
in Figure 6-1, there was little pre-Columbian development of the temperate
grasslands and of areas even further south. This pre-Columbian emptiness
was mirrored in a lack of Spanish attention to what is now Uruguay, Paraguay and Argentina. Only at a later stage in their colonial history when they
were obliged to defend the small outposts of Empire they had created, at places
like Buenos Aires and Asunción, from the dangers of Portuguese expansionism from bases further north along the east coast of the continent, was
their level of interest increased. Even then little effort was made to exploit the
resources of the vast region which remained dependent on Lima even for its
contacts with Spain. Spanish interests also largely failed to seek out opportunities east of the Andean divide in areas further north for there, too, there
were few Indians and no readily usable land. Thus, throughout this region at
a later period in its development, Brazil was able to expand its national
frontiers to take in territory that had been made nominally Spanish by the
Treaty of Tordesillas. In Central America neither the resources of Indians
nor those of metals were sufficient to justify other than a limited development
of the area and Spanish activities there remained, as in the Caribbean islands
to an even greater extent, at a relatively low level.

There were, of course, a few important exceptions to this geographical correlation of Spanish interests with pre-existing Indian activities. Perhaps the
most important was Panama City, the most influential Spanish settlement
between Mexico and Lima, in an area which had been virtually devoid of
Indians. But Panama was essentially a strategic and trading city responsible,
until a much later stage in the colonial history of Latin America, for the
transhipment of goods between Lima and Spain. In its rapid emergence to a
role of economic importance, as a result of the first political and commercial
links between Latin America and the Old World, lies a first hint of the later,
and even greater, economic and strategic importance of this 'crossroads-of-
the-world' location.

Another example was Santiago de Chile. This was an outpost of Empire
as far as Spain was concerned and was one which rose to importance only in
part because of the attractive environment in which it was located. The region
around Santiago consisted mainly of the type of land on which the Spanish
system of land tenure could most effectively be established and it had a climate
not dissimilar to that of Southern Spain, thus making familiar agricultural

ECONOMIC GEOGRAPHY: ITS ANTECEDENTS

practices possible. In part, too, its growth resulted from the military function which it fulfilled in a frontier region where the Indians were the only ones never to be conquered by the Spanish in the whole of their area of interest in the continent. The combination of these two factors led to Santiago being developed as an important nucleus of Spanish settlement and activity.

The limited extent of Spanish migration to Latin America following the Conquest, together with the continued dominance of the motivations already described for Spanish rule in the continent, meant that succeeding decades in Spanish America produced few fundamental changes in the basic pattern of the continent's economic geography. The Spanish American Empire had its economic base in the production of high-value minerals with the limited local profits from this being mainly invested in the development of the main administrative centres such as Mexico and Lima. The mining activities also produced the growth of more local but still significant urbanization including such important 'silver' towns as Potosí, in present-day Bolivia, and Taxco, some 120 kilometres to the south west of Mexico City. The cities themselves produced a demand for commercial agricultural products but such influences were felt only within a very limited radius of the main centres of population. Outside these limited zones of more intensive agricultural development around the cities, 'agriculture' was organized, in general, on the basis of the hacienda system within which the non-economic motivations were stronger than those of an economic character. Thus the hacendados followed up their ownership of land only, in the main, to establish their prestige and their position in the hierarchy. As a result, commercial agriculture failed to develop to any large extent in response to possible economic opportunities presented by external markets. There were some minor exceptions to this, and locally they produced significant developments. One good example was the commercial production of indigo in favourable (viz. near coastal) locations in Middle America. Another example, on a somewhat larger scale, was expansion in the production of sugar—again mainly in the Caribbean area—for sale in the expanding markets in Western Europe. But this first of the great plantation crops of Latin America was, in fact, more effectively developed in those parts of the continent outside Spanish control.

The Portuguese settlement of Brazil was always more broadly economically motivated than the Spanish conquest of the rest of Latin America. In particular, the way in which the Portuguese colonies were organized did at least allow for the possibility of individuals making effective economic use of the territory which they were awarded by the Crown. Moreover, Brazil did not have much of the mineral wealth which was financing development elsewhere in the continent. This, coupled with a much less urban-oriented outlook on the part of the Portuguese settlers in contrast with their Spanish counterparts, produced a need and a desire on the part of the colonists to use their lands for agricultural products which could be exported back to Western Europe. Thus, the coastal fringe of Brazil was developed as an area of relatively intensive land use under the stimulus of export potentials for tropical crops from the markets of Europe. For such crops, especially sugar which was introduced in 1552, the favourable environmental conditions of the region gave it a comparative advantage over competing areas.

But an even greater response to the existence of European markets for sugar and other tropical products emerged in the case of those limited parts of Latin America which fell to the domination of other European powers. The most important example of this arose from the agricultural enterprise of the Dutch in the coastal fringes of the north-east corner of South America, where the economic motivation provided by the rapidly growing European markets for sugar lay behind their expansionist ventures into territory which was nominally Portuguese. Having extended their area of influence from the region of the present-day Guianas to coastal areas well to the south of the mouth of the Amazon, they set about the exploitation of the suitable climatic and soil characteristics of the region for large scale sugar production (by Latin American colonial standards). In the Caribbean itself they were rivalled by the enterprise of the British whose political colonization successes there were quickly followed by the commercial exploitation of islands such as Jamaica and Barbados etc.

At a later period (from the mid-19th century onwards) plantation agriculture was to become an important element in the land-use patterns and economic systems of Latin America. The antecedents to the development can be seen in these early colonial efforts to exploit the agricultural export potential of parts of the continent. The fact that Britain and Holland, and the British and Dutch colonies, thrived as a result of this activity was as much a function of the Spanish lack of interest in such matters as it was of the particular abilities of the nations concerned. Had Spain really been interested in developing the use of the land for commercial purposes, and had the organization of its colonial system made this possible, then Britain and Holland would have had a much harder fight to secure the positions they achieved. The plantations in their colonies might well have been much less effectively developed and less profitable than they were, as a result of competition from the same crops produced from the large areas of Spanish America which were environmentally suited to such developments.

Thus, by the time the colonial period came to an end in Latin America (that is, by the mid-19th century if we ignore the small remnants of the Spanish Empire in the Caribbean and also the relatively unimportant non-Iberian colonies in the Caribbean) there had been relatively little extension geographically of the areas of economic significance compared with the precolonial situation. Economic activities were, in the main, still concentrated around those areas which had enjoyed relatively high levels of development at the earlier period: Central Mexico and the Northern and Central Andean region. Though mining activities for gold, silver and other high-value minerals had been intensified, it is possible to argue, on the other hand, that the establishment of the Spanish hacienda system had had the opposite effect on the level of agricultural activities except in the zones of more intensive cultivation around the cities. The great decline in the numbers of Indians as a result of Spanish rule and European diseases had relieved population pressure on the land in areas which had previously had to provide sustenance for much larger numbers. Moreover, as shown previously, this pre-Columbian motivation for as intensive a land use as possible had not been substituted by any strong motivation for high agricultural productivity on the part of the Spanish landowners. Their holdings were sufficiently large to enable most of them to achieve an entirely satisfactory and acceptable standard of living without needing to put their land to anything like its fullest possible use. Nor were they under any effective obligation to Spain to produce agricultural exports.

Overall, therefore, the use of land in the Spanish Latin American Empire was a function of other than economic forces. Only elsewhere in the continent, where other colonial regimes were established, did economic motivations produce large new areas of agriculture on the largely coastally located development of tropical plantations whose products were orientated to the export markets.

The economic geographical effects of the colonial period had another facet arising from the fact that the continent's political system depended on the external relationships of the Latin American territories with their respective metropolitan powers. This necessitated locational developments orientated to this political situation. Hence the economies in most parts of the continent were organized, in spatial terms, around a coastally located most-important point of contact between the metropolitan power and the local administration. Thus one can argue that what would today be termed tertiary economic activities became, in most cases, concentrated in the main point of seagoing contact with the metropolitan power. When this point did not also happen to be the capital of a colony, its functions enabled it eventually to emerge as a rival centre of no little importance. One example, on a relatively small scale, is the establishment of Guayaquil as the port through which the audiencia city of Quito maintained its contacts with Spain. On a somewhat larger scale was the role of Veracruz, which served as the port for Mexico City, and which therefore began to rise to a high position of administrative and commercial importance. Panama City has already been mentioned in this respect and it, of course, had continental rather than local importance.

In cases where the capital city was near-coastal, the point of external contact was established at the nearest suitable coastal site with the port settlement functioning very much as a satellite town of the capital and specializing only in those activities which demanded a port location. The most outstanding example of this was Callao in its relationships with Lima and, to a lesser degree because of the greater distance between them, Valparaíso and Santiago in Chile. Maracay, the colonial capital of Venezuela, was also near enough to the coast to enable it to inhibit the growth of a port which could rival it in status. Later, however, one factor which enabled Caracas gradually to assert its dominance over the original colonial capital might well have been its greater degree of accessibility to the main coastal point of contact with Spain and the outside world, viz. La Guaira.

Elsewhere in South America, however, one notes two strongly contrasting spatial responses to the need for contact between colonies and the metropolitan power. The Colombian capital, Bogotá, was just about as isolated from the outside world as it was possible to get: a journey of well over a week by river and land transport from the Caribbean port of entry. In spite of this situation, however, Bogotá maintained its absolute supremacy in the economic, as well as the political and social life of the country, with the ports providing only the essential maritime services in much the same way as Callao did in Peru and Valparaíso in Chile. The ability of Bogotá to maintain its leading role in Colombia in this way is one of the still unexplained problems of the economic geography of the colonial period.

At the other extreme lies the great reversal in the geographical pattern of development in what now constitutes Argentina. As already pointed out, early Spanish interest in the lower River Plate region was very limited and though Buenos Aires was established in the 16th century, it languished at the end of a very long supply route coming over the Andes from Lima and down through a series of relatively fertile intermontane basins in what is now North-Western Argentina where cities such as Salta, Mendoza and Córdoba were founded and which for much of the colonial period far exceeded Buenos Aires in importance. This relative position in the status of the inland cities on the one hand and Buenos Aires on the other changed with the Spanish need to protect their claim to Argentina from the expansionist tendencies of the Portuguese in the direction of the River Plate estuary. As a result, Spanish interest in Buenos Aires was heightened. Initial military interest soon widened into other interests and permission was ultimately given for the city to trade directly with Spain across the Atlantic Ocean rather than continuing to trade across the continent via Lima. The continuing absence of much Spanish interest in the grassland areas behind Buenos Aires limited its potential for growth but, nevertheless, it was made an Audiencia city and it did become a transhipping point of minor importance for the southernmost parts of the Spanish Empire. These developments were sufficient to enable it to become the single most important settlement in the south of the continent and in the last half-century of the colonial period it had risen in importance and status beyond those of the previously more important inland Argentine cities.

Independence and the Geography of Economic Activities

Thus during the colonial period in Latin America economic development was geographically limited. It was from such limited areas of development that the newly independent Latin American states of the 19th century had to build their own national economies. It turned out in most cases, however, that the fundamental political change from colony to independent nation had only limited social and economic, and geographical, effects. The new rulers were almost invariably imbued with Spanish traditions and their interests lay in maintaining the structure of society as established and in which they usually occupied a privileged position. Thus ownership of land remained as a mark of social standing and not primarily as a means of making money. Moreover, ownership was so concentrated in a few hands that those that had land could make more than enough profits—still utilizing the low-cost labour which was part and parcel of the system—by a far less than complete use of the resources. Thus, even into the independence period one of the main reasons for the under-utilization of the continent's land resources continued to apply.

In one respect, however, independence did make one important difference even in this sector. As they became sovereign states each country had to make a choice in the economic strategy to follow. Each newly independent country had to decide whether to associate itself economically with a nineteenth-century world in which trading and other commercial interests were then expanding rapidly, or instead be content merely with what it could produce nationally, for, of course, Spain would no longer accept responsibility for providing imports within the framework of its own currency and exchange system. In fact, given a situation in which the national leaders of the new countries were already well used to the wealth and variety of an exchange economy and unlikely, therefore, to forgo the advantages stemming from such a system, a choice in favour of participation in the international economic system was fairly self-evident. Moreover, to hasten this choice of strategy along there were outside interests very anxious to get footholds in the economic systems of the newly independent states. Thus, the Independence period is marked by the beginnings of investment by foreign, non-Spanish entrepreneurs and companies anxious to make money out of exploiting the continent's resources required by the industrializing nations of North America and Western Europe. In doing so they thereby provided the Latin American nations with foreign exchange and domestic revenues so that the imports of consumer goods needed by the 'aristocracies' could be financed and, more important from the standpoint of the continent's economic geography, they also financed the development of elements of a modern, 19th century economic infrastructure, such as railways, public utilities and other aids to city life.

We shall return to examine, in more detail, the structure and geographical effects of this exploitative economy in the next chapter, rather than dealing with it here, for it is possible to argue that it does not form an antecedent to contemporary patterns of economic life but is, in fact, in many respects still part of the economic pattern on which the existing economic geography of the continent is based! At this point it will suffice to point out that amongst the phenomena involved in bringing about major change in the geography of the continent were activities such as the development of plantations, the building of the railways, the construction of ports, and the effects of the migration of large numbers of Europeans to Latin America (particularly to the southern part) so as to provide, in the main, the labour supply for the economic activities arising in the exploitative economy.

In the next chapter, moreover, we shall also try to differentiate between migration and settlement which was an integral part of the process of exploitations as defined, and that which was more closely related to pushing back the frontiers of the occupied territory as an objective in its own right on the part of some of the new nation-states. In respect of the latter development one thinks in terms of the attempts to extend the occupied area of Chile into the forested south using both domestically available manpower resources and foreign immigrants: or the settlement of Antioquia in Colombia: or agricultural expansion from the core area of San Juan in Costa Rica. Overall, however, we shall see these developments as having had a relatively minor impact on the geography of the continent compared with the much greater impact of resource exploitation for foreign trade purposes. Even this in its turn, however, with the exception of the development of the Pampas of Argentina and Uruguay for agriculture, still affected only relatively limited areas of the countries of the continent. Even by the middle of the 20th century the situation as far as most countries were concerned was still one in which most of them had the larger parts of their national territories either unused or underused: in marked contrast with the effects of exploitation and settlement in North America over the same period.

Finally, as an antecedent to contemporary patterns in the continent's economic geography one must note the effects of the emergence of the system of sovereign states. The political geography of this development is not our objective, but what does need to be emphasized here is the economic-geographical effect of such nationalism. As successor states to the Spanish Empire, almost all the new Latin American nations were bequeathed a highly centralized form of administration and a tradition of capital city living by the élite groups. Thus tertiary economic activities were usually concentrated almost exclusively on the capital city, or, at best, and in a few cases, on one or more cities in addition. This spatial concentration of non-agricultural activities within nations established the first conditions for the emergence of the modern imbalance between regions in the Latin American nations. In this respect, therefore, the historical accidents of the emergence of states and the choice of their capitals have been important economic geographical antecedents.

One or two examples will demonstrate the validity of this argument. With the overthrow of Spanish control, which had administered Central America as a single political unit with authority being exercised only through Guatemala City and Panama City, the Central American isthmus soon broke up into a set of separate sovereign states. Guatemala City was left with only a small national territory (like Vienna after the fall of the Hapsburg empire). Panama suffered an even more ignominious fate; it became a province of Colombia and was, therefore, ruled from Bogotá which cared little for its welfare. But, on the other hand, what had been small provincial towns in the Central American Viceroyalty (e.g. San José, San Salvador) now became capital cities of new sovereign states, with all the attendant advantages which such status gave in terms of the possibilities of attracting a range of secondary and tertiary economic activities.

Further south, post-independence rivalry between Argentina and Brazil had ultimately led to the formation of a separate sovereign state of Uruguay whose territory was, in most other respects, in the same relationship to Buenos Aires as that of half-a-dozen other Argentinian provinces. Had Uruguay remained an Argentine province, then Montevideo would have been just another provincial capital like Rosario or Córdoba. Instead it became a national capital and ultimately one of Latin America's 'million' cities. At the other end of the continent one has evidence by which to judge what might have happened to Montevideo if Uruguay had not become a separate sovereign state. If Guadalajara, an audiencia city since 1548, had succeeded in its efforts to secure its independence of Mexico City, it would have become the capital of another successor nation. Instead it continued in a subordinate status to Mexico City and only after a period of more than 100 years of Independence has it just managed to develop into anything much more than a sleepy, provincial, colonial town. This could well have been Montevideo's fate as well, given a different political solution to the Uruguayan problem. Thus, in the capital cities of the successor states to colonial rule, we see the main antecedents to the establishment of these selected cities' 'initial advantage' for development, on the basis of which emerged the 'core regions' in the contemporary economic geography of Latin America.

Bibliography

There have been few studies of the historical geography of Latin America. However the following books and articles are most useful in achieving an understanding of the historical background to the exploitation of Latin America.

SAUER, C. O., 'A geographical sketch of early man in America', *Geographical Review*, **24**, 1934.
Background to the initial human occupation of the Americas—in part on South and Middle America.

STEWARD, J. H. and FARON, L. C., *Native Peoples of South America*, McGraw-Hill, New York, 1959.
This contains very useful sections on the distribution and organization of different societies in South America in the pre-Columbian period.

KELLY, K., 'Land Use Regions of the Central and Northern Portions of the Inca Empire', *Annals of the Association of American Geographers*, **55**, 327–338 (1965).

KOSOK, P., *Life, Land and Water in Ancient Peru*, Long Island U. P., New York 1965.

SIMPSON, L. B., 'Exploitation of the Land in Central Mexico in the 16th Century', *Ibero-Americana*, no. **36**, Univ. of California, 1952.

WILLEY, G. R., *Prehistoric Settlement Patterns in the New World*, Johnson Reprint Corp., New York, 1956.
The above four publications are concerned with interpreting the patterns of economic activities in various parts of the continent prior to colonization and are amongst the most geographical of the studies of the pre-Colombian period.

WOLF, E., *Sons of the Shaking Earth*, U. of Chicago Press, Chicago, 1959.
An anthropological interpretation of the indigenous cultures of Middle America which is very helpful in explaining their relationships with the colonial system.

HERRING, H., *A History of Latin America*, 3rd Edition, Cape, London, 1968.

PENDLE, G. A., *A History of Latin America*, Penguin Books, Harmondsworth, 1963.
These two general texts, the first one long and the second short, on the history of the continent are more geographically orientated than alternatives.

BOXER, C. R., *The Portuguese Seaborne Empire 1415–1825*, Hutchinson, London, 1969.

HARING, C. H., *The Spanish Empire in America*, O. U. P., Oxford, 1947.
The two standard texts on the history of the empires in Latin America.

WHITTLESEY, E. A., *The Earth and the State*, Holt, New York, 1944.
Chapters 13 and 14 present a political geographical interpretation of the colonization of Latin America and of the development of the independent states of the continent.

CHAPTER 7

The Economic Geography of the Exploitative Economy

As shown in the previous chapter, the achievement of political independence by most countries of Latin America in the first half of the 19th century coincided with the increasing interest of the industrializing nations and their entrepreneurs in exploiting the resources of the continent. Their interest was a response to the rising demand for imported foodstuffs by their urbanizing populations and the demands for industrial raw materials, both vegetable and mineral, by the growing number and variety of factories in Western Europe and North America. This chapter is concerned with a description and evaluation of the economic geographical effects of this development which is principally characterized by the system of the commercial exploitation of the land. Our hypothesis is that the geography of Latin America's economic development in the second part of the 19th century and up to at least the First World War (much later in some areas) can be explained in terms of such exploitation and its secondary effects.

The Acceptance of Foreign Capital

We have already pointed out that, given the circumstances of independence and of the interests and motivations of the groups that achieved political control in the newly independent countries, governmental acceptance of the idea of 'development' by foreign capital was never really in doubt. Moreover, at this time the Latin American countries had brotherly feelings towards the United States on account of its recent successful anti-colonial fight, and this persuaded them of two things. Firstly, that U.S. capital for development purposes was welcome. This was because the U.S., with its fifty years of post-independence experience behind it, would surely know exactly what it was that the Latin American countries wanted and would be prepared to show them how to achieve the same mighty economic progress that it had made since Independence. Latin American governments were, therefore, readily able to persuade themselves that in welcoming U.S. capital to their countries they were taking positive action to ensure that their countries would follow the U.S. example and pattern of expansion. Secondly, the Latin American governments were also aware that capital originating from the newly industrialized nations in the north-west of Europe had helped the U.S. to achieve economic growth. During this time they had been languishing under the handicap of being part of the economic system of Spain which, as they saw, had suffered a serious relative decline in its status amongst the European nations. Spanish rule had severely circumscribed investment in Latin America by other European countries but this barrier was now out of the way. The United States offered an example of what could be done by making use of investment capital from Britain, Germany and other European powers.

From the point of view of the capital surplus nations, particularly Britain and the United States, the opportunity to invest in Latin America was welcome. And such investment opportunities lay either directly in resource development or indirectly in infrastructure such as railways, which would then facilitate resource development. Large scale investment was thought likely to offer the promise of high returns, for the 'el Dorado' attitude towards the continent persisted in spite of Spain's earlier inability to maintain its wealth from this source. Moreover, Latin America also presented the types of physical environment from which many of the growing requirements of industry and of industrial, urbanized populations could be met. Thus, North American and European capitalists were prepared, and indeed anxious, to go out to seek investment opportunities in Latin America.

Thus, in both political and economic terms, Latin America was 'ripe' for commmercial exploitation and both individuals and companies went to it with enthusiasm. The varied fortunes of those involved do not concern us here except to note that a lack of familiarity with some of the difficulties of working in Latin American environments was responsible for some of the fortunes that were lost. We shall return later to consider the phenomenon of the failure of the exploitative economy to affect other than a small part of the continent. As we shall then see, there were important social and institutional, as well as physical environmental factors, which caused this geographically limited impact of resource development.

Space considerations alone, apart from other factors, make it impossible to present a systematic and chronological account of the changes in the continent's economic geography arising from the impact of the forces of exploitative capitalism. Instead we shall pick out a few of the outstanding examples of the changes that were brought about, and in discussing three cases we shall also be introduced to some of the main issues involved. The most important case was the commercial development of the pampas of Argentina and Uruguay. Another significant development was the massive expansion of the plantation system involving both new crops and new areas. And a third has resulted from the impact of the search for mineral wealth in Latin America.

The Economic Development of the Pampas

In the previous chapter we saw how Spanish interests in the temperate grasslands of the southern part of the continent to the east of the Andes remained largely unaroused except, at first, in response to a political/strategic threat from the Portuguese pushing down from the north and, later, in the establishment and development of Buenos Aires as a new and more convenient coastal point of contact between Spain and the southern part of its Latin American empire. As a result of these limited Spanish interests in the region, the pattern of Argentina's economic geography at the time of independence consisted of the relatively new main urban centre of Buenos Aires surrounded by a very limited area of agricultural development, concerned principally with raising food for the city, and a more extensive area of horse raising on the unimproved native grasslands. These coastal or near coastal activities were both geographically and structurally separate from the longer developed economic activities of the interior basins, in the foothills of the Andes, where the local economies had been expanded on the basis of traditional Spanish patterns of agriculture in environments not dissimilar from those of the central parts of Spain. Each basin was organized socially, economically and politically around its central city: Mendoza, San Juan, Tucamán etc. Each was jealous of its independence and, although collectively they could have offered strong opposition to the dominance which Buenos Aires sought, they were unable to work effectively together. As a result, Buenos Aires was able to assert its absolute dominance in all spheres of national life and Argentina thus achieved a centralized political system which provided an ideal framework within which the economic revolution noted below could take place.

By this time, in the middle of the 19th century, some element of appreciation of the potentiality of the pampas as an area which could supply industrializing Western Europe with part of its growing food requirements was beginning to emerge. The political domination of the country by the 'porteños' of Buenos Aires provided a political environment within which this potentiality could be realized. As a result, the next thirty years or so proved to be a long enough period for the complete transformation of the pampas under the stimulus of changed geographical values. This transformation has been succinctly described and explained in the following words: 'The transformation . . . was the result of a combination of factors. Some of the more important were the coming of political stability in the new Argentina after the overthrow of the dictator Rosas in 1852; the expanding markets offered in the industrialized nations of Western Europe; the elimination of the nomadic Indian hunters to the south-west; the introduction of agricultural and pastoral techniques such as barbed wire, fences, windmills and machinery; the influx of capital from a prosperous and expanding British economy; the immigration of Italian labour . . . to till and harvest the new lands; the spread of the railway network over the region; and last, but not least, speedy trans-oceanic transport with refrigerated facilities to bridge the gap of 6,000 miles between producer and consumer.' (Butland, G. J., *Latin America*, Longmans, London, 1960, p. 259)

The only significant omission in this brief quotation lies perhaps in the absence of any reference to the impact of the system of land tenure which was evolved following the success of Buenos Aires in achieving control over the country's affairs. Most of the pampas were not, at that time, under formal ownership which thus became vested automatically in the state. But state power was more or less identical with the power of a few score leading families of Buenos Aires and, in spite of legislation which was specifically designed to prevent the lands of the pampas becoming privately owned, these families managed to obtain the right to use the land on terms which, sooner or later, secured them ownership of the title. Once this transfer of ownership to private hands had been achieved, the way was open to the rapid exploitation of the land. This was achieved largely within the framework of a system of short-term tenant farming. Immigrants to Argentina, largely from southern Europe, were 'given' the right to use an area of virgin land within one of the large landholdings. In return for their expenditure of labour and expertise in improving the land they shared the crops with the landowners for a few years. Thereafter, the immigrants had to leave (either to find unimproved land elsewhere on which they could become short-term tenants or to become urban dwellers in a rapidly expanding Buenos Aires). The landowner was left with additional hectarage of improved land suitable for extensive agriculture and dedicated to the production of food crops for export.

These fundamental land-use changes thus achieved were not only of importance in terms of agriculture. In addition they produced a region of economic growth and strength certainly unrivalled in the southern Hemisphere and surpassed only in the northern one by a few important manufacturing regions such as the Ruhr and the North-East United States. Buenos Aires itself developed into one of the world's biggest cities and ports of the period, while the rail transport network of the whole region—and particularly of areas within a 300 km radius of Buenos Aires—achieved a density of route development and of services which rivalled those of the world's main industrial regions. The continuing strength of the external demand for the wheat, maize, meat and other agricultural products that could be grown so cheaply in the near ideal physical conditions of the pampas, and under a system in which the exploitation of the immigrant workers also ensured low production costs, produced so much wealth that Argentina as a whole was numbered among the top ten nations in income per head from the later part of the 19th century through to the Great Depression of 1929. In that Argentina outside the pampas, moreover, remained largely undeveloped and relatively poor, one can judge that the pampas themselves, and Buenos Aires in particular, achieved standards of development well up to those of the world's industrial powers at this time. Thus, exploitation of the potential of the pampas, arising out of an external demand for its agricultural products and financed largely by foreign capital, produced the most important change in the economic geography of Latin America in this period of economic colonialism.

The Expansion of the Plantation Economy

The massive expansion of the plantation system in Latin America, involving both new areas and new crops, is the second aspect of the geographical impact of exploitative capitalism that we must examine. Plantations had, of course, long been part of some colonial systems, most particularly the British, with sugar as the most important plantation crop. But such agricultural land use in Latin America had been restricted by the great geographical extent of Spanish rule. As shown in the previous chapter, Spain's peripheral position in the process of industrialization in Europe, together with its deteriorating economic and financial position in the crucial 19th century meant that it had neither the incentive nor the ability to make use of those of its possessions with suitable environmental conditions for plantation agriculture on a large scale. And, as also shown previously, it was not prepared to allow exploitation of its colonies by capital and entrepreneurs from other countries. Following the establishment of independent nations in former Spanish America, this restraint on the development of plantations disappeared and concessions were sought and obtained by foreigners in response to the rising demands for tropical products. In contrast with the mainly European investment in Argentina and Uruguay, the financing of plantations in tropical or sub-tropical regions of ex-Spanish America was mainly American. The major European powers had much less need for plantations in former Spanish possessions since they retained their own colonial territories in Africa and Asia, many of which had appropriate tropical climatic conditions for plantation crops. Thus their relative lack of interest in the potential offered by the newly-independent tropical South and Central American republics for the expansion of plantation agriculture left the field open for entrepreneurs from the United States. By this time the United States was experiencing sufficient growth in industry, income and in population to justify foreign investments designed to secure overseas supplies of foodstuffs and raw materials which could either not be produced at all or not be produced cheaply enough within its national territorial limits. Thus, U.S. capitalists sought land concessions on a large scale for the plantation production of sugar, cocoa, coffee, bananas and, at a later stage, with the growth, in particular, of the automobile industry, rubber.

The alienation of large areas of the coastal plains of the small countries of Central America by a few U.S. companies, anxious to produce bananas for the American market, perhaps provides the most outstanding example of the impact of the plantation system in newly-independent Latin America (see Figure 7-1). Large-scale American interest in bananas in Central America dates from the 1870s when lands physically suited to banana production on the Caribbean coastlands, generally at altitudes of less than 500 feet, were opened up for cultivation by the development of railways such as that from Puerto Limón to San José, the capital of Costa Rica. In fact, for this railway (as with others in Central America such as the line from Puerto Barrios to Guatemala City) the need for a basic income from freight traffic provided the stimulus for the use of the land along their rights of way as banana plantations.

In other areas it was the rapid success of the banana industry, following its

Figure 7.1 Central American economies, ports and stations, and the major areas of banana and coffee production

establishment to supply fruit to the American market, that provided the in-centive for further railway construction and for the development of port facilities and other items of infrastructure. An example of this is seen in the case of the Caribbean coastlands of northern Honduras, for which no earlier incentive to development had existed, in the light of the country's orientation to the Pacific ocean, mainly because Tegucigalpa, the old, inland capital, had its external connexions in that direction. The development of bananas along the Caribbean coast now had the effect of reorientating its spatial economy in a completely different direction: with Tegucigalpa consequently isolated from the new geographical pattern of development in the country.

Thus banana plantations in the period from 1870 through to the second decade of the 20th century, when expansion was thwarted by the onset of disease which necessitated the progressive abandonment of plantations, pro-vided the means whereby the economic geography of these areas was trans-formed. The transformation was significant even though the area affected in no case amounted to more than 7% of the total crop land of any one of the countries concerned. The impact was sufficient to make bananas the mainstay of the countries' economies and to cause these nations to be dubbed 'the banana republics'. This, however, was not so much a description of the actual land use in the Central American countries, as it was a manner of indicating the apparent potential of the foreign companies concerned to secure first refusal on any and all land which they considered was potentially suitable for the production of bananas. Moreover, the ability of the companies in this re-spect was one aspect only of their more general ability to mould government action in whatever directions were acceptable to and needed by the compa-nies. Thus, the importance of the development of banana plantations in Central America was a function of the combination of very small countries, lacking the abilities to sustain competent or even adequate governments, with the incidence of one very powerful company, the United Fruit Company, with access to far greater resources of funds and expertise than all of the Central American countries put together. Thus wherever it operated in the region it could be certain of securing whatever conditions for exploitation of the land were necessary to ensure its profitability.

Much the same line of argument can be used when examining the conver-sion of Cuba to a sugar-plantation-based, economic colony of the United States, following the end of Spanish rule over Cuba after the Spanish-Amer-ican War of 1898. The excellent physical conditions, both climatic and phys-iographic, for the production of sugar in Cuba had ensured its importance in the economy of the island even under Spanish rule. But in the late 19th century, after most of the former Spanish colonies had gained their independence, Spanish political and economic conditions did not do much to stimulate the development of its plantations. Thus, production remained relatively small-scale in comparison with sugar plantations elsewhere in the Caribbean where more active colonial powers were encouraging development of the crop. Production was therefore largely concentrated in the western part of the island where the economic infrastructure, particularly in transport facilities, was sufficiently developed to enable use to be made of the highly favourable physical conditions. Levels of production were also affected by highly unstable political conditions in Cuba from the mid-19th century onwards—conditions which deteriorated into virtual civil war over quite long periods. Thus, whilst in 1860 there were reported to be some 2,000 small sugar mills in Cuba, the number had been reduced to 1,200 by 1878 and to only just over 200 still in operation by 1899 when sugar production was under half-a-million tons. Thereafter, the 'Pax Americana', with the stimulation it gave to U.S. capital and expertise to seek opportunities for profitable investment in the island, rapidly changed the situation and converted Cuba into a land of sugar plantations and an economy largely dependent upon the greatly expanded sugar mono-culture. Considerations of profit maximization on the part of the U.S. corporations involved, together with similar motivations for those Cuban companies and individuals which managed to survive the modernization of the industry, now emerged as the sole criteria by which decisions on land use in Cuba were taken. Thus, the excellence of the physical conditions for sugar cultivation, plus the low transport costs involved in getting the sugar away to the U.S. markets, combined to give Cuba a significant comparative advantage in the production of the commodity. Only a quarter of a century after the Americans took over the sugar economy, output had multiplied to nearly 20 times its 1900 level and production had been pushed to all areas of the country where climatic and other conditions were suitable: except where, locally, a more highly valued crop, most particularly tobacco, could be produced (see Figure 7-2).

Ultimately, land dedicated to sugar cane came to involve not far short of 50% of the total land area of Cuba; though it should be noted that not all this land area would actually be producing sugar at any one time. The actual area in use depended, firstly, on the rotational requirements of the crop in different areas (soil and climatic conditions affect the length of the period of recuperation required for the land following its use for cane production) and, secondly, on the price level for the commodity on the world and U.S. markets. With high prices, as in World War II, investments in fertilizer could be substituted for

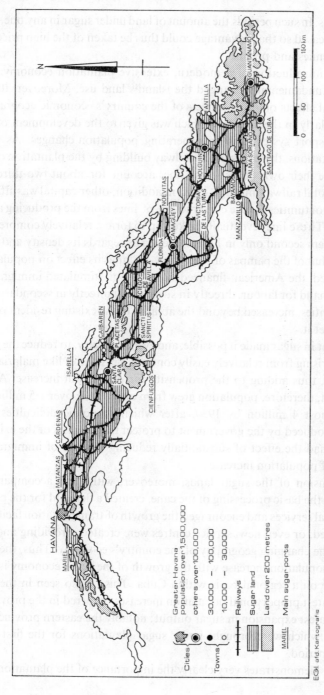

Figure 7–2. Cuba: land set aside for sugar production and associated transport facilities

fallow periods. In such periods the amount of land under sugar in any one year could be increased so that advantage could thus be taken of the high prices to increase revenues and profits.

Thus, the introduction of a modern, extensive plantation economy into Cuba quite fundamentally changed the island's land use. Moreover, it had consequential effects on other aspects of the country's economic geography, most particularly in the incentive which was given to the development of the island's transport system and in generating population changes. As with banana plantations, there was much railway building by the plantation operators to serve their own needs—such lines account for about two-thirds of the island's total railway mileage—but, in addition, other capital was attracted to the opportunities for the construction of lines from the producing areas to the ports. These lines eventually linked up to form a relatively comprehensive rail system second only in Latin America as regards its density and connectivity to that of the pampas of Argentina. As far as its effect on population was concerned, the American-financed sugar boom stimulated immigration since the demand for labour, directly in sugar and indirectly in secondary and tertiary activities, increased beyond the abilities of the existing resident population to meet it.

Investment in sugar made it possible, and even necessary, to reduce the mortality rates arising from relatively easily controllable diseases like malaria and yellow fever, thus adding to the propensity for population increase. As an overall result, therefore, population grew from only a little over 1·5 million in 1900 to almost 4 million by 1930, after which economic difficulties and controls introduced by the government to protect the interests of the existing population had the effect of substantially reducing the rate of immigration and hence of population increase.

The expansion of the sugar lands, moreover, with their accompanying centrales for the basic processing of the cane, created a demand for the provision of central services and encouraged the growth of transportation facilities. Thus enlarged, or even new, service centres were created, providing another element in the changing geography of the country's economy. Thus, the correlation of population increase with the growth of the sugar economy is also recognizable on a regional basis within Cuba. This is also seen in the fact that the greatest proportional population increases occurred in the provinces with the greatest expansion in sugar output: notably the eastern provinces of the country which were brought under sugar plantations for the first time during this period.

Cuba thus demonstrates very clearly the importance of the plantation system in changing the economic geography of a hitherto underutilized territory. Though it is strictly beyond the scope of this section of the book, the opportunity must not be missed for pointing out that sugar plantation development in Cuba —largely financed from the United States and designed to produce a commodity to be consumed in the United States—led to social and political problems which contributed greatly to the revolution in Cuba in 1959. Such a high degree of foreign control over the very basis of a country's economy, and thus over its political development too, at least as far as the main strands of policy are concerned, constitutes an extension of colonialism which has become unacceptable in the modern world. Further attention will be given in the next chapter to the geographical implications of this unacceptability of the plantation system in its traditional form.

Meanwhile, however, it would be incorrect to leave the impression that the plantation system was invariably based on foreign ownership. Plantations were, most frequently, foreign-owned in that plantation agriculture was an inevitable geographical extension of the economic systems of the advanced industrial nations of the time. These nations provided the capital, expertise, ocean transportation and markets and their functions outweighed in importance the land and labour provided, almost incidentally, by the host countries. However, one important Latin American plantation crop did not develop in this way to anything like the same extent. This is coffee, which up until 1945 was provided for world markets almost exclusively by Latin American countries. In this case the enterprise has often been indigenous and where it has been imported, as in the case of the German cultivators of Guatemala, Costa Rica and other Central American states, the foreign entrepreneurs involved have become residents of the country concerned and thus involved in its national life, rather than remaining merely the local representatives of foreign-owned companies. The case of Brazil, traditionally responsible for about half the world's total supply of this commodity, illustrates the situation.

As shown in the previous chapter, exploitation of Brazil under the Portuguese was concentrated on the northern and north-eastern coastal lands where sugar could be produced with slave labour on the large landholdings of those to whom land grants had been made. The boom in sugar had worked itself out before the end of the colonial period, however, as a result of competition from other colonial areas and main economic interest had moved further south, with particular attention focused on the extraction of gold and other precious metals and stones. The lands in this new area of interest were divided into fazendas providing the foodstuffs required by the relatively small population but the fazendeiros' income arose mainly from the sale of cattle. Needless to say the system generated little wealth (compared with that which had been generated out of the sugar plantations in the north at an earlier period) particularly after 1800 or thereabouts, when gold production began to diminish. In spite of this, and in spite of expanding market opportunities, attempts to introduce and expand coffee as a cash crop at this time within the framework of the existing system were not very successful. There was insufficient motivation for change on the part of the landowners. However, as the land was already under some form of use, it was not open to coffee exploitation by foreign enterprise. Thus, the expansion of coffee to the status of Brazil's most important economic activity, and one which successively occupied most of the suitable (and some unsuitable) land in the south and southeastern parts of the country, had to await the acceptance by the fazendeiros of the idea that their land should be utilized in a new way.

Coffee cultivation necessitated, first, land clearance and then continuing high inputs of labour over a period of several years into the establishment of a plantation. Coffee trees take from four to six years to reach bearing age, during which time they must receive constant attention. Such a large demand for labour was beyond the capability of Brazil to supply, as population numbers were still small and most of them had interests which lay mainly in the towns and cities. At the same time international pressure and action had eliminated any likelihood of the introduction of large supplies of slave labour. The solution to this labour problem in the development of coffee cultivation did not begin to emerge until the second half of the 19th century and labour availability only reached the level necessary for the rapid exploitation of the land for coffee plantations after 1885. The solution was found in the encouragement of European immigration on a similar basis to that which we have already examined in the development of the Pampas in Argentina. The immigrants were offered short-term tenancies on the fazendas during which period they cleared the land and established the coffee plantations in return for the right to grow food and certain other crops between the immature coffee trees. Their tenancy was terminated at the beginning of the period in which the trees started to bear fruit and the tenants then had to seek similar opportunities elsewhere.

Utilizing labour in this way enabled coffee plantations to spread over the states of São Paulo, Rio, Minas Gerais and Espirito Santo in response to the rising demand for coffee by the outside world. Though coffee cultivation thus remained almost entirely under national ownership and control, the use of the land remained essentially exploitative in the crudest sense, as there was little effort to conserve the ability of the land to continue to produce the commodity. As land quality was depleted below the level demanded by coffee so the frontier of exploitation moved on, with the speed of advance, and of abandonment, functions of the fluctuating price levels for coffee on the international market. This was a phenomenon which was essentially outside the ability of the Brazilians to control except partly through some half-hearted measures to curb the flow of coffee to the market in time of glut. This generally unsuccessful action depended on governmental purchases of some of the crop either for destruction or for release at a later, less-depressed state of the market. As the first centenary of the large-scale exploitation of coffee in Brazil approaches, one notes that the coffee plantation and its product remain the key to Brazilian economic well-being though, as we shall see later, even a nationally-owned, plantation-type crop has been condemned as an inappropriate base for the agricultural economy of a modern state.

Foreign Exploitation of Latin America's Mineral Wealth

There are few countries in Latin America where the economic geography, in the later 19th and first half of the 20th centuries, was not radically affected by the types of agricultural development described so far in this chapter. There is, however, another somewhat different aspect of the geography of economic colonialism to which we must give some attention: and more particularly because it applies most of all to those countries of Latin America which were least affected by the agricultural developments of the economic colonial system. This is the economic geography of the extraction of mineral deposits from Latin American countries for export to the manufacturing nations of Europe and North America. The system closely parallels that of the plantation economy as it also involves the use of national territory at the behest of external forces with, traditionally, the host government having no control over, or even any say in, decisions on developments—or retrenchments. It is, of course, sometimes argued that developments of these activities do, in fact, lie entirely within the control of the host government which has an initial right to decide whether or not any concession shall be made to the exploiting company. The government can, of course, also lay down the conditions on which the exploitation shall take place. Until quite recently, however, all Latin American governments were unwilling and/or unable to negotiate effectively with the large foreign companies seeking conces-

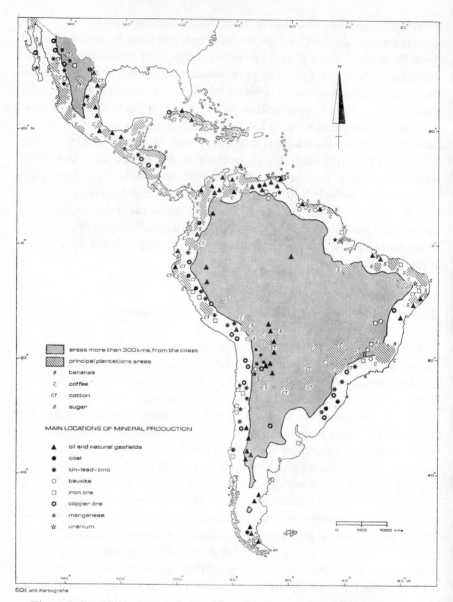

EGI. afd. Kartografie

Figure 7–3. Latin America: the location of extractive industries and plantations.
This demonstrates their near-coastal general orientation

sionary rights to work minerals, particularly as, almost always, the companies sought their concessions with the tacit, or open, support of either the U.S. or the British government.

In addition, all too often in the past, some Latin American governments have been concerned too little about the longer-term interests of their countries in such negotiations. This was because the sale of concessionary rights to foreign companies created possibilities of personal gains on a considerable scale by unscrupulous politicians. Thus, one can hypothesize that the geographical pattern of extractive industry in Latin America principally and simply reflects the foreign exploiting companies' evaluation of the relative profitability of the products from different locations when sold on the world markets.

In that most of the products involved are of a great bulk with a low value per ton, a prime consideration determining the profitability of particular deposits has been, and, to a large degree, still remains, their location in relation to points of export. By and large, this has created a significant advantage for coastal or near coastal deposits such that even today extractive industry is largely confined to locations within 300 kilometres of tidewater (see Figure 7-3).

The most important 19th century development of mineral resources was that of Chilean nitrates, whose occurrence and low-cost working was a function of the particular physical conditions of the Atacama Desert. Their location, in turn, meant that low-cost transport to the coast was possible in spite of the harsh and arid environment. Once the political problems between Chile, Bolivia and Peru had been settled, albeit only at the cost of a war between the three countries caused partly by their anxiety to secure some of the benefits likely to arise from the exploitation of the nitrates, then the rapid expansion of the industry was assured, and large parts of the Atacama Desert region of Chile secured a transport infrastructure unmatched in the world's arid regions (see Figure 7-4).

The railways were either built by the nitrate companies themselves or by other companies which responded to the opportunities for profitable investment created by the traffic generated by the nitrate companies. They were thus designed essentially to provide the shortest or lowest-cost route from the 'oficinas' (the locations where the nitrates underwent preliminary primary processing) to the ports, which were constructed at the nearest possible points of access on the coast. Thus, their general orientation was across the narrow width of Chile but, nevertheless, some parts of their routes could often be incorporated into the northward extension of the country's longitu-

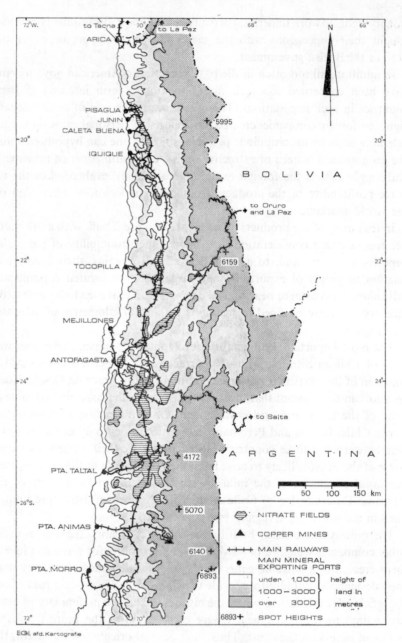

Figure 7–4. Chile: railway development and the location of extractive industry
in the arid North of the country

dinal railway. Without the incentive of nitrate development in the desert this would probably never have penetrated north of the northern end of the Central Valley of the country. The demand for rail transport facilities created by the extraction of nitrates, and, somewhat later, of copper, ensured its completion to Antofagasta and Iquique. Moreover, from Antofagasta it was continued across the Andes into Argentina and Bolivia, thus providing a means whereby the Chilean government could exercise its authority over its northern regions. (In contrast, one can note in passing the absence of any incentive to build a railway south into forest and Atlantic Chile. The absence of a railway there coincided with a continued concern for the security of the southern provinces.)

Apart from the consequential transport linkages achieved as a result of the development of the nitrate industry, there were few other local multiplier effects arising out of its development and, for most other intents and purposes, what happened in the desert north of the country remained a matter of indifference to the mainstream of Chilean development, except in as far as the Chilean government was eventually able to collect revenues from the companies concerned and with these was better able to pursue development policies elsewhere in the country through bodies such as the state-financed Chilean Development Corporation, whose activities have included oil developments and investment in manufacturing industry. But this was an effect which had its geographical impact elsewhere in the country, whilst northern Chile was in essence run from Britain and the United States: from whence came the capital and expertise for the extraction and export of nitrates (and copper). The development of the extractive industry there seems likely to have produced more favourable results for their economies than it did for that of Chile itself. This is certainly a view widely held in Chile which, in recent years, proceeded first to the 'Chileanization' of the copper industry (under President Frei) and then (under President Allende) to its nationalization.

But it can be argued that Chile really lost nothing by having the development of nitrates and copper undertaken by foreign enterprise. Without such foreign-financed development the whole of the northern part of the country would just have remained so much unused, and unusable, land basically without people. In as far as Chile would have taken any interest in it at all, it would have been a burden rather than an asset to the nation by virtue of the costs of maintaining contact with it and the costs of keeping out neighbouring powers possibly anxious for territorial expansion. Economic colonialism in Northern Chile made the territory, in fact, irrevocably Chilean and also provided the means whereby it could be defended.

However, in looking at similar developments of extractive industry elsewhere in Latin America, not even this 'justification' for economic colonialism can be advanced. Tin in Bolivia or copper and lead in Peru both provide examples of the geographical, as well as economic and political, separation of the foreign-controlled extractive industry from the mainstream of national life. But it is the petroleum industry in Latin America which provides not only the most widespread, but also the most blatant, examples of 'enclave' development arising from foreign ownership and control. It is worth noting first that the dangers considered likely to arise from foreign-owned and controlled oil exploration and development were recognized very early in the history of the industry in some Latin American companies. Chile, for example, after allowing foreign oil companies to investigate the geological possibilities for oil occurrence in the extreme south of the country, in Tierra del Fuego, then decided in 1923 not to grant them concessions to exploit the resource. This decision was made on the grounds that such foreign-controlled activites in an area so remote from the effective centre of government could lead to a situation in which there would be encouragement of collusion with Argentina whereby the latter could take-over the region. Chile decided to work the deposits through its own national efforts and went on to establish a national, state-owned monopoly for the exploitation of oil and gas. A similar policy towards oil exploration and development was adopted by Argentina at about the same time; by Brazil more recently in 1950, and by Peru as recently as 1969.

In part these, and other Latin American nations with state-controlled oil sectors, have been responding to the earlier Mexican experience with foreign oil companies. There, oil companies from the U.S. and Britain, within the framework of the highly favourable opportunities established for foreign enterprise in the country by the regime of Porfirió Diaz in the last quarter of the 19th century, acquired vast land concessions for petroleum exploitation in the Gulf coastal areas of the country.

Exploration efforts were successful and the companies concerned began to produce oil not mainly for distribution in Mexico, whose demands were still small, but for sale overseas. The oil concession areas became tantamount to states within the state. Within the petroleum enclaves the law which mattered was that according to the company concerned and was upheld by 'armies' operated by the companies. The exploitation of the oil reserves was, the companies argued, a matter of concern only to them. For this privilege the companies had to pay little more than a nominal sum to the Mexican government and in return secured the ownership of the country's oil. Even after the Mexican Revolution of 1910 which arose in part because of Porfirió Diaz's 'sale' of Mexico to foreign companies, the oil companies were powerful enough not to have to take much cognizance of the fact and, given the market opportunities of the early post World War I period, took anti-Mexican action by deliberately over-producing the fields in search of short-term profits at the cost of the longer-term viability of the reserves.

Neither at the political nor an administrative level were the companies prepared to come to terms with the revolutionary governments which naturally had stronger feelings over such matters than did previous administrations. Finally, in 1938, the government felt strong enough to act. In order to re-establish state sovereignty over alienated territory and also to establish conditions in which the petroleum industry could be made an instrument for the development of the Mexican economy, the oil companies were expropriated and the whole of the petroleum industry was placed under national ownership. In a later chapter we shall examine the significance of this step for the economic geography of the country. At this point we need only to emphasize that the country took over several enclaves of development very largely unrelated economically, or even politically, to the rest of the national territory.

The expropriation of their producing fields in Mexico was the part cause why the oil companies, anxious to secure control over new supplies and potential supplies, strengthened their interests in Venezuela where the petroleum industry, worked entirely by foreign companies, had been slowly but steadily increasing in importance since the mid 1920s. Now, following Mexican expropriation, the companies eagerly sought to expand their activities, particularly in the proven prolific areas around Lake Maracaibo. The Venezuelan government of the time raised no objections to this development and, in spite of events in Mexico, laid down no conditions on the future exploration and development of oil which would prevent a recurrence of the Mexican situation. As it turned out however, wartime opportunities for bringing pressure to bear on the companies, and their countries of origin (the U.S. and the U.K.), and a changing politico-economic environment within which international business has had to be carried out, combined to make oil colonialism in Venezuela less objectionable and unfavourable to the host country. In most recent years, in fact, the pressures have been such as to turn the ventures virtually into company/government partnerships with the bulk of the benefits flowing to Venezuela rather than to the companies. This will be discussed in a later chapter.

In the meantime oil development in the period from 1940 through to 1958

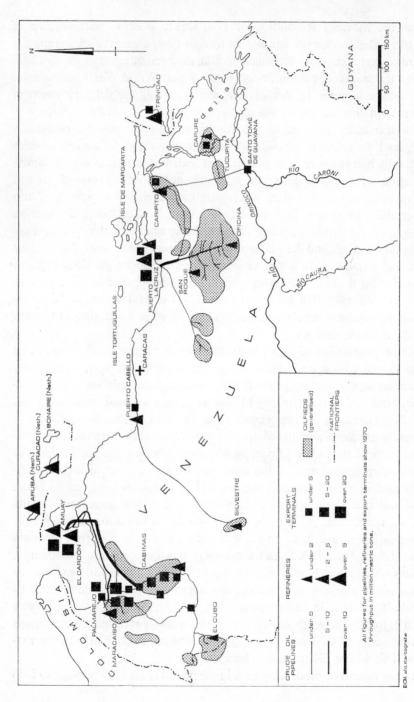

Figure 7–5. Venezuela: the location of oil industry activities. Note the isolation of Caracas from the oil producing, refining and exporting regions

had geographical implications arising from the essentially colonialistic nature of the economic relationship between Venezuela and the companies concerned. Having secured their concessions from the government for exploration and production rights in extensive areas of the country (see Figure 7-5), the companies' way and speed of working them, and the development of facilities associated with the production and export of petroleum, were determined solely by reference to the international requirements of the companies and not at all to the needs of the Venezuelan people or economy. Thus, exploration and oilfield development facilities and settlements, developed to house and serve the staff and workers of the companies, were established as enclaves of modernization—and even luxury— within a generally underdeveloped part of the country. The modernization influence of these developments ceased abruptly at the enclaves' fences, only spilling over, at best, into a marginal settlement of occasional workers on the far side of the company road. This was a situation which made for easy visual comparison of the wide gap in living standards between those in the enclave and those outside it. Moreover, petroleum, unlike most other mineral developments, does not even produce a transport infrastructure which is generally available. Except for a limited number of access roads to the developments it produces only pipelines which are not only useless for anything but the movement of oil but which, of course, are also invariably directly controlled by the companies which built them. Thus, the movement of tens of millions of tons of oil from producing areas around and under Lake Maracaibo over the 300 kilometres to the new export terminals, which were constructed on the Paraguana Peninsula, produced no jobs (other than the short-term opportunities involved in laying the line) and no entrepreneural possibilities for the provision of services en route. Petroleum pipelines do not, by their very nature, produce transportation service centres and so the country between production points and export points remained undeveloped and outside the geographical enclaves of modernization created by oil exploration activities and also at exporting/refining locations.

Nor did the growth of the oilfields themselves produce much effect on the development of local services in that the oil-company-owned communities aimed to achieve as high a degree of self-sufficiency as possible. They provided everything from utilities such as electricity and water to social services such as primary and secondary education and health services up to and including hospitals. Thus, overall, the Venezuelan oil industry's exploration, development and transportation facilities produced a series of isolated islands of economic development in areas where the general level of development was either that of subsistence agriculture or, at best, the commercial cash cropping, on a relatively small scale, of products like cacao from the forests of the Maracaibo basin.

Furthermore, even these separate islands achieved little by way of functional relationships with each other in light of their separate ownership by different oil companies, and the fact that more or less the same services were provided in each of them. There was, in other words, no element of specialization in service provision or the development of a hierarchy of settlements as there would have been in an open system.

In 1943 the Venezuelan government negotiated a new agreement with the oil companies. Amongst other provisions, this obliged the companies to expand their oil-manufacturing activities in Venezuela and there was a consequent rapid expansion of refining facilities particularly by Shell and Esso, the two most important oil companies operating in Venezuela, on the Paraguana peninsula. The two refining complexes with their associated export facilities soon came to extend over several square miles of this arid and hitherto little used part of Venezuela. Inevitably, alongside them were developed the company towns to provide living space, etc. for their employees. Perhaps one should not be surprised that these, too, became just two more islands of development for which the perimeter fences marked the geographical extent of their influence to a very high degree. Their location was a function of their anticipated relationships with outside, foreign markets and not a function of their relationship with other parts of the Venezuelan economy. Their geographical contacts with the latter were no more than accidental. Such a divorce from the domestic economy ensured that there would be no forward or backward linkages into other sectors and the refineries still remain almost as isolated as when they were first built. And again, as with the oil fields themselves, the complexes are self-sufficient for services and offer little traffic, either in or out, on which an enhanced local transport structure could develop.

Thus, partly by the very nature of oil industry operations, in terms of their strong locational ties to the resource itself and of their independence of any public system of transportation, but partly also by virtue of their foreign ownership, control and operation, with the effect that this has had on attitudes to the indigenous role and responsibilities of the industry, the geographical pattern of the development of the oil industry in Venezuela has been mainly as described so far in this chapter. But at least a hint must be given at this stage of another side to the picture: even though we shall return to these considerations in more detail in a later chapter. First, one should note that the oil industry did produce a local multiplier effect as far as the city of Maracaibo was concerned. At the beginning of the oil period this capital city of the

State of Zulia had under 20,000 inhabitants and served as the administrative, marketing and collecting/exporting centre for the west of the country which had remained relatively little developed (see Figure 7-5). Now, by virtue of its location in the main area of oil exploitation, it became the centre from which all the companies co-ordinated their field activities as well as the centre for the required transportation facilities. For example, some of the early export terminals were located in the vicinity of the city. As a result it gained both in population and in functions and rapidly grew to become the second city of the country. In this case, development by the individual companies was impossible and Maracaibo enjoyed the stimulus offered by an open system in which both public and private capital were involved, with the latter coming not only from the oil companies but also from other entrepreneurs.

Ironically, in more recent years Maracaibo has suffered a series of setbacks to its development as a result of the rationalization of their Venezuelan activities by the oil companies. Increasingly effective telecommunication links and the growth of air transport made co-ordination of their activities at a regional level in Maracaibo unnecessary and inappropriate. Fields, company towns, refineries and terminals were now linked directly into national headquarters at Caracas, thus enabling them to achieve cost reductions largely at the expense of Maracaibo's local economy. In parenthesis one notes here that the retrenchment of activities affected the regional, rather than the national, capital and thus further emphasized the fact that the single most important geographical effect of oil industry growth in Venezuela lay in its influence in Caracas. Though this has partly arisen from the companies' expenditure and activities there (in head office developments etc.), a much more important aspect has been the influence of government. In the first place, the high degree of centralization of government activities in Venezuela was in large part responsible for the decision of the companies to locate their head office activities in Caracas. In the second place, the expenditure of government revenues arising from oil industry activities, and these rose quickly after the renegotiations of the concessions in 1943, has been heavily skewed in favour of the Caracas area. In this way revenues earned by Venezuela out of the resources of the oil-producing regions have been geographically shifted away from the regions to benefit the centre.

We shall return to consider this theme more closely in the next chapter, for it is a phenomenon that is not restricted to Venezuela, though it is demonstrated there most clearly as a result of the scale of revenues secured by the government from the oil industry. The point that needs to be made here is that the blame for the phenomenon can hardly be laid on the oil companies themselves as a consequence of their neo-colonialist activities in the country. This is an indication that the hypothesis we have examined in this chapter, that the geography of Latin America's economic development can be explained in terms of the effects of the system of economic colonialism, has, throughout the independence period, been only a partial explanation of the geography of the continent's economic development. Moreover, as the 20th century has progressed, it has decreasingly explained the geographical pattern of economic activities in Latin America and it is, therefore, now time to turn to describe and examine other phenomena and considerations involved in our study of Latin America's contemporary economic geography.

Bibliography

a) Some of the general texts recommended for chapter 6 also provide background reading for the ideas presented in this chapter. More specific interpretation of the relationship between the world capitalist economic system and the exploitation of Latin American resources can be found in

FRANK, A. G., *Capitalism and Underdevelopment in Latin America*, Monthly Review Press, New York, 1967

FURTADO, C., *Diagnosis of the Brazilian Crisis*, U. of California Press, California, 1965.

b) The idea of the economic exploitation of Latin America within the framework of an inequitable world economic system provided much of the motivation for the enthusiastic activities of the U.N. Economic Comission for Latin America in the 1950s and early 60s and its publications, particularly the annual *Economic Survey*, provide useful reading in this respect. For a critique of E.C.L.A.'s work see:

BAER, W., The Economics of Prebisch and E.C.L.A. *Economic Development and Cultural Change*, Vol. X, No. 2, 1962.

c) There are several publications which deal with the theme of foreign investment in Latin American agricultural and mineral development. See, for example

BERNSTEIN, M. D., *Foreign Investment in Latin America*, Knopf, New York, 1966.

GRUNWALD, J., Resource Aspects of Latin American Economic Development in CLAWSON, M. (Ed.) *National Resources and International Development*, J. Hopkins Press, Baltimore, 1964.

MAY, S. and PLAZA, G., *The United Fruit Company in Latin America*, National Planning Association, 1958.

ODELL, P. R., 'The Oil Industry in Latin America' in Penrose, E., *The Large International Firm in Developing Countries*, Cass, London, 1968.

PAN AMERICAN UNION, 'Plantation Systems in the New World', *Social Science Research Monograph no. 7*, Washington, 1959.

d) For books which analyse the consequences of exploitation of land and/or mineral resources in particular countries see,

BERNSTEIN, M. D., *The Mexican Mining Industry 1890–1950*, Antioch Press, New York, 1965.

CRIST, R. E., *The Cauca Valley, Colombia: Land Tenure and Land Use*, Waverley Press, New York, 1954.

FERRER, A., *The Argentine Economy*, U. of California Press, Berkeley, 1966.

GUERRA Y SANCHEZ, R., *Sugar and Society in the Caribbean*, Yale U.P., New Haven, 1964.

JEFFERSON, M., *Peopling the Argentine Pampa*, American Geographical Society, New York, 1926.

LIEUWEN, E., 'Petroleum in Venezuela', *California U. Publications in History*, Vol. III, 1954.

MCBRIDGE, G., *Chile: Land and Society*, American Geographical Society, New York, 1936.

PARSONS, J. J., *Antioqueño Colonisation in Western Colombia*, U. of California Press, Berkeley, Revised Edition, 1968.

YOUNG, B. S., Jamaica's Bauxite and Alumina Industries, *Annals of the Association of American Geographers*, **55**, 1965.

Only a few of these publications are specifically geographical in authorship and/or objective but they all provide valid background from which to extract implications for the spatial structure of the economies concerned.

e) Finally, here is a short selection of articles which look in greater detail at particular cases of land and/or mineral exploitation.

DYER, D. R., 'Sugar Regions of Cuba', *Economic Geography*, **32**, 1956.

GALLOWAY, J. H., 'The Sugar Industry of Pernambuco in the Nineteenth Century, *Annals of the Association of American Geographers*, **58**, 1968.

HUTCHINSON, H. W., The Transformation of Brazilian Plantation Society, *Journal of Inter American Studies*, **III**, No. 2, 1961.

JONES, C. F. and MORRISON, P. C., 'Evolution of the Banana Industry in Costa Rica', *Economic Geography*, **28**, 1952.

PARSONS, J. J., 'Bananas in Ecuador', *Economic Geography*, **33**, 1957.

PRESTON, D. A., 'Changes in the Economic Geography of Banana Production in Ecuador', *Transactions of the Institute of British Geographers*, 1965.

CHAPTER 8

Regional Imbalance in Economic Development

In the last chapter we examined the geographical significance of a situation in which economically and politically weak Latin American governments had to face up to the greatly superior resources and expertise of foreign companies and corporations seeking concessions for development opportunities. This 'unfair' situation was made even worse in that the private entrepreneurs were often backed-up diplomatically, and sometimes in other more questionable ways, in their search for profitable investment, by the governments of the United States and Britain (and other European nations). As a result, Latin American governments were, until very recently in most cases, either content or obliged to see the speed and patterns of their development shaped by the forces of international commerce.

The Geographical Impact of the Exploitative Economy

The most strongly-growing sectors of the national economies of all Latin American nations under this system of economic colonialism were those which produced primary commodities for export markets. Usually, as we have seen, this created a need for extensive areas of land which could be used for the production of plantation crops or minerals. However, the degree to which the land or the mineral resource was developed at any given moment in time was a function of the state of world demand for the product concerned and the relative strength of the competition from other supplying areas of the world. The degree of development was not determined by competition from other sectors of the local economy. Given these conditions, the question of the location of these activities within national territories and their intensity of development was a matter over which national governments had, even if they might have wished otherwise, no control. The governments could deny the use of certain lands to such enterprise, perhaps for political or strategic reasons, but they had no means of ensuring that the enterprises developed the resources concerned or that they developed them at a rate preferred by the government. This depended on decisions taken by the companies in London or New York. As they almost always operated in more than one country they could choose instead a development in some other country, either within or outside Latin America, where similar climatic, soil or geological conditions enabled them to produce the commodities they wanted. They were used to doing what they wanted, without let or hindrance from awkward governments.

These considerations, moreover, applied as well to the development of industries concerned with primary processing of the food-stuffs, agricultural raw materials and minerals. The companies evaluated internationally the lowest cost/maximum profit locations for such secondary economic activities and, if they were not allowed to locate them in their chosen area of a given country, then, as likely as not, they would take the investment elsewhere in the world. This meant a loss of jobs and, possibly, even the loss of an opportunity for an industrial growth point through the forward and backward linkages that could be created by such location decisions.

The development of oil refineries in Venezuela by Shell, Esso and other international oil companies is an example of the lack of any national control over the activities of such foreign companies. At first almost all Venezuelan oil was taken out of the country for refining (to off-shore islands belonging to the Netherlands: viz. Aruba and Curaçao) and even when refineries were at last built in Venezuela they were located in a region wholly eccentric to the pre-existing areas of development in Venezuela, and in a way wholly unrelated to the internal spatial structure of the national economy. This arose because the locations were chosen to minimize costs on an international, rather than a Venezuelan, scale since the companies concerned sold over 95% of the refineries' production overseas and thus had no need or incentive to take note of Venezuelan requirements and wishes. Another example is seen in the locations in Argentina and Uruguay of the meat-packing and freezing factories. These were established at points convenient for exporting the products from the countries concerned rather than in locations related to the needs of their spatial-economic development. Given this situation throughout Latin America, one can argue that each of the national economies was 'out of control' and this applied as much to the geographical or spatial aspects of development as it did to any other aspect. In that the locational decisions were based on conditions external to the national economy, they were thus unrelated even to considerations of maximizing national income, let alone to considerations of maximizing national welfare or some other less quantifiable objective like that. Thus the 'bodies' of many Latin American economies were wagged by what should have been the 'tails', and even if national governments might either have wished or have wanted to do anything about the matter, all they were in fact able to do was to make little more than the most of a fundamentally adverse situation.

However, as it was few of them either wished or sought to do much about the economic geographical implications of the situation, except when they were political and strategic issues at stake in their relations with neighbouring countries. In such special cases they might seek control over the actions of foreign companies in border areas. Their increasing efforts to contain the impact of economic colonialism and the exploitative economy were instead normally limited, as pointed out in the previous chapter, to concern about the share of the profits which they could secure from the companies concerned. This was not, of course, an unimportant consideration, for in achieving a larger share of the profits arising out of exploitative ventures, governments secured revenues which could be used for other purposes. Those purposes might be the creation of personal fortunes for members of such governments whereby, amongst other results, they could ensure that they continued in office through the power of patronage this conferred on them. On the other hand, profits could mean the availability of funds for possible investment in a country's basic economic and social infrastructure. In the case of governments which were made up of individuals concerned with securing personal fortunes, increased governmental revenues from foreign companies were likely to have their geographical expression in the intensification of the small islands of conspicuous consumption which had already been brought into existence by the geographically concentrated expenditure of the considerable profits which were made in most countries from traditional land holdings. Firm witness to such use of profits are the elegant suburbs and richly endowed avenues and paseos of cities like Buenos Aires, Rio de Janeiro and Santiago and the sophisticated, and almost equally elegant, developments of summer resorts such as Mar del Plata, the Chilean Lake District and resorts of a like nature, but on a smaller scale, in almost every other Latin American country. Needless to say, the conspicuous consumption of the income arising from shared profits or from land ownership which found its expression in the grand tour of Europe or a season in Paris did not leave any imprints on the economic maps of Latin American countries!

For governments with some or even, as in a few cases, an overriding interest in using revenues arising out of the exploitative economy for investment in the country's economic or social infrastructure, the geographical results are much more significant. However, an examination of the geographical pattern of investment that has emerged from this form of use of these revenues reveals that there was an almost continental-wide propensity to invest the funds at the principal pre-existing national centres of economic and social activities. Such centres were, almost always, the capital city of each country.

The background to this geographical pattern of infrastructure investment emerges out of the predeliction of the Spanish rulers and settlers in Latin America for life in urban centres and for the consequential evolution of highly-urbanized and urban-orientated colonial societies. This was briefly described in chapter 6. The successor governments following independence from Spain were constituted by people who had basically similar attitudes and outlooks. These new rulers were, moreover, in the main able to satisfy their material desires out of the profits from their land holdings and, to an increasing extent in the later part of the 19th century, from the concessions which they granted to foreign companies and corporations in 'outlandish' areas: about which they cared very little and of which they often had even less knowledge. When revenues started to flow to the governments from these concessions, so providing an opportunity for investment possibilities in infrastructure developments, what could be more in keeping with their interests and inclinations than to make the investments in the centres which they knew and from which they worked or, if it was to be investment in transportation facilities, then on roads and railways leading to the centres. In that governments of most of the Latin American countries at that time were highly centralized, such decisions by the national governments took care of most of the revenues which became available from the plantation and mining companies etc. Local government was weak (and in many countries it was deliberately kept that way so as to avoid any possibility of local independence movements). Local authorities were, therefore, in general not endowed with any rights to collect revenues from concessionary companies operating in their province, department or municipality. What money they were permitted to expend was usually made available from the national government, which almost invariably acted as an intermediary between the companies which paid the revenues and the local governments which would have welcomed the chance to collect it! As a result of these politico-economic arrangements there were significant regional differences in the degree of public investment and a consequential spatial imbalance in the development of the Latin American countries' infrastructure. The geographical emphasis in such infrastructure investment was generally on expenditure on the needs of the primate city which, as a consequence, achieved an even higher degree of primacy within the nation's space economy.

Nor was this development just a matter of central government decisions concerning the location of the expenditure of government revenues. Private investment decisions were also locationally related to that of government, for several reasons. In the first place, most finance available for private investment originated at the centre which was the most likely residence of individuals wealthy enough to have savings available. Even when they made their money out of land holdings or out of agriculture in other parts of the country, this was largely remitted by them or their agents to the capital or central city where banking and financing institutions were developed to a high enough degree to enable those with capital available to participate in the local opportunities for investment. Similarly, capital coming in from abroad for investment, (in sectors other than organized plantations and extractive industries for which financing was usually arranged internationally rather than locally) came first into the primate centre, through local branches of European or American-based banks, where it could be merged with the flow of domestic funds. Finally, on the demand side, the opportunities offered for investment in the centre were safe, easy and profitable enough for both political and economic reasons to inhibit interest in possible investment opportunities elsewhere in the national territory.

Moreover, politically, many governments were interventionist, and particularly so as far as the development of industry was concerned. Therefore, in order to secure all the necessary permissions for private development in this field, early and effective liaison with appropriate (often many) government departments and ministers was essential in order that the investor could succeed in ironing out all the continuing difficulties. To isolate geographically any investment in the private sector from the bureaucracy was a sure means of accentuating the problems. Thus, politically there was much to be said for locating private investment in the centre rather than at the periphery of the national space-economy.

This political motivation for a primate city (or near primate city) location for private enterprise developments in the secondary and tertiary sectors was, moreover, strongly backed up with an economic motivation. Most private investment was in those sectors of a Latin American country's economy concerned with the production and transportation of goods and services for final consumption. Thus, investment was important in sectors such as the construction industry, the servicing of vehicles and machinery and, a little later in the development process, the production or assembly of goods already being consumed locally but which had hitherto been imported. The bulk of the markets for such goods and services were, again, almost invariably geographically concentrated in the core region which usually contained the only sizeable group of potential consumers. Such potential customers could only be found among those sectors of the population which had sufficiently good incomes to place them in the market for such goods. These were essentially those people whose strong urban orientation has already been mentioned earlier in this chapter. Thus, lowest cost/maximum profit locations for investment in these sectors were also at the centre. To have located elsewhere in the country would have involved the firm or entrepreneur in additional transport costs in getting his goods back to the main market area, with very little likelihood that other than a small part of those additional costs would be offset by lower costs in other parts of the production processes.

The Core/Periphery Phenomenon in Economic Development

Thus, the core/periphery phenomenon in the economic geographical patterns of Latin American countries emerged and became marked by a major contrast in the degree of economic development achieved in different parts of the national territory. The developed core areas, moreover, still reflected, in the main, the locational preferences of the Spanish conquistadores for their most important administrative centres whilst areas in which the Spanish had been uninterested remained, even now, outside the main loci of economic activities. However, before going on to look more closely at this fundamentally important component in the contemporary economic geography of Latin America, it seems necessary to define rather more precisely what is meant by the 'periphery' of an economy and to relate it geographically to another important phenomenon in the economic geography of Latin America. This is the so-called 'empty heart' of the continent. This must be done because although one can, and should, be very concerned about low standards of development, and the absence of opportunities, in large areas and regions of Latin American countries with significant populations, it is difficult, and often inappropriate, to worry in the same way about the mere existence of empty lands where low levels of economic activities merely reflect the fact that there are very few people living there. If the peripheries of the spatial economic structure of Latin American countries coincide with the empty, unpopulated areas then this is not necessarily a matter for concern or even for attention. Our concern and attention in these cases will be to evaluate whether or not the empty lands represent 'resource frontiers' capable of potential development. This, however, is a distinct issue in the geography of development and must be dealt with quite separately from the problem of regional imbalance in the levels of development within those parts of the national territories that are already populated.

The Economic Periphery and the 'Empty Heart' of Latin America

As previously shown, the idea of a Latin American 'el Dorado' dies hard, and is part and parcel of the concept of the limitless opportunities waiting to be exploited in an 'empty' continent in which man's colonizing activities have barely penetrated beyond the coastal margins! Figure 8-1, showing the relationship between the geographically limited areas with a density of population of at least 10 people per square kilometre and the national territories of the largest Latin American countries, is an example of the sort of evidence that is often produced to demonstrate the existence and size of the empty heart of the continent. But the description of the main elements in man's use of Latin America which has been presented in the last two chapters will already have indicated that this sort of evidence hardly represents a profound analysis of the reality of the situation as far as the potential for development is concerned.

Empty lands, other than the semi-deserts of the northern part of Mexico, rarely exist on a large geographical scale in Middle America. Parts of Honduras and Nicaragua are empty but these largely unpopulated lands are in close juxtaposition with the very overcrowded rural areas of El Salvador and Costa Rica. This situation has already given rise to unofficial immigration across the frontiers: as well as to political difficulties between the countries concerned, of which a recent example was the so-called 'Football War' between El Salvador and Honduras in 1969. There is a similar situation in parts of the Caribbean. The Dominican Republic does have unused but usable areas within its frontiers, but these are in many cases almost within hailing distance of land-hungry Haitians, who, like the landless Salvadoreans,

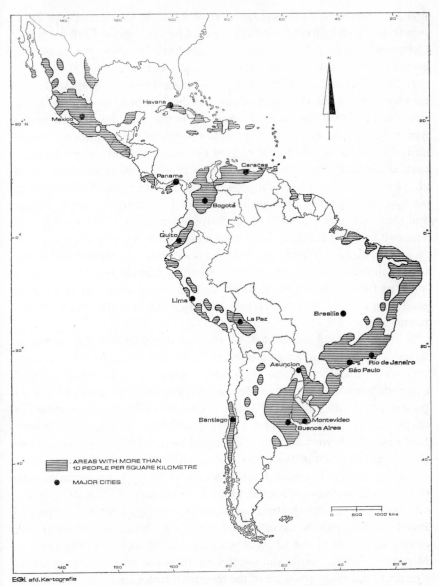

EGI. afd. Kartografie

Figure 8–1. Latin America: national frontiers and populated areas. Note how the frontiers run mainly through non-populated areas giving most countries a share in the 'empty-heart' of the continent

find their way across political frontiers in search of subsistence-type hold-ings from which to meet their basic needs. Elsewhere in the Caribbean only Cuba could be described as underpopulated in relation to the known re-source base for sustaining primary economic activities.

In South America perhaps the most significant feature of the settlement geography is not the emptiness of parts of the continent, but the continued pressure of population on land resources in parts of the Andean region where the cumulative effects of a lengthy period of out-migration to lower altitudes and/or to urban centres have not yet reduced the populations of parts of Central Peru and Bolivia to levels at which living standards much above the subsistence level are possible. On the other side of the continent we have already noted the transformation of the previously empty pampas and their settlement by millions of European migrants. This has led to a situation in which the area, in spite of more recent out-migration, still has an average density of rural population almost twice as high as that of the U.S. prairies; a comparison which is surely a relevant one to make as it indicates that increasing living standards in areas of extensive agriculture, producing commodities for export, lead to a smaller rather than a larger population.

North-East Brazil, as we shall see in more detail later in the chapter, is increasingly becoming an area of excessive human demands on its limited resource base and as a result constitutes a major area of difficulty, and of overpopulation in relation to the region's potential for development, in present-day South America. Further south, the coffee boom described in chapter 7 has taken agricultural settlers well into the interior of South-East Brazil far beyond an area which could be described as a 'coastal mar-gin'. Although much of the land has been effectively worked out as coffee-producing land, it has more recently been utilized for other forms of agri-culture. Such agricultural activities have been increasingly stimulated by the growing food and raw material demands (e.g. sugar, meat and cotton) of Brazil's rapidly expanding urban/industrial cities which are concentrated, of course, largely in the adjacent southern coastal regions of the country. Moreover, further south and south-west than coffee was ever grown in significant quantities (because of the recurrent, rather than occasional, dan-gers of winter frosts), the 'frontier' of agricultural settlement was gradually pushed inland, away from the original coastal settlements, from the begin-ning of the 20th century onwards. This has progressed most effectively since the 1920s as a result of the search by former coffee plantation tenants for more permanent land holdings. This internal migration to new areas was, moreover, accompanied by a flow of new migrants to Brazil from both Europe and Japan. The agricultural use of this southernmost part of Brazil brought settlement there up to the frontiers with Uruguay. Almost the whole of Uruguay's territory has, of course, been effectively settled since job opportunities offered by its expanding agricultural sector in the second half of the 19th century stimulated the same kind of migration of agricultural workers from Europe that we examined in the case of Argentina. Thus, moves that have already begun towards the rationalization and modernization of agriculture in parts of south Brazil, Uruguay and the extensive pampas of Argentina would seem more likely to lead to a *reduction*, rather than to an increase, in the present level of the rural population. This is a situation and a prospect which necessarily excludes this vast region from the 'empty heart' of the continent.

Further south, the emptiness of Argentina beyond the pampas appears very obvious on Figure 8-1. This is so in spite of the fact that southern Argentina also was an area of immigration in the late 19th and early 20th centuries. Then, certain groups of foreign settlers, either unwilling to accept the uncertain opportunities offered by the short-term tenant farming, which was all they could secure on the pampas, or else unfamiliar with the climatic conditions and agricultural practices required in those areas, sought opportunities in the more southerly parts of the country. The valleys of Patagonia provided the preferred areas of settlement and were soon occupied by farmers utilizing the locally variable physical environments which thus provided initial opportunities for diversified, largely subsistence agriculture. Later, when they were firmly established, and with the improvement in transport facilities, they were able to specialize in fruit farming in the more northerly valleys and in the production of wool from areas further south. However, much of the upland area of Southern Argentina between the more fertile and less exposed valleys remained empty because it could not be profitably utilized. This was the case even half a century ago when the farmers' expectation of returns on their labour was at a much more modest level than it is today. More recently, growing populations in the valleys have exerted considerable pressure on the limited agricultural resources of these areas and there has been consequential out-migration to the north. Their description today as 'empty areas' is true only in the same sense that the southern uplands or the highlands of Scotland can be described as empty areas. Any possibilities for resource frontier development in Southern Argentina lie only in the field of mineral exploitation and even that seems unlikely to produce great possibilities for population expansion.

12

Across the Andes (which are themselves also empty areas in the south of the continent for very obvious physical reasons!), it is difficult to find areas of Chile which can be considered as 'empty' when seen in relation to the lack of opportunities offered for the agricultural use of the land, given the prevailing adverse conditions of climate, soils and topography. The impossibility of agricultural development in the Atacama Desert, covering about the northern third of Chile, has already been demonstrated in our earlier discussions on the establishment and growth of the nitrate industry there. At the other 'end' of the country lie forest and Atlantic Chile which together form another one-third of the area of the country. In these regions, collectively accounting for over two-thirds of the area of the country, are found only a little over 30% of the country's total population of 9 million and they can certainly be correctly described as empty in any crude comparison of people with area. But again, given the conditions of the physical geography of these regions, in terms both of topography and climate, which are, in most parts, extreme even by the standards of the most rugged, wettest and windiest parts of north-west Europe, perhaps it is the extent to which colonization and settlement have been pushed, rather than their absence, which is the more surprising attribute of the human geography of Chile south of Concepción and the River Bió-Bió.

19th century colonization across this river, south from the Mediterranean heartland of Chile, followed the Treaty in 1883 with the Araucanian Indians. This Indian nation, the only one in Latin America which did not submit to the Spanish, had made its homeland in these forested areas some 300 years earlier following their tactical retreat in the face of Spanish expansionism from areas further north. The late 19th century settlers now brought large areas under a type of peasant farming with a high degree of local self-sufficiency consequent upon the relative isolation of the region from national, let alone world, markets. The colonists were, in part, landless labourers who moved south to get away from the absence of economic opportunities on the large estates of Central Chile. Of more importance, however, in settling the region were the new immigrants from Central Europe who brought with them the traditions and practices of an agriculture more suitable for the forest zone. But the difficulties of the Chilean forest environment were such, and the consequences of isolation from markets so great that even by the standards of the 19th and the earlier parts of the 20th century, it could not really be said that the colonization thrived. At best, just acceptable standards and minimally viable populations were maintained. Since the first decade or so of the 20th century, however, throughout the world of European-type civilizations (and as much in Europe itself as well as in the areas of colonization overseas) such environments and such conditions have given rise to strong out-migration movements on the part of the peoples concerned. The fact that this has happened in 'forest' Chile is in line with the general phenomenon and it explains why this part of Latin America must also be excluded from those parts of the continent where further colonization might well be directed. Thus, any future settlement in southern Chile seems likely to be orientated only to the industrial exploitation of its forests for wood products and, more especially, for pulp and paper and to the even longer-term possibility of its utilization for its tourist attractions. Neither of these developments are going to fill the region with permanent settlement on a large scale and they are, in any case, dependent upon the construction of a high-cost network of transport and communication facilities.

Thus, for good and continuing reasons the population of Chile is concentrated in the central 30% of the national territory and here there is little empty land. Much of the upland in this central region is, in fact, overpopulated with reference to its agricultural development and potential, and any hopes for increases in living standards seem likely to require a continuation of existing out-migratory trends. And in the lowlands themselves, only the acceptance of a labour-intensive agriculture (to replace the traditional haciendas), of a type that has long been practised in Mediterranean Europe, can create new opportunities for settlement. The chances of this approach providing other than a short-term solution to unemployment and underemployment in Central Chile seem remote. In the longer term, development in the region will probably become increasingly dependent on the sort of mechanized 'Mediterranean-style' agriculture now utilized in California, Australia and southern France and lead to a further need for a rural–urban migration to bring down the population densities to a level at which reasonable living standards can be achieved for the remaining people.

Thus, around much of Latin America, the 'empty' lands remain empty for very good reasons. Moreover, as we have seen, in many cases these good reasons are becoming even better; particularly in light of the rising expectations of an essentially European-orientated population in the second half of the 20th century. In other words, the 'emptiness' of much of Latin America is a rational human reaction to the occurrence of many adverse environments for human occupation and to the possibilities of developing productive agriculture without a locally resident high density of agricultural workers and their families. 'Emptiness' does not, in other words, always indicate the existence of limitless resource frontier regions waiting and asking to be opened up!

It will not, however, have escaped the reader's attention that so far in this discussion of the concept of Latin America as an empty continent, we have more or less 'skated' around its periphery. In doing so, we have, of course, successfully avoided coming to the issue of the continental interior of South America which consists essentially of the basin of the Amazon and its numerous tributaries. In all, this massive river system basin covers about 30% of the total area of South America and includes parts of the national territory of every South American country except Argentina, Uruguay, Paraguay and Chile. And, as in pre-colonial days (see Chapter 6, pages 118 to 120), the basin is still very empty with a total population not exceeding 10 million: under 6% of South America's total. Moreover, in none of the countries within which part of it is located, does the section of Amazonia in that country form part of its developed core area. It is, in fact, always highly peripheral to the central zone of development. In many cases, however, it is represented as a resource frontier in which expansion can and should take place and, in some cases, as an area potentially able to provide living space through which national problems of imbalance between man's growing demand for land and the supply of land can be solved.

This latter attitude is most clearly demonstrated in the cases of Bolivia, Peru, Ecuador and, to a lesser degree, Colombia. There, as we have seen, the Andean highlands are overpopulated. Colonization of the upper areas of Amazonia immediately to the east will, it is argued, provide the solution to this problem. But the facts of this situation have been thus for many decades. And the arguments for migration eastwards have been put forward now for almost half a century during which period of time the techniques for effecting colonization have been steadily improved: as, for example, in the growth of knowledge as to how tropical soils should be used for productive purposes. During this period also, man's ability to exploit unused regions has increased through the increasing availability of mechanical equipment and means of transportation. In spite of these favourable developments, there has still been relatively little effective colonization. Even many officially sponsored, and often relatively well financed, schemes for the resettlement of people from the Andean regions have, after reaching the stage of implementation, soon foundered in the face of social and economic difficulties.

The social difficulties have emerged from the traumatic experience of the groups which have had to move from a long-established, well-structured society in a familiar, if somewhat inhospitable, environment in the Andes to profoundly different societal and environmental conditions for which none of their accumulated knowledge and experience offered any guidelines for action. The economic difficulties have arisen not out of the inherent unproduc-tiveness of the areas of colonization, but firstly because most of the colonies failed to become economically self-sustaining and secondly because of the high capital cost of creating an effective settlement pattern. In as far as the government or other sponsoring body concerned naturally tries to recover part or all of the capital costs from the settlers, the first reason for lack of success is, in part, a function of the second. The settlers become too over-burdened with capital debts to permit them to earn enough surplus from their agricultural activities either for investment in improvements in their holdings or even to achieve an acceptable level of consumption. Moreover, the loca-tion of their colonies in relation to the markets for their products and the sources of their wants has meant not only low sales prices for the commodi-ties they produce but also high delivered prices for their imports: both as a result of the high transports costs involved.

So far too little has changed in this general situation to indicate a greatly increased likelihood that settlements in the Oriente of the countries concerned will become economically self-sustaining in the foreseeable future. The exis-tence of a very small number of apparently successful settlements would not appear to negate this general conclusion concerning the overall settlement possibilities for the vast areas involved. Part of the reasoning behind such an assertion lies in the inability of settlers adequately to service the capital that must be invested in large quantities in such schemes. In that there is neither expectation nor hope that these capital costs could or should be recovered in the short term from the settlers themselves, then expenditure on the necessary roads, communication systems and the provision of social and other facili-ties invariably becomes a charge on the funds of the central government. In the absence of any significant income from taxes either from companies or people in the areas which are being opened up, the expenditure thus represents a drain on the financial resources provided by other regions of the country concerned. Government revenues in none of these countries, however, have been, or are, noted for their buoyancy and plentitude. Indeed, exactly the opposite is the case at most times, for the demands on government revenues far exceed their availability as the normal order of events. Thus, any funds spent on opening up areas of a country for colonization through the provi-sion of basic infrastructure and social services in the new regions, diminish the money available for investment in the already populated areas of the countries concerned. And, in each case, the populated areas are in desperate need of whatever development funds the government can make available out of revenues or borrow from abroad.

Thus, the question of opening up the empty areas of the 'East' has, in every case, become a political issue. It involves a tug-of-war between those who would have significant resources devoted to the development of the Oriente, in the long-term interests of the country, and those who argue that the short-er-term needs of the populated areas of the country are the more pressing. This latter group sometimes also argues that resources put into the populated areas will, in any case, produce a better return on investment. Because of such political attitudes towards the investment of resources in the areas to the east of the Andes one finds that policies have often been inconsistent and lacking in continuity such that periods of road building and other infrastructural development have alternated with the non-availability of funds for continued investment in such projects. The process of 'opening up' the east has thus been patchy and irregular. In the particular physical environment of the selva, where the climate and vegetation characteristics tend to depreciate untended and incompleted man-made projects very quickly, such irregularity in the flow of funds has really meant the misuse of what capital has been invested. A road that stops in the 'middle of nowhere', or a power or water supply system which does not reach the majority of the potential consumers produces no return on the investment made. But even where particular projects have been successfully completed, their scale has been so relatively small as to ensure that the results are almost lost in the immensity of the area involved. Moreover, they have produced too little by way of a cash flow, either in the public or the private sector, to make investment in their expansion possible, without further recourse to external capital sources.

Thus, the Orientes of Colombia, Ecuador, Peru and Bolivia, formed by the upper reaches of the Amazon and its tributaries, remain almost empty of population and largely unused, except for developmental efforts, mostly only tentative, in the areas immediately to the east of the Andes. They are still largely outside the effective national territories of the countries concerned. In the mid-20th century the effective colonization and settlement of this pioneer fringe appears to demand a massive and continuing capital investment on a scale far beyond the present capabilities of the countries concerned, even if they could agree on jointly planned, directed and implemented efforts whereby the economies of scale generated could help towards making the investment worthwhile. Peru has formulated such a plan, orientated around the so-called Andean 'marginal highway', and this will be evaluated in the final chapter of this section of the book when we look at the emerging themes in the economic geography of the continent. In the meantime, the individual efforts of the separate countries concerned have had basically no impact on the general patterns of the spatial distribution of economic activities in the region.

To the east, in the main part of the Amazon basin lying mainly in Brazil, the area as a whole is not quite as empty as it was or quite as limited in the degree and extent of economic activities achieved. However, one must still emphasize that what has been happening in the centre of Brazil is still relatively small–scale; both in terms of capital involved and of job opportunities created when compared with the development of the Brazilian economy in the growth areas of the country in the south and south-east. Investment in buildings alone, in just the city of São Paulo in the last twenty years, appears to exceed the total capital invested in the whole of the interior (except for that which has gone into Brasilia and its road system)!

As described earlier in this chapter, migratory movements in Brazil have taken settlers well inland in the south and south-centre of the country in search of land to use and occupy on a permanent basis in preference to an uncertain existence as insecure tenant farmers in the older-established areas. Recent investigations show that such spontaneous movement of peasants is now taking place even into the Amazon basin, with settlements and landholdings for agriculture being carved out of the selva ahead of the developing road system in the interior of the country. Then, as the road system is expanded and extended, so the degree and effectiveness of this settlement increases.

Apart from these peasant-scale, unsponsored and unsupported ventures, the establishment of which is still too recent to make possible any evaluation of their degree of success, there has also been development of a very different sort in even more remote valleys of the northward-flowing tributaries of the Amazon and in the upper Parana valley. Here, again, however, the development is so recent as to make evaluation of its long-term significance impossible. Largely as a result of tax incentives offered by the Brazilian government to companies and entrepreneurs willing to put money into the interior of the country, large-scale investors have begun to investigate the possibilities of commercial cattle raising in the selva. The first ventures have involved the clearance of thousands of hectares of forest and the establishment of a grass cover. Such work very obviously involves a high investment in the purchase of heavy machinery and also in its transportation to and within an area basically without roads. This is a situation, moreover, which will, at least in the early stages of production, also involve the airlifting out of any cattle that may be raised for sale in the distant national markets. The scale of the operations, however, appears to be so large that it will, if successful, quickly produce an increased incentive and motivation for the completion of a road system which in its turn will further stimulate the development of the enterprise. Though some of the capital flowing into these ventures is Brazilian (as a result of the tax advantages noted above), the speed and extent of the development also appears to be a function of an increased flow of West German capital to Brazil, a country which appears to have captured the imagination of those Germans looking for investment opportunities overseas. The German entrepreneurs have also been encouraged in such investment by the existence of favourable German tax laws which, a few years ago, were changed to encourage overseas investment in the developing world. Thus, as a result of the combination of Brazilian and German fiscal encouragement for investment in the interior of Brazil, it appears that the ventures there could soon approach the critical minimum size which we have suggested is needed to make the development of a resource frontier an effective and self-sustaining possibility. If and when they achieve this, then these colonization developments could well turn out to be the largest in terms of areas and the quickest in terms of time of any, anywhere in Latin America. The next few years are the really critical ones in this respect.

However, in spite of such dramatic changes taking place in parts of the Amazon and Parana basins in Brazil, most of the vast area remains untouched; or even in some cases, as with Manaus and the now largely-abandoned rubber industry of its region, still looking back with nostalgia to an earlier period of a higher level of economic activity. In these cases, the higher levels of activity were not sustainable in the face of competition from similar products coming from other more favourably located parts of the world. This description of the situation in the Amazon basin is valid also for the less extensive basin of the Orinoco and its tributaries and the even smaller and less developed northward-flowing rivers of the Guayanas, where effective occupation is limited to areas within 250 kilometres or so of the coast. Brasilia on the eastern fringe of the Brazilian selva, and Ciudad Guyana, on the fringe of the Venezuelan selva, constitute developments which can be considered separately from the question of the use or otherwise of the continent's 'empty heart'. Their significance will be examined in the next chapter dealing with the future economic geographical aspects of Latin America's development.

The intention in presenting this brief evaluation of the 'empty lands' of Latin America has been to put the situation into perspective. Three aspects of the situation need to be stressed. Firstly, one must note that the continent is not quite as empty as it is sometimes made out to be. Secondly, it is seen that many of the 'empty' areas are virtually unpopulated or have a very low density of population for very good reasons and that in many of these cases there is a trend towards the outward movement of population for social as well as economic reasons, thus further denuding such areas of people. Thirdly, it is clear that the empty areas which could well have potential for development are often proving difficult to develop, if for no other reason, and this is in itself a very good one, than that investment in such areas is less rewarding and less urgent than investment elsewhere in the countries concerned. Only in the special case of Brazil—with a strong non-economic motivation for colonizing effectively all its national territory (a kind of 'manifest destiny' attitude to national frontiers)—have we noted a really strong and effective movement to extend the area of occupied territory. Even there, however, the great bulk of 'empty Brazil' remains empty and seems likely to do so for most of the rest of this century.

Thus, having evaluated the current position as far as the empty areas and the resource frontiers of the continent are concerned, we must now return to the current, and, for-the-foreseeable-future, more important economic geographical problems of the populated and utilized areas of the Latin American nations and examine further our hypothesis that the geographical pattern of economic development can be effectively described in terms of a centre-periphery model for each nation.

The Geography of Underdevelopment

Earlier in the chapter we presented a set of factors which, it was suggested, caused Latin American economies to become spatially concentrated around a central, usually the capital, city location whilst the rest of the national territories, even the effectively occupied parts, were largely ignored in terms of their developmental possibilities beyond the stage of traditional agricultural activities, plantation agriculture and mineral extraction. We must now demonstrate that such a description of the geography of secondary and tertiary economic activities in Latin America is justified. Before doing so, however, it appears worthwhile to note briefly that we are dealing here with an issue which is relevant and, indeed, fundamental to the whole problem of economic development and underdevelopment.

An earlier virtually *exclusive* concern by economic planners for ways of attacking nationally aggregated problems of economic growth has now been rejected as an approach which can satisfactorily ensure that the welfare of the population in all parts of a country will benefit from economic development.

Thus in Western Europe we have become increasingly familiar with the additional attention which has been devoted in recent years to the spatial patterns of economic development within national boundaries. However, this increasing concern for the geography of economic development in mature industrial countries has not yet been matched by a similar degree of interest in such matters in the developing countries. Even apart from what is, or more usually is not, presented in governmental planning exercises in this field, one must also note that the theoretical and descriptive literature on 'development economics' largely ignores the problem!

A recent textbook (dating from 1966) on development planning, written by Professor Lewis, one of the world's leading advisers in this field, devotes a mere seven pages to the question of 'regional balance' in a developing economy, out of 121 devoted in total to plan strategies. And in contrast with his proposals on other aspects of economic development planning, where recommended strategies are based on a wealth of analyses, his conclusions on strategies for the regional problem appear to be extremely tentative and hesitant. For example, he concludes that 'a workable approach to regional balance is to treat suspiciously all proposals for development in towns whose population exceeds 500,000 or has not yet reached 5,000.' Such a conclusion appears to be based on little more than preconceived notions of doubtful validity. A present minimum town size restraint on the location of development is a particularly bad indicator for the potentiality for growth when one is concerned with countries with a 'resource frontier' and which have only relatively small parts of their national territories in effective occupation. Such advice given to the United States even less than 100 years ago would have effectively prevented the development of most of its national territory and of many centres of industry and commerce which today exceed the 500,000 population mark! Nor is suspicion over planning new growth in cities already having over half-a-million people necessarily wise, as much evidence from the United States and Europe indicates the critical importance of large cities in creating the right conditions for the cumulative growth of secondary and tertiary economic activities.

However, while such advice may not be appropriate in its specific recommendations, it does at least recognize that there is a geographical aspect to development planning which needs attention simultaneously with that given to other aspects. But there is another school of economists which still argues that developing countries cannot afford the 'luxury' of regional planning. These economists see such regional planning as a device whereby maximum rates of growth are constrained by the need to locate activities in 'economically undeserving areas'. They argue that such uneconomic location of activities adversely affects the speed of economic growth because scarce resources (particularly capital) are used less efficiently than would otherwise be the case. In the longer term, these economists suggest, the spatial problems of the developing countries will either 'sort themselves out' or the countries will become rich enough to be able to afford to divert some resources to dealing with their depressed and undeveloped regions.

With reference to Latin America, even if not to other parts of the developing world, such a view seems naive in the extreme since it ignores both the economic and the socio-political realities of the contemporary situation. Regional disparities in per capita well-being (measured by means of income-per-head or through indices presenting social as well as economic criteria) of the order of 10 to 1 exist in most Latin American countries. This is the case even in Mexico where there has been some concern for backward areas of the country over the whole of the revolutionary period since 1910. In other countries the regional disparities appear to be even greater. This is not only fundamentally divisive for a country in political and social terms, and hence certain to hinder modernization efforts, but is also significant in economic terms. Economically, such disparities put almost all the population in the poorer area of a country outside the ranks of the consumers of anything but the simplest and cheapest goods, and thus act as a major restraint on the creation of an economy diversified away from the production of primary commodities for export into one in which manufacturing industry has continued scope for expansion.

One can find many examples of such restraints on industrial growth in Latin American countries over the last two decades. New factories have not been able to produce to their full capacity because there was insufficient demand for their output due to the inadequate purchasing power of many people in the poorer parts of the country. This phenomenon of less-than-capacity use of factories has again even affected Mexico, which has proceeded further and faster than most of its Latin American neighbours in the industrialization process. The continuation of this situation, in which there is a lack of a sufficiently strong increase in the growth rate of effective demand for industrial products as a result of the continuation of wide discrepancies in income between the core area and the periphery, would seem to ensure that the degree of industrialization can never rise above a modest level. This will inevitably frustrate development plans: a phenomenon which is not unknown in Latin America where, as we shall see below, there is good evidence of chronic regional imbalance in all the national economies.

Dual Spatial Economies in Latin America

However, it is easy to say that Latin American countries exhibit the features of a dual spatial economy. Nor is it difficult to suggest that such an economy is marked, on the one hand, by a developed core region or limited areal extent, with an important industrial component contributing to its degree of development, and on the other, by an extensive undeveloped 'periphery' with few secondary economic activities. It is much more difficult to present adequate quantified evidence to demonstrate the validity of the description. Paucity of spatial statistics and information creates difficulties in describing the situation adequately, or accurately, even for a single country, let alone for all the countries of Latin America on a comparable basis.

Even in the case of Venezuela, where the spatial structure of the economy has been more thoroughly subjected to analysis than elsewhere in the continent, the presentation of the pattern of regional imbalance has been principally in terms of the degree of urbanization of the population in different parts of the country. But in Latin America the degree of urbanization and the distribution of urban population is not necessarily an adequate indicator of the distribution of economic activities. Elsewhere in the continent there are broad regional figures of incomes per head (generally on a provincial or departmental basis) but these mask significant spatial variations which occur within the large administrative areas concerned. Moreover, in that the administrative units concerned vary in size and scale within, as well as between, countries, comparisons based on such evidence are difficult to justify. Statistics of employment by regions and sectors are either unavailable or unreliable and, in any case, are not necessarily a particularly good measure of spatial variations in the level of economic activities for they fail to distinguish contrasts in productivity arising from the variable application of capital or energy to the activities concerned.

In an attempt to overcome the lack of readily available and comparable data for examining the geography of economic activities within the countries of Latin America, an analysis has been made of the spatial distribution of available electricity–generating capacity. It is self-evident that a more appropriate indicator of geographic patterns of economic development would have been provided by an examination of the spatial distribution patterns of electricity consumption by industry and other economic sectors, but such data is not available on a sufficiently wide and standardized basis, whereas continental-wide information for roughly the same period of time (the early 1960s) was available on the location

Figure 8–2. Latin America: the distribution of electricity-generating capacity

and capacity of all electricity-generating stations, except the very smallest ones (see Figure 8-2).

Two factors, however, permit us to assume that the distribution and size of generating stations indicate the quantities of electricity consumed in different locations. Firstly, all of Latin America is short of electricity-generating capacity. Where capacity exists, therefore, it will be run at maximum possible output so that the quantity of electricity produced (and therefore consumed) depends mainly on the size of each station. Secondly, long-distance transmission systems for electricity hardly exist in Latin America. This means that electricity consumption is spatially concentrated around the production points and as the areal basis for the analyses of the data is by grid squares as large as 100 km × 100 km, there can be little movement of electricity across the graticule. Where long-distance transmission systems are known to exist, as in south central Chile and from the hydro-electricity stations on the River São Francisco in eastern Brazil, appropriate adjustments have been made to the allocation of generating capacity in the grid squares affected.

Using the data for each of the nine largest countries of Latin America, a cartographical and statistical presentation of the geographical pattern of electricity production is given in Figures 8-3 to 8-11. Cartographically these provide a clear visual impression of the high degree of geographical concentration of activities in all the nine countries and this impression is confirmed, ranked and measured by simple statistical analyses of the mapped patterns. Each map includes a graph showing the minimum number of grid squares required to account for 25%, 50% and 75% of total activities. The position in the nine countries is summarized in Table 8-1.

Table 8–1. Distribution of electricity–generating capacity in the nine largest Latin American countries

Number of grid squares needed to locate each quartile of national capacity	25%	50%	75%	100%	Total number of grid squares in country
Argentina	1	2	5	31	299
Bolivia	1	2	4	22	151
Brazil	1	2	6	30	908
Chile	2	4	8	34	134
Colombia	2	4	7	22	160
Mexico	3	8	20	64	217
Paraguay	1	1	1	5	71
Peru	2	3	7	29	178
Venezuela	1	3	6	30	128

KEY TO MAPS SHOWING SPATIAL PATTERNS OF ELECTRICITY
GENERATING CAPACITY IN LATIN AMERICAN COUNTRIES.

●   Capital City (point of origin for the 100 x 100 km. graticule)

✛   Mean Centre of Electric Production derived from the formula:

$$\bar{\Delta} = \begin{cases} \bar{x} = \dfrac{\sum (x_i c_i)}{C} \\[2ex] \bar{y} = \dfrac{\sum (y_i c_i)}{C} \end{cases}$$

where x_i = vertical co-ordinate of the i'th area

         y_i = horizontal co-ordinate of the i'th area

         c = capacity of the i'th area

         C = Total Capacity

Spatial Distribution of Electricity Generating Capacity – The Capacity has been totalled for each square
of the graticule and the totals ranked in descending order. Distribution is shown thus –

     Minimum squares required to locate 25% of country's total capacity

     Minimum additional number of squares (if any) required locate next 25% of capacity

     Minimum additional number of squares (if any) required locate next 25% of capacity

     All other areas with generating capacity

     No generating capacity

Graph: This plots cumulative capacity by ranked order of squares shows also number of squares
            required to achieve 25%, 50% and 75% of total capacity

Index: Index of Spatial Concentration of Electricity Generating Capacity This falls within the range
            0 to 1 and is derived from the formula

$$1 - \frac{\sum\limits_{i=1}^{m} c_i r}{\sum\limits_{r=1}^{n} r\left(\dfrac{C}{m}\right)}$$

where c_i = capacity of i'th square

         C = Total Capacity

         r = radius in 50 km. intervals from the mean centre

Key page. This refers to Figures 8-3 to 8-11 on pages 182-185. Also see text for
explanation.

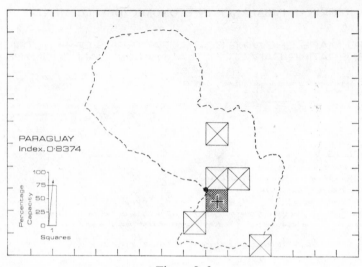

Figure 8–3

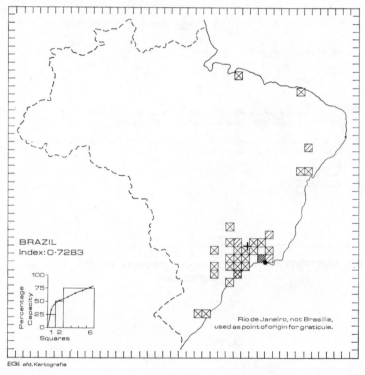

Figure 8–4

Each map shows, for the country concerned, the spatial pattern of electricity-generating capacity. For an explanation see the Key on page 181 and the text

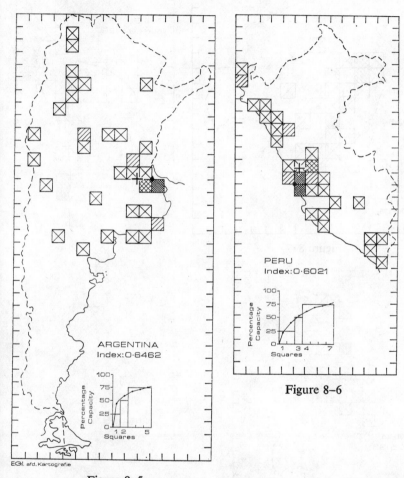

ARGENTINA
Index: 0·6462

PERU
Index: 0·6021

Figure 8–6

Figure 8–5

Each map shows, for the country concerned, the spatial pattern of electricity-generating capacity. For an explanation see the Key on page 181 and the text

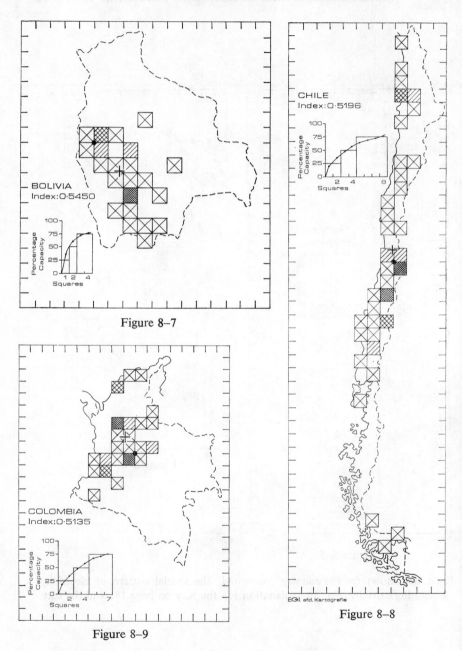

Figure 8–7

Figure 8–9

Figure 8–8

Each map shows, for the country concerned, the spatial pattern of electricity-generating capacity. For an explanation see the Key on page 181 and the text

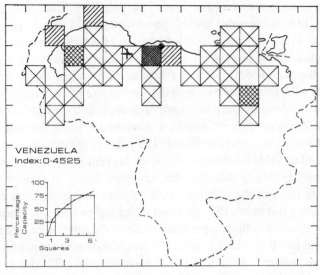

Figure 8–10

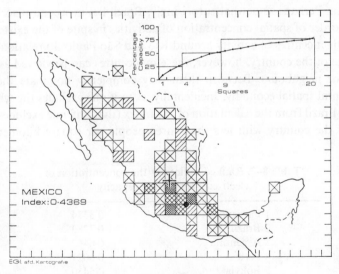

Figure 8–11

Each map shows, for the country concerned, the spatial pattern of electricity-generating capacity. For an explanation see the Key on page 181 and the text

This shows that in five of the nine countries at least 25% of activities are located in a single square and in three of the remaining four countries in only 2 squares. In four countries half of the activities are in 1 or 2 squares and in four others in 3 or 4. Even the third quartile of activities is spatially highly concentrated, taking place in no more than four more squares for any country except in the case of Mexico. Taking the analysis a little further, so as to relate the degree of concentration of activities to the size of each country, and to take into consideration the relative importance of different centres of activity, an *Index of Concentration of Capacity* around the previously determined Mean Centre of Production was calculated. The index is recorded in each case on the map and in Table 8-2 the nine countries are ranked by their indices.

This analysis clearly indicates the very high degree of concentration of activities in most of the countries with only the indices for Venezuela and Mexico falling just below the mid-point in the scale whose limits are 0 and 1. A score of 0 would indicate a perfectly uniform distribution of activities over the national territory whilst a score of 1 would indicate the concentration of all activities within a radius of 50 km of the mean centre. This latter situation is, in fact, closely approached in the case of Paraguay where, as Figure 8-3 shows, there is only very limited development of activities outside the Asunción area. Perhaps somewhat surprisingly, Brazil lies in second place in the ranked order of spatial concentration of activities in spite of the existence of two distinct centres of activity around Rio and São Paulo. In relation to the total size of the country, however, these two centres can be viewed as being next-door neighbours. Between them they completely dominate the non-agricultural spatial economy. Incidentally, even if one excludes the whole of 'empty' Brazil from the calculation of the Index (that is if one excludes those parts of the country with less than three people per square kilometre, or

Table 8–2. Ranked indices of the concentration of electricity-generating capacity

1 Paraguay	0·8374
2 Brazil	0·7283
3 Argentina	0·6462
4 Peru	0·6021
5 Bolivia	0·5450
6 Chile	0·5196
7 Colombia	0·5135
8 Venezuela	0·4525
9 Mexico	0·4369

roughly all the country west of a line linking Uruguay and Fortaleza), then the Index of Concentration for the remaining part is still as high as 0·6.

At the other end of the ranked order of the nine countries Venezuela and Mexico, as already mentioned, have indices of slightly under 0·5. The results for these countries quantify special features in their spatial patterns of electricity generation. In Mexico, a planned programme of rural electrification extending back over almost 25 years, together with the use of electricity for pumping irrigation water in some of the large-scale agricultural projects in areas along the west coast and adjacent to the boundary with the United States, accounts for the much more widespread availability of electricity.

In spite of this, however, the concentration of capacity around Mexico City still stands out very clearly. This confirms the other available evidence that we have of the great concentration there of non-agricultural activities. In Venezuela, the use of electricity in the oilfields of the Maracaibo region and in the large refineries of the Paraguana peninsula, coupled with the first stages in the development of electricity-generation capacity in the Guayana project in the eastern part of the country, introduces an element of country-wide dispersal in the spatial pattern. In the light of these aspects of the country's economic geography it is rather surprising that Venezuela's index is as high as 0·45. This gives an indication of the dominance of the Caracas metropolitan region in non-oil industry activities.

Thus, the maps and the statistical analyses of the geographical distribution of electricity production within the nine countries clearly indicate, providing one accepts the validity of the use of this spatial variable, the existence and high relative importance of the 'core area' of development in each country and the co-existence of such an area in each country with a far more extensive 'periphery' of either very limited, or even non-existent, degree of development as far as non-agricultural activities are concerned.

From this country-by-country examination of the core/periphery phenomenon within the largest nations, we may move on to examine the position from the viewpoint of the whole of the continent: again using the distribution of electricity-generating capacity as a means of establishing the picture. Locations where at least a modest 50 MW of electricity-producing capacity are sited are ranked in Table 8-3 and are designated as the centres of non-agricultural economic activity in Latin America.

The descending importance of each centre in the rank order is a function of its generating capacity and its importance is, moreover, shown relative to that of the centre in the first position—Buenos Aires. The geographical distribution of these centres over the continent is shown in Figure 8-12. In

Table 8-3. Ranked centres of economic activity in Latin America

Rank	Centre	Country	Rank within country	Size (when Buenos Aires = 100)
1	Buenos Aires	Argentina	1	100
2	São Paulo	Brazil	1	63
3	Mexico City	Mexico	1	50
4	Rio de Janeiro	Brazil	2	34
5	Santiago	Chile	1	25
6	Havana	Cuba	1	18
7	Caracas	Venezuela	1	17
8	Lima	Peru	1	17
9	Rosario	Argentina	2	15
10	Montevideo	Uruguay	1	13
11	Antofagasta	Chile	2	9·1
12	Mar del Plata	Argentina	3	8·9
13	Belo Horizonte	Brazil	3	8·6
14	Maracaibo Oil Towns	Venezuela	2	8·4
15	Concepción	Chile	3	7·5
16	Veracruz	Mexico	2	7·0
17	Monterrey	Mexico	3	6·8
18	Medellín	Colombia	1	6·6
19	Ciudad Guayana	Venezuela	3	6·5
20	Mazatlan	Mexico	4	6·3
21	Córdoba	Argentina	4	5·8
22	Recife	Brazil	4	5·7
23	Bogotá	Colombia	2	5·7
24	Panama	Panama	1	5·3
25	Cali	Colombia	3	5·0
26	Mendoza	Argentina	5	4·8
27	Paraguana	Venezuela	4	4·7
28	Maracaibo	Venezuela	5	4·5
29	Salvador	Brazil	5	4·4
30	La Paz	Bolivia	1	3·8
31	Porto Alegre	Brazil	6	3·7
32	Guadalajara	Mexico	5	3·6
33	Tampico	Mexico	6	3·1
34	Barranquilla	Colombia	4	2·9
35	San José	Costa Rica	1	2·7
36	San Juan	Argentina	6	2·6
37	Chihuahua	Mexico	6	2·5
38	San Salvador	El Salvador	1	2·4
39	Santiago	Cuba	2	2·4
40	Cajamarca	Peru	2	2·4
41	Bahia Blanca	Argentina	7	2·3

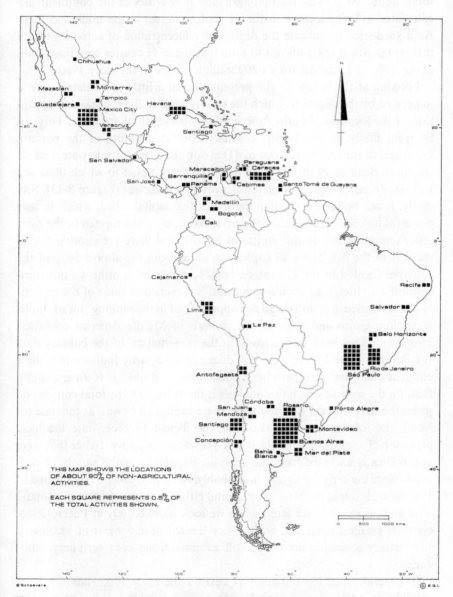

THIS MAP SHOWS THE LOCATIONS
OF ABOUT 90% OF NON-AGRICULTURAL
ACTIVITIES.

EACH SQUARE REPRESENTS 0.5% OF
THE TOTAL ACTIVITIES SHOWN.

Figure 8–12. Latin America: the main centres of economic activity. See the text
for the explanation of their derivation

total, about 90% of all the non-agricultural activities of the continent are calculated as being located in the 41 centres shown in the table and map. As a yard-stick to indicate the degree of concentration of activities which this represents, it is significant to note that these 41 centres contained only about 25% of Latin America's 200 million people in the early 1960s.

Looking at the results of the presentation in a little more detail, one is impressed by the degree to which the results confirm the traditional description of the location of Latin America's non-agricultural activities. This can be seen, firstly, in the highly coastally-orientated nature of the pattern. Over half of the centres (22 out of 41) are on the coast (or tide-water) whilst the mean distance of the other 19 from the nearest port to which there is a railway or paved-road connexion is only 75 kilometres (Figure 8-13). Secondly, it can be seen in the domination of the capital cities, which is very powerful indeed. Capital cities comprise eight out of the top ten in the rank order (counting Rio as the capital of Brazil), and there are another five in the rest of the list. These 13 capitals in all account for almost 58% of the activities located in the 41 centres, or 52% of all the continent's non-agricultural activities. One should point out, however, that some of the capitals of Latin American countries do not appear at all in the ranking: for example, Asunción, Quito and some of the capitals of Middle America countries. However, as we have seen already in the presentation of the country data for Paraguay (see Figure 8-3), this does not necessarily indicate that these countries lack the core/periphery phenomenon. Rather is it an indication that, on the scale at which this analysis is made (that is, the total continental scale) the development of activities in these capital cities was, at the time for which the information was available, insufficient to necessitate the local provision of even 50 MW of electricity-generating capacity. Hence they were automatically excluded from the analysis. Expansion in the supply of electricity since the early 1960s has, in probably every case except Tegucigalpa in Honduras, brought the remaining capital cities up to this minimum demand level and, as we shall see later, when we look more closely at Puerto Rico, even the smallest countries, with a very limited development of secondary and tertiary economic activities, still exhibit strong core/periphery tendencies.

In general, updating the analysis beyond the early 1960s has not been possible as only incomplete information is available on the growth of electricity-generating capacity since then. However, what information has become available does suggest that the pattern already depicted is being accentuated rather than weakened. Details of newly developed or planned

Figure 8–13. Latin America: the centres of economic activity (from Figure 8.12) and their location with reference to ports and/or other transport facilities. Note the coastal or near-coastal location of nearly all the centres

generating capacity show much of it to be in areas of existing high capacity, as, for example, in the 1968 commissioning of a 500 MW station in Buenos Aires. Most of the rest is in locations suitable, as far as the physical geographical conditions are concerned, for the development of hydro-electricity. These locations, however, are also convenient to allow for the electricity's transmission to areas of existing demand.

The Continued Geographical Concentration of Economic Development

This continuation of the process of the spatial concentration of non-agricultural economic activities indicates that the limited and modest attempts by Latin American countries to achieve a broader geographical spread of economic growth and employment opportunities have not yet, in general, been very successful. This suggests that the 'play of market forces', relatively unhampered as far as location policies are concerned in most Latin American countries, is, in fact, having the effects that the Swedish economist, G. Myrdal, suggested it would have. He hypothesized that such market forces would have a tendency to increase inequalities between regions of a country as industrial production, commerce, banking, insurance, shipping and, indeed, all those economic activities which tend to give a higher than average return, cluster in certain localities. At the same time, he argued that the expansion of activities in the favoured locality has 'backwash effects' elsewhere in the countries concerned. These effects include denuding the other localities of capital, of their resources of skilled labour and of benefits from intra-regional trade. In other words, there is a continuation in the development of the particular spatial pattern of economic activity which, we suggested earlier, typifies the geography of contemporary economic development in Latin America.

We have since defined the 'favoured localities' and have noted the high degree of concentration of economic activities in these localities in almost every country of the continent. More detailed studies of particular situations serve to confirm and elaborate this general view. In Argentina, the Buenos Aires region, already the foremost centre of the whole continent (see Figure 8-5 and Table 8-3) continues to grow as it attracts most of the new secondary and tertiary industries that are created in the country, thus more than maintaining its estimated share of almost two-thirds of total national value-added in manufacturing and commerce. Around Buenos Aires, relatively proximate cities such as Rosario and Mar del Plata (both about 300 kilometres from Buenos Aires) achieve expansion through 'overspill' tendencies from the 'core city' as some entrepreneurs decide that the benefits of a Buenos Aires location are offset by the costs likely to be incurred by locating in a city of over 6 million people with its consequent transportation and congestion problems. Further away, however, Córdoba, some 600 kilometres from Buenos Aires, has only succeeded in securing some share in the expansion of industry in Argentina by dint of considerable local efforts on the part of the city authorities, local businessmen, trades union leaders and other influential parties. They formed a group for stimulating new investment in the locality and attempted to achieve this aim both by publicity for the city's advantages for industry and by offering help over the provision of sites and their development for industrial purposes. The fact that Córdoba succeeded in attracting industry—most notably by securing important factories connected with the motor car industry—seems to have been due more to its own efforts than to any really positive commitment on the part of the national government to the expansion of the region. In less favourably located parts of Argentina for industrial development, for example Misiones, Formosa and Patagonia, there have been no similar concerted local efforts to secure development. Nor has the national government paid little more than political lip-service to the need for, and the desirability of, stimulating local regional economies through their diversification away from agriculture and other primary activities. There is thus, as yet, no evidence of the creation of a situation in which these other areas appear to have any propensity for sustained economic expansion based on the growth of economic activities 'which tend to give a higher than average return'.

The inclusion of proposals for regional development in the election programmes of political parties and statements by national governments that such development is, indeed, a fundamental part of their economic policies, are very common throughout Latin America. In Mexico, regional development, albeit directed from the centre, was virtually a 1910 revolutionary warcry. In terms of the spatial patterns of infrastructure development since then, as, for example, in the provision of rural electricity, the nationwide supply of oil and natural gas, the construction of roads and the spatial extension of welfare services, attention to parts of the country away from the capital city can be numbered among the achievements of successive Mexican governments. But these same governments have taken no really effective steps over the same period either to encourage the dispersal of established manufacturing and other secondary and tertiary economic activities away from Mexico City, or even to discourage its further concentration there. In fact, their policies in this sphere of activity have evolved such that they have exactly the opposite effects. These policies thus tend to strengthen the already strong market forces which favour the location of everything in the centre!

This has come about because government policies have deliberately aimed to keep down the costs of the factors of production in Mexico City. Amongst the measures that have been taken in furtherance of these policies are, firstly, the subsidization of freight rates on foodstuffs and agricultural and other raw materials moved to Mexico City from other parts of the country. (Note that there has been no compensating subsidization of the cost of transporting manufactured goods in Mexico, thus effectively discouraging location away from Mexico City which, for most such goods, provides some 80% of the total market) Secondly, there has been the subsidization of certain items of consumption (particularly basic foodstuffs and gasoline) in Mexico City, aimed at containing the pressures for wage increases which might otherwise have priced this location out of the market for certain industries. In taking such action the Mexican governments concerned, and they are by no means the only Latin American governments to act in this way, indicate their acceptance of the importance of two separate considerations. Firstly, they have accepted that it is entirely 'natural', and more than fully expected, that any industrialist would want to locate in Mexico City. If he cannot do this with a reasonable chance of success, then he may decide not to proceed with his plans. In other words, the governments believe that they do not have an ability to make industrialists locate elsewhere in the country away from Mexico City. If they did choose to try to force a factory away from the capital city region then the entrepreneur concerned would, in turn, choose not to build his plant in Mexico at all. This is a risk that governments consider they cannot afford to take.

Secondly, in spite of all the political platitudes expressed about the need for, and desirability of, ensuring that citizens in all parts of the country have an opportunity to participate in the nation's development, national leaders know that they are 'made' or 'broken' by their ability or otherwise to sell themselves to the most articulate, best organized and politically most conscious pressure group in the country. The national leaders are fully aware that this group occupies the tenements and shanty towns, as well as the elegant suburbs, of the Federal District and its immediately surrounding area. If there is legislation, or threat of legislation, that is likely to reduce the ability of Mexico City to continue to attract jobs and income, then large numbers from this group can be outside the parliament buildings or the presidential palace within a matter of a few days, at most, or even a few hours, if necessary. Their abilities to pressurize governments are recognized clearly. By contrast, the failure of a government to match its electoral promises to less articulate, ill-organized, less politically conscious (and much smaller) groups in the distant states is unlikely to produce anything much more serious than a spot of local trouble outside the offices of the government's representative in the area concerned, or possibly the 'threat' of a delegation which will travel from the area affected to Mexico City in order to present the grievances of the people it represents. Such a delegation can, on arrival in Mexico City, easily be overawed and overshadowed by the appropriate Minister and his city-based experts who will, if it is necessary to convince the delegates that all will be well within the 'foreseeable' future, usually be able to argue effectively even that black is white. Political reality in other words, even in Mexico and much more so in most other Latin American countries, lies in the dominance of the central government whose actions can easily and usually do have the effect of strengthening the development of the core region at the expense of the country's unprivileged periphery.

The Role of Transport Facilities

Mexico also illustrates nicely another aspect of the regional development problem within the framework of the core-periphery situation for the spatial economic organization of society. Transportation developments, especially the construction and improvement of roads, are frequently held to be the key to regional expansion. In that the absence of transport facilities, or the existence of only inferior ones, obviously means that any economic activity which depends on contact with the outside world (for example, for obtaining supplies of raw materials and components, and/or for marketing the goods produced) will never be located in areas so affected, this is something of a truism. Even in this context, however, one should recall that the development of certain economic activities in isolated locations does in itself sometimes produce the transport infrastructure required. We saw examples of this in the previous chapter, when we were examining the growth of plantation systems and of extractive industry in Latin America and we have seen another example in this chapter in our discussion of the embryonic growth of a cattle-raising industry in the interior of Brazil. Apart from this relationship between transport facilities and the growth of new economic activities, the hypothesis stated above, on the role of transport in development, appears to imply that if only the road and/or rail facilities in those parts of a country which lie beyond the boundary of the developed core were to be improved, then the development gap between 'core' and 'periphery' would start to close as entrepreneurs rush to locate their investment in the latter area rather than the former.

But this 'law' of development assumes that all else is equal. However, from our knowledge of the contrasts between core and periphery we know that this assumption is as far from being realistic as it is possible to get! And because it is so unrealistic, the hypothesis as stated is invalid. There would, in fact, appear to be sound theoretical reasons, as well as much empirical evidence, to suggest that an alternative, almost in fact a contradictory, hypothesis more nearly represents the truth of the situation as far as transport developments are concerned. This can be stated as follows: where there is a development or improvement of a transportation infrastructure within a country already marked by strong regional imbalance in development amounting to the existence of a core/periphery situation, then the effect is to strengthen the market forces which favour the development of the core region. This is because the cost of getting raw materials and other factors of production into the centre, and the cost of getting the finished goods back to whatever markets may exist in the periphery, are both reduced. Thus the centre's products can now compete with alternatives which had previously been locally made. So small-scale industries, using primitive or intermediate technology only and located in the towns of the 'periphery', fall victim to the products of the more advanced technology located in the 'centre'. Similarly, the marketing and wholesaling functions of the peripheral towns can now be superseded, in part at least, by similar activities in the centre where increasing economies of scale in the growth of these functions are such as to enable them to more than offset the transport costs involved in delivering goods to a much wider area. This is so because the improvement of transport facilities has led to a reduction in the per kilometre transport costs, whilst increasing size of shipment arising from the greater throughput also reduces the unit cost. Such consequences seem to have arisen from the considerable investment of funds in Mexico's road network, the development of which has significantly enhanced the competitiveness of many capital cities' activities. Similarly in Venezuela, where, until the 1960s, virtually the only large element of investment of government revenues from oil, outside investment in Caracas and its immediate region, was in the field of road construction. But all roads built led to Caracas which could thus be fed with its requirements more cheaply, whilst the outward-bound lanes of the same roads could carry mass-produced articles from the factories in the Caracas area to all parts of the country: to the detriment of the level and range of economic activities in the country's smaller towns.

This preceding argument could be interpreted as an attack on the utility of transport-infrastructure improvement in helping economic development. To attempt to sustain such an argument would so obviously be ludicrous in the face of all the evidence that better transport facilities not only encourage growth but are, indeed, a prerequisite for it. This, however, is not the point at issue. What needs to be established is where the main economic growth will occur, given transportation improvements in a developing country. The degree of growth will certainly be locationally related to the new facilities. Thus, within the periphery, areas near to the new road or railway will do better than those further away. There is evidence of this from Venezuela, for example, where there have been differential rates of growth between those towns in the periphery on or near one of the new roads, and those still remote from them. But this distinction is a relatively minor one compared with the unequal division of benefits from the new transport facility as between the favoured core city and its region, on the one hand, and the undeveloped periphery, on the other. In this relative inequality in the sharing of the benefits we see the real role of new transport facilities connecting a pre-existing core region with the lesser-developed peripheries within an underdeveloped country which already exhibits strong geographical contrasts in levels of economic and social well-being. Such new facilities further accentuate these contrasts between the rich and the poor regions.

Clearly then, investment in roads or railways to 'improve' the accessibility of the periphery with the centre is not enough in itself to secure the objective of economic advance in the depressed regions. Such investment, though necessary in itself, must be accompanied by other measures designed to ensure that the benefits of transport construction flow into those areas lagging so far behind the centre in well-being per capita. One effective way would be to introduce physical controls on the use of the road: prohibiting, for example, any flow of certain consumer goods along the road from the centre towards the periphery in the hope of stimulating thereby the development of factories to make the goods at some point in the periphery itself. But such physical controls invariably raise more problems than they solve, as well as being difficult to administer. They almost inevitably invoke an ever-widening degree of direct control over economic decision-making, something which only Cuba among the Latin American nations has, so far at least, incorporated into its economic system. A more acceptable and hence more practical possibility within Latin America arises from the introduction of positive measures of various kinds to encourage the dispersal of economic activities away from the core region. The implementation of such measures could ensure that the new road, or other new transport facility concerned, was used as a determinant of the geographical directions and patterns that such dispersal shall take. But such an approach implies a comprehensive evaluation of the propensity for, and the need of, development in various parts of the 'periphery' before the transport development programme is finally determined. To date, however, few Latin American governments have enough real interest in, or effective motivation for, the introduction of a more dispersed geographical pattern of non-primary economic activities so as to make an approach to the problem of priorities in investment in transport facilities based on these considerations likely to outweigh the many other interests in, and motivations for, improved transportation facilities.

Looking around Latin America to-day one sees much evidence of the vast investment that has gone into transport facilities over the last 25 years. These include the improvement and electrification of the railways of the central valley of Chile centred on Santiago; the reconstruction to modern standards of the highway system radiating from Buenos Aires; the creation of an intensive network of new roads in the Brazilian state of São Paulo: the building of the Atlantico Railway designed to give Bogotá a direct connexion with the Caribbean coast; the linking of the capitals of the Central American countries by the Inter-American highway; the construction of a super-highway system in and around Mexico City and linking it with the port of Veracruz and the building of airports equipped for the latest intercontinental jets at every capital city in the continent. In other words, no matter where one looks in the continent, one sees that almost all of the investment in transport developments has been made in capital city regions or in locations leading to and from the core areas. If our foregoing argument is valid, then such investment can only have had the effect of strengthening the position of the core regions relative to other ports of the national territories. Thus the investment will have made it even more difficult to make a start to reducing the wealth and welfare gap between the richest and the poorest regions.

It is, therefore, hardly surprising that there is little evidence to date that the gap between average per capita well-being in 'core' and 'periphery' is starting to close; and some evidence, as we have seen, that it is continuing to widen. This is the case, for example, in the battle between north-east and south-east Brazil. The latter core region continues to forge ahead, in part because it appears to secure a net gain from intra-regional trade with the north-east, which is obliged by national regulation to buy its industrial goods requirements more expensively from the factories of south-east Brazil than if it had the freedom to buy them in foreign countries, but which in return is required to sell its agricultural production at government-controlled prices. On the other side of the continent the same sort of relationship emerges between the core region of Lima and the country's periphery set in the harsh conditions of the Sierra. The 'backwash' effect on the Sierra of the continued development of Lima through the migration of higher-quality labour and capital from the former to the latter, and the latter's lack of choice in buying its import requirements of consumer and other goods (these can only be bought from the factories of Lima rather than from potential lower-cost suppliers overseas) has, it has been calculated, been sufficient to reduce the rate of growth in the Sierra by some 4 or 5% per annum. This has depressed the Sierra's rate of growth in many years to one below the rate of growth of the population, thus ensuring a stagnating income per capita, whilst that of Lima's inhabitants continues to move ahead at a not unreasonable rate. Hinterlands (or peripheries) of Latin American countries are, in other words, even subsidizing growth at the centres and producing a situation in which Latin America is becoming a continent of widely-scattered developed zones, feeding on and keeping down standards of living in the remainder of the national territories. There are a few significant exceptions to this situation and they will be examined in the next chapter, together with future possibilities for geographically more extensive and nationally integrated patterns of economic development. Meantime, at the beginning of the 1970s, our hypothesis that the economic geography of Latin America's secondary and tertiary activities is described adequately by the core/periphery model appears to have virtually general application through from the Rio Grande, in the north, right to Tierra del Fuego some 10,000 kilometres away to the south.

Bibliography

a) The approach to the economic geography of Latin America followed in this chapter is not one which can be supplemented by very obvious additional reading material. For many readers, however, the first requirement will be further literature on the concept of regional imbalance in economic development. The following books are recommended:

FRIEDMANN, J., *Regional Development Policy*, M.I.T. Press, Cambridge, Mass., 1966.
Note that the sub-title to this book is *A Case Study of Venezuela.* This provides the most comprehensive study of regional imbalance for any Latin American country.

JOHNSON, E. A., *The Organisation of Space in Developing Countries*, Harvard U. P., Cambridge, Mass., 1970.

STÖHR, W., *Regional Development—Experience and Prospects: Latin America*, Moutons, Den Haag, 1972.
Note that this is one of many publications sponsored as part of the Regional Development Programme of the United Nations Research Institute for Social Development in Geneva. Many of the other publications are highly relevant.

UNITED NATIONS: Economic Commission for Latin America, *Annual Report for 1968*, Published 1970, Geneva.

b) The geographical 'core' areas of national economies have involved the development of very large cities and city regions and an understanding of their structure and problems is important. See:

BEYER, G. H. (Ed.), *The Urban Explosion in Latin America*, Cornell U. P., Ithaca, 1967.

HAUSER, P. M. (Ed.), *Urbanization in Latin America*, UNESCO, 1961.

MORSE, R. M., 'Latin American Cities: Aspects of Function and Structure' in Friedmann, J. and Alonso, W. (Eds.) *Regional Development and Planning: a Reader*, M.I.T. Press., Cambridge, Mass., 1964.

c) This might be followed up by case-studies on particular Latin American cities. For example,

BIRD, R., 'The Economy of the Mexican Federal District', *Inter-American Economic Affairs*, **17**, 1963.

FITZGIBBON, R. H., The Economy of 'Montevideo', *Inter-American Economic Affairs*, **6**, 1952.

FRIEDMANN, J. and LACKINGTON, T., 'Hyperurbanisation and National Development in Chile', *Urban Affairs Quarterly*, **3**, June 1967.

MORSE, R. M., 'São Paulo in the 19th and 20th Centuries,' *Inter-American Economic Affairs*, **5**, 1951 and **8**, 1854.

d) Studies of the peripheries of national economies tend, in the main, to see them in isolation from the core areas but the following publications do relate them,

BAER, W., 'Regional Inequality and Economic Growth in Brazil', *Economic Development and Cultural Change*, **12**, 1964.

FRIEDMANN, J., 'The Future of Urbanisation in Latin America. Some Observations on the Role of the Periphery', *Papers of the Regional Science Association*, **23**, 1969.

GRIFFIN, K. B., 'Reflections on Latin American Development', *Oxford Economic Papers*, **18**, March 1966.

ODELL, P. R., 'Problems of Regional Economic Planning in Developing Countries', *Proceedings of the British T.C.P.A. Summer School*, Belfast, 1967.

SMITH, C. T., 'Problems of Regional Development in Peru', *Geography*, **53**, 1968.

e) Problems of the peripheral areas of various Latin American countries are treated in the following selection of books and papers:

FLORES, E., 'The Significance of Land Use Changes in the Economic Development of Mexico', *Land Economics*, **XXXV**, May 1959.

ROBOCK, S. H., *Brazil's Developing North East*, Brookings Institution, Washington, 1963.

BUTLAND, G. J., 'The Human Geography of Southern Chile', *Institute of British Geographers' Publication* no. 24, 1957.

UNITED NATIONS, 'Rural Settlement Patterns and Social Change in Latin America', *Economic Bulletin for Latin America*, **X**, 1965.

UNITED NATIONS, 'Geographical Distribution of Population in Latin America and Regional Development Problems', *Economic Bulletin for Latin America*, **VIII**, 1963.

WILSON, A. CURTIS., *The Central American Area*, The Caribbean Conference Series, **11**, U. of Florida Press, 1961.

WHETTEN, N. L., *Guatemala: the Land and the People*, New York, 1961.

f) Colonization of the empty heartland of Latin America has attracted much attention mainly on the basis of studies of particular projects or groups of projects. See, for example:

CRIST, R. E. and GUHL, E., *Pioneer Settlement in Eastern Colombia*, Smithsonian Institute, Washington, 1956.

CROSSLEY, C. R., 'Santa Cruz at the Cross-Roads: a study of Development in Eastern Bolivia', *Tijdschrift voor Economische en Sociale Geografie*, **52**, 1961.

EDELMAN, A. T., 'Colonisation in Bolivia, Progress and Prospects', *Inter-American Economic Affairs*, **20**, 1967.

EIDT, R. C., 'Pioneer Settlement in Eastern Peru', *Annals of the Association of American Geographers*, **52**, 1962.

SIEMENS, A. H., 'Recent Spontaneous Settlement in Southern Veracruz', *Canadian Association of Geographers' Occasional Paper*, No. VI, 1964.

STEWART, N. R., 'Japanese Colonisation in Eastern Paraguay', *Publication 149*, *N.A.S.*, Washington, 1967.

g) The role of transportation in the structuring and re-structuring of the geographical pattern of societies is of fundamental importance. The following publications present in more detail some of the issues involved,

GAUTHIER, H., 'Transport and the Growth of the São Paulo Economy', *Journal of Regional Science*, **8**, 1969.

MOMSEN, R. P., *Routes over the Sierra do Mar*, Rio de Janeiro, 1964.

SOBERMAN, R. M., *Transport Technology for Developing Regions: a Study of Road Transport in Venezuela*, M.I.T. Press, Cambridge, Mass., 1966.

STOKES, C. J., *Transportation and Economic Development in Latin America*, Praeger, New York, 1968.

STOKES, C. J., 'The Freight Transportation System of Colombia', *Economic Geography*, **43**, 1967.

WILSON, G. W. et al., *The Impact of Highway Investment on Development*, Brookings Institution, Washington, 1965.

CHAPTER 9

Emerging Themes:
Towards a New Economic Geography
of Latin America

In the two preceding chapters an attempt has been made to isolate, describe and explain the major components in the contemporary economic geography of Latin America. We turn now to indulge in some geographical prediction on the likely trends in the spatial patterns and ordering of the economy of Latin America, based on our understanding of the processes out of which the current economic geography has emerged and on an interpretation of the way in which these processes will work in the future, when they will undoubtedly also be influenced by new forces and new restraints.

In descending order of probability we can predict four distinct, but not altogether unrelated, prospects for the future. Firstly, the geographical expansion of the 'core areas' at their fringes: secondly, the strengthening of development trends in second-order cities and even some other lower-order towns: thirdly, the deliberate encouragement of major, new growth areas within the framework of national developmental planning which pays greater attention to spatial aspects of economic development; and fourthly, some efforts directed towards the opening-up and colonization of parts of the empty heart of the continent. Most of this chapter will be devoted to an examination of these possibilities, and their implications for Latin America's economic geography but, finally, we shall discard the assumption of continued full national sovereignty on the part of the continent's individual nations and evaluate the likely spatial impact of Latin American economic integration.

The Geographical Expansion of the Core Areas

To predict the geographical extension of the core areas at and around their fringes does not involve a very intensive use of the 'crystal ball'. It involves only the prediction of a continuation of the process of central city growth which has been readily apparent for periods of up to fifty years and which has already produced some of the world's largest urban agglomerations. This is an aspect of the human geography of Latin America which has been discussed at length elsewhere in the sections on the urban environment and urbanward migration (see chapters 4 and 5). As shown too, in chapter 8, such a growth process has, in part, been a function of the concentration of secondary and tertiary economic activities in these cities. This is a phenomenon of great current importance, given the almost continental-wide insistence on industrialization as an appropriate policy for development. It is a process, moreover, which will continue to be important unless and until there is very positive government intervention in the location decision-making processes of private entrepreneurs (both domestic and foreign) and state capitalists.

In the meantime, however, there is great pressure of demand for land in these cities. This arises not only from the need for space in which to carry out the economic activities themselves but also from the derived demand for land for new residential areas, for wholesaling and retailing functions, for educational, social and medical facilities and for transport developments, particularly new roads. All this creates physical, as well as technical and economic, problems in the expansion of the continuously built-up areas. This is demonstrated time and time again in the great cities of the continent.

The expansion of Mexico City, for example, has created problems associated with the difficulty of building on badly-drained land susceptible to flooding during the rainy season. Caracas lies in an elongated intermontane basin and its expansion has literally 'filled up' the limited space available. Similarly, Rio de Janeiro has come to occupy the suitable, and even some inherently unsuitable, terrain in its hill and mountain-girt location around the Bay of Guanabara. Even a much smaller city such as La Paz is finding that the expanding needs for living and working space are necessitating developments up on the general plateau level (at around 4,000 metres), below which the city has traditionally sheltered as its inhabitants sought out an altitude somewhat less demanding on the abilities of both men and machines. Similarly, San José in Costa Rica has its growth potential adversely affected by the high probability of repeated pollution by volcanic ash from one of the several nearby still-active volcanoes.

Such physical problems associated with particular sites do not, however, frustrate the geographical expansion of all Latin American core cities. Buenos Aires and Montevideo, for example, could, in theory, carry on expanding outwards from the centre over the pampas for as far ahead as one can possibly visualize and even Bogotá still has the bulk of its intermontane basin to cover with the paraphernalia of urbanization! But even for these cities—as well as for the others which are affected directly by the problems of the physical attributes of the site in which they are located—there are immense technical and economic problems associated with growth. These problems, although insufficient in themselves to overcome the lethargy and unwillingness of governments to take sufficient action to restrain the growth of the primate and other large cities, do cause them to think more seriously of the possibilities of the dispersal of population and other time-honoured physical planning approaches to the phenomena of congestion and over-crowding. Unfortunately, even in this respect the efforts at physical planning have usually been copies of measures taken in the quite different economic and social circumstances of North American cities and hence quite inappropriate for tackling the problems of the largely pre-industrial cities of Latin America. The provision of urban motorways in cities like Caracas and Mexico on a grand scale, à la Los Angeles, is probably the most blatant example of the misuse of foreign technology and of a most inappropriate approach to investment priorities in capital-scarce situations. Such urban motorways do little to improve the lot of the overwhelming majority of Latin American city dwellers who are forced to make increasingly difficult journeys to and from work in inadequate public transportation facilities. In these two cities, where urban motorways have been a favourite way of using up scarce capital resources over the last 25 years without their having made much difference to urban congestion, attention and resources have only recently been directed to the possibilities of constructing rapid mass-transit facilities. So far, their development has been on a very limited scale though the sheer pressure of demand for urban transport from the rapidly growing populations now seems likely to lead to their continuing expansion into city-wide systems.

Increasing government interest in physical planning approaches to the core city problems is one reason for the attention that is now being given in several Latin American countries to the concept of the greater Metropolitan region. Another reason for this, and probably an even more important one in the present circumstances, emerges from concern for the increasing inefficiency of the core cities as locations for secondary and tertiary industry. This inefficiency, which is reflected in higher costs of production and lower profits for the entrepreneurs concerned, arises from infrastructure deficiences of a serious nature in most of the cities concerned. These include the inadequate provision of water and drainage facilities; an excessive pressure of demand on public electricity systems with consequential off-loading of some consumers at peak periods, and an unpunctual work-force as a result of traffic congestion and overcrowded, inefficient public transport facilities. Thus, on the part of both public and private authorities there is now a recognition of the need for the core city to be expanded into a core region involving either the creation of a multi-nucleated metropolitan region or the development of a linear form of urbanization along the main lines of communications: particularly along inter-urban motorways in which large investments have been made in recent years in many Latin American countries.

Three examples of this type of spatial transformation of the core area stand out already in Latin America. The first is in Mexico where the country's core region has expanded outside its area of origin: the Federal District (see Figure 9-1a). As the combination of demands for living, working and recreational/cultural space rose rapidly under the impact of industrialization and a burgeoning bureaucracy in the 1940s and early 1950s, so a greater Mexico City spilled over into the surrounding state of the same name. Expansion has continued until the continously built-up area now extends over a radius of up to 20 kilometres from the city centre in most directions with all the inevitable problems for mass-transport facilities and deficient public utilities as mentioned above. This expansion, moreover, occurred even before the industrialization process there moved into a later phase in which manufacturing plants with a need for extensive areas of land were built in Mexico for the first time. These are the modern, single storye plants which are concerned with the assembly of consumer durable goods ranging from the simplest, such as mass-produced cooking pans, through commodities like cookers and refrigerators, and up to the most complex, the motor car assembly plant. In addition to their land-in-plenty requirement, however, the nature of the organization and operation of such factories demands first-class access to good transport facilities so that they can be constantly fed with the components needed in assembly-line techniques. Some of these types of plants managed to find adequate space for establishing their production facilities and good transport connexions on the fringe of the built-up area of Mexico City. Many others, however, became convinced that, given the problems of Mexico City itself, an extra-Mexico City location was essential to efficient operation.

Coincidentally, but fortunately, by this time the first stages in Mexico's super-highway system were approaching completion (see Figure 9-1b). As these were essentially capital-city focused, rapid freight transport facilities to and from Mexico City in several directions became possible. This meant that a continuing flow of component parts to new assembly plants from older established component suppliers in the City could be assured. Thus, several large towns, notably Puebla, Cuernavaca, Querétaro, all within two hundred kilometres of the capital, could be considered as possible locations for this type of industry. Puebla, for example, was served by one of these new highways and it lay, moreover, on the route between Mexico City and Veracruz; the country's main port through which the imported components for the French and German cars (to be built in Mexico under licences from the firms concerned) would be shipped. This combination of favourable location factors resulted in Puebla's choice as the site for the largest assembly plant for motor vehicles.

This decision was perhaps the single most important one in producing a major geographical 'breakthrough' in industrial location possibilities in Central Mexico. This breakthrough consisted of the prospects which were opened up for a spatially more extensive economic growth zone (based on secondary and tertiary activities) extending over much of the eastern part of the Central Valley of Mexico, and over the eastern edge of the plateau to link with Veracruz, to replace the geograpically much more limited growth zone of Mexico City and its immediate environs (see Figure 9-1b). In that motor vehicle assembly plants have strong backward linkages to component suppliers, the opportunities for further related industrial development in Puebla and its vicinity are obviously good, and there is evidence already of new factories, functionally related to the assembly plant, deciding to locate there. Veracruz, at the end of this line of development from Mexico City, should simultaneously enjoy the advantages of forward linkages from its traditional port industries coupled with the juxtaposition there of industries based on locally produced oil and gas. Thus, Mexico City, Puebla and Veracruz become nodes of development along the main axis of transportation facilities served both by modern road and rail systems. The extension of the economic growth zone westwards beyond Mexico City is so far less evident and, at the moment, less compulsive, but some industrialists have already found locations in Querétaro, Léon and even as far west as Guadalajara, some 400 km from Mexico City. Such locations are attractive on the basis of a more readily available, and possibly lower cost, labour force and by virtue of their having fewer problems of services and space than in Mexico City. In addition, however, as a result of promotional efforts by the states and cities

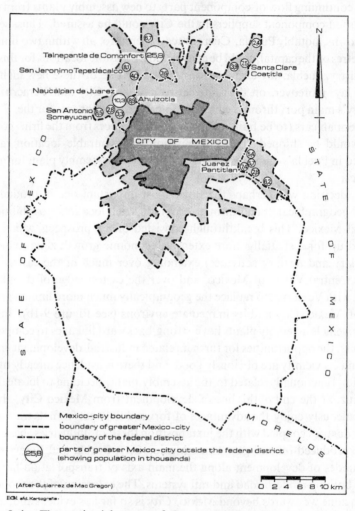

Figure 9–1a. The territorial extent of Greater Mexico City, showing its growth outside the Federal District

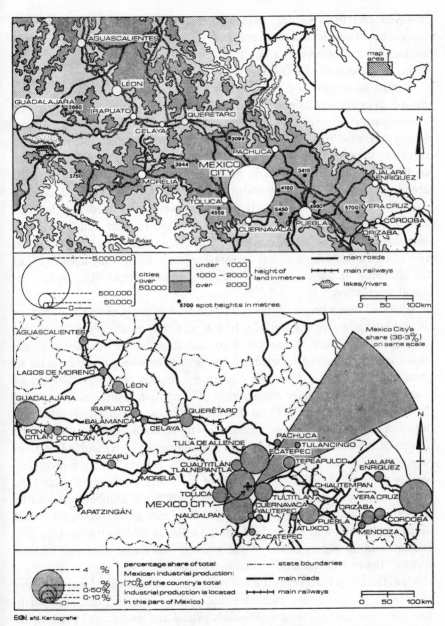

Figure 9–1b. Aspects of the economic geography of Mexico's Core Region, showing development along the axis, Guadalajara, Mexico City, Puebla and Veracruz

involved, certain advantages have been created for industrialists locating in these cities. These include the remission of local taxes for new industry over periods of up to ten years and a greater willingness by the local authorities to provide the kind of infrastructure that the companies need.

It must be emphasized, however, that the growth zone described here is not yet in existence except in a tentative or, at best, an embryonic form. The concentration of secondary and tertiary economic activities is still almost totally Mexico-City-orientated (Figure 9-1b) and there are still powerful forces at work to keep it that way. But the dice are no longer loaded quite so heavily in its favour and it now seems highly likely that we shall be able to talk quite accurately about a Mexican 'Central Valley Industrial Zone' by the end of the 1970s. It must, however, be pointed out that this embryonic more extensive economic industrial growth zone still represents a high degree of spatial concentration of high-value economic activities when viewed in the Mexican national context, for it constitutes only about 12% of the land area of the country and presently contains about 40% of the national population.

A second case where a spatial transformation of the core area is occurring is in Venezuela (see Figure 9-2). In this country, as already pointed out, the capital city, Caracas, has grown to such an extent as virtually to fill the small intermontane basin where it was first established. Possibly more so than any other Latin American city except Brasília, the physical form of Caracas approaches most closely that of a modern, motor-car-orientated North American city. It lacks an effective centre and the functions that more traditionally assemble in and around the city centre are scattered along the length of the urban motorway which runs along the intermontane basin in which Caracas lies. In addition an airfield (for private flying), a large university campus, the extensive grounds of the military officers' club and the big houses in extensive gardens of the relatively large numbers of wealthy Venezuelans and foreigners eat up the remainder of the desirable spaces along the bottom and lower slopes of the valley, whilst on the flanking hills the flats and the shanty towns of the workers and the unemployed take up most of the rest of the land available for building.

Manufacturing industry is a more recent phenomenon in Venezuela than in Mexico, partly because of contrasting governmental attitudes and partly because American manufactured goods gained and maintained preferential entry to Venezuela in return for certain privileges which were given to Venezuelan oil in U.S. markets. Both factors inhibited the effective development of other than small-scale industry until the early 1950s. It is only

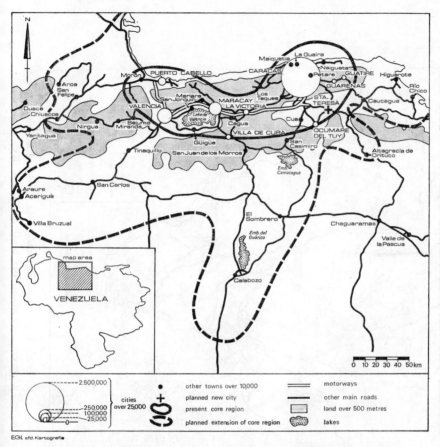

Figure 9–2. Venezuela: the core region and its possible expansion

since then that government incentives have been introduced in order to encourage the substitution of imported manufactured goods by domestically produced products. Such producers naturally sought Caracas locations, for reasons given in the previous chapter (see p. 192 to 199), and the city quickly achieved a manufacturing sector making goods for local, i.e. mainly Caracas, consumption. However, dispersal soon became something of a necessity because of the physical problem of the lack of room for industrial expansion. As the physiography of the immediate environs of Caracas prevented expansion at the periphery to anything but a limited degree, potential industrialists had to seek sites for their enterprises in the formerly important colonial towns of Maracay and Valencia, 80 and 130 kilometres respectively

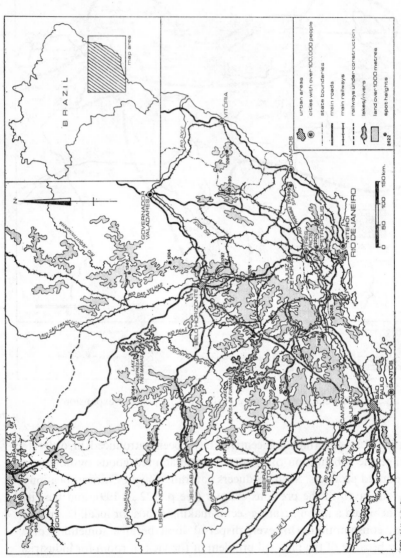

Figure 9–3. Brazil: cities and transport facilities in the Core Region. Note the large absolute size of the region even though it covers only about one-tenth of the country

to the west of Caracas along a motorway giving direct access to the capital. In the other direction, the port of Caracas (and also the location of the capital city's main airport), La Guaira, provided another alternative location for new industries anxious to remain as close as possible to the market provided by Caracas but unable to find building space actually in it. Thus, the core area of Venezuela can now be extended from a geographical identification with the capital city itself to a zone, roughly 200 kilometres long (but without any significant depth) stretching from the coast, through Caracas, over the intervening mountains to the shore of Lake Maracay along which the former colonial towns are being converted into manufacturing cities, and then back to the coast at the refining and petrochemical city of Puerto Cabello. And, as with Mexico, a motorway forms the axis of this new growth zone, thus providing a facility for the fast interchange of products by interdependent firms and for the low cost marketing of articles for final consumption. Further geographical extension of this core region is planned as shown on Figure 9-2.

The third example of this type of development is in Brazil (See Figure 9-3) which has a bi-nuclear core region, focused on Rio de Janeiro and São Paulo. Using European geographical standards we would describe these two multi-million cities as widely-separated poles of growth but in Brazilian terms the 400 kilometres between them makes them virtually next-door neighbours. Their inter-urban connexions by rail, modern highways and air services (The Rio–São Paulo link is one of the 10 busiest air routes in the world) are close and effective. Referring back to Figure 8-12, one will see that a third city, Belo Horizonte, located inland and about the same distance again from both Rio and São Paulo, also emerges as one of the forty-one centres of economic activities in Latin America. It remains, however, well behind the other two in its scale of development. Recently, however, the locational attractions of Belo Horizonte, particularly for the metal industries including iron and steel developments, have been significantly enhanced by the establishment of Brasília as the new capital of the country (replacing Rio de Janeiro). Its growth—to be discussed later in the chapter—as a centre of the 'government industry' (an important part of the tertiary economic sector) has already had the effect of 'pulling' some development inland. This pull was important for Belo Horizonte, which was a 'natural' location for such new activities, in that it had already achieved importance as the main inland centre of industrial development, and in that the improved transport facilities built between the coast and the new capital enhanced its locational attractions.

Thus, Belo Horizonte becomes the third point in the emergence of Brazil's triangle of development. It now stands to increase its size and standing, and its ability to attract industry, more quickly than either Rio or São Paulo. Following on this, it is reasonable to hypothesize that urban industrial development will no longer be restricted to the three nodes in the network, but will also tend to occur along the routes connecting them. This produces the possibility, therefore, of a geographically extended, multi-node core area taking up developments that might otherwise have been almost entirely concentrated on Rio and São Paulo. It is interesting to note that the geographical scale of this potential multi-node core region is roughly the same as that of 'Boswash': the United States great north-east coast urban industrial area. By the year 2000 'Sãoriobelo' could be a megalopolis of equal importance. Paradoxically, in the shorter term of the next decade or so, the growth of this 'development triangle' seems likely to be the main economic geographical effect of the establishment of Brazil's new capital. Only after that is the geographical impact of Brasília itself on the interior likely to become the more important element in Brazil's changing economic geography.

Elsewhere in Latin America the dynamism of the geography of the core regions is still basically expressed in the continued peripheral expansion of the primate cities which grow outwards and overwhelm smaller surrounding settlements; as demonstrated very clearly in the cases of Buenos Aires and Montevideo. A possible exception exists in Chile where the separation of the capital from its port by a distance of some 100 kilometres suggests the likelihood of an axis of development with major nodes at each end. But so far this seems to have happened hardly at all, for Valparaiso does little more than maintain its status based on handling the country's external trade and on the limited development of port industries. Greater Santiago continues to secure the bulk of activities and employment in the country's progress towards industrialization though this may now be effectively contained to some degree by recently introduced planning mechanisms which aim to stimulate expansion elsewhere in the region.

Growth Possibilities in Second-Order Cities

The second trend which appears to be shaping a new economic geography of Latin America lies in the strengthening of development possibilities in second-order cities and other existing centres, apart from those which enjoy the benefits of 'spread' or 'overspill' effects from the primate city. As we have previously tried to demonstrate, there is not usually much national concern for the fate of second-order cities at an official level: for good political reasons. In spite of the lack of official encouragement, however, they have sometimes come through to achieve economic success: in terms of attracting modern manufacturing and tertiary industry. One notable case of this has been the success of Guayaquil in Ecuador in challenging the earlier dominance of Quito. It should be noted, however, that its economic advantages of a coastal location were, in themselves, not sufficient to give it the edge over Quito. Its local élite group also had to indulge in efforts to achieve sufficient political power at a national level to curb the influence of the capital. This it did so successfully that the government has been run over long periods of time essentially by Guayaquil-sponsored politicians for, of course, the benefit of Guayaquil. Thus, its achievement of parity of status with, and of more rapid economic growth than, Quito lies fundamentally as much in political considerations as in economic ones. Had it also been the capital city then it is not difficult to imagine that Guayaquil would have achieved as high a degree of primacy within Ecuador, as Lima has in neighbouring Peru or as Buenos Aires has in Argentina following the mid-19th century success of the porteños (the inhabitants of Buenos Aires) in winning quite convincingly their political struggle with rival inland cities.

In Argentina the second-order cities have had an almost impossible task in keeping up, even relatively speaking, with the expansion of the capital. As shown in the previous chapter, even Córdoba's success in attracting industry has depended to a large degree on the significant local efforts which its leading groups of citizens made to achieve this end without much encouragement from Buenos Aires. But now, with the attraction to Córdoba of part of Argentina's motor-car industry, the city has been propelled into what should be a period of self-sustaining industrial growth.

However, Córdoba is something of the exception in this respect, for although Argentina has a number of largish, second-order cities, mainly provincial capitals, they remain for the most part as essentially marketing and administrative centres (Figure 9-4). The industrial components of their economies are mainly limited to processing locally available raw materials (for example, sugar, as in the case of Tucumán) and to producing bulky products required locally but which have to be made from imported raw materials of much smaller bulk: for example, the ubiquitous coco-cola bottling plant. Rosarió and, to a lesser degree, Bahía Blanca have enjoyed some industrial growth; but, rather surprisingly, little beyond the industries engendered directly by their exporting functions as far as Argentina's food and agricul-

EGI afd. Kartografie

Figure 9–4. Argentina: the distribution of second-order cities. Note that the most remote provincial capitals have populations of less than 100,000

tural raw materials crops are concerned and by their status as important rail-way centres. In that even these two advantageously located cities have largely failed to participate in the broader patterns of Argentina's industrialization, based particularly on the growth of industries producing goods to substitute for imports over the past 25 years, it is quite clear just how much difficulty has stood in the way of the industrialization of the country's other provincial cap-itals, leading towns and cities. However, there are some indications that the real costs of the continued expansion of Buenos Aires beyond the 6 million inhabitants' level are, at last, being recognized and the chances of effective moves to stimulate the dispersal of economic activities to other cities appear to be growing, though there is, as yet, certainly no accepted national strategy for this fundamental change in the geography of Argentina's economy.

A country showing a major contrast in this respect is Colombia, where the spatial patterns of development in the post-independence period have diverg-ed markedly from the model which has been demonstrated to apply to Latin American countries in general. The Colombian economy has developed with a group of quite distinct and geographically separate centres of secondary and tertiary activities. Although the capital, Bogotá, has always been the largest centre in terms of population, it has never had the same degree of primacy as has been usual in Latin America. In fact, as Table 8-3 shows, in terms of economic activities, as opposed simply to population size, it does not even now stand in first place. This is still occupied by Medellín, the provincial capital of Antioquia, the economy of which, for reasons which have never been very adequately explained, developed an industrial component, initially in textiles and then in other goods, from the third quarter of the 19th century onwards. It thus stood well ahead of Bogotá which remained without a significant modern industrial sector until the 1930s. Since then both cities have succe-eded in attracting new industry, though Bogotá, starting from the lower base, has enjoyed a more rapid rate of increase and, in particular in the 1960s, appears to have secured the largest share of the expansion in the country's newest industries, possibly because rapidly improving transport facilities during this period have made much wider areas of the country accessible to Bogotá (Figure 9-5).

But in this period the rivalry between Bogotá and Medellín has been accompanied by other major developments in the geography of the Colom-bian economy. Cali, the country's third city, was, until the earlier 1950s, mainly functioning as a departmental and regional centre and as the centre for the sugar-refining and other agricultural-processing industries of the fer-tile Cauca Valley. It has since succeeded in establishing itself as a significant

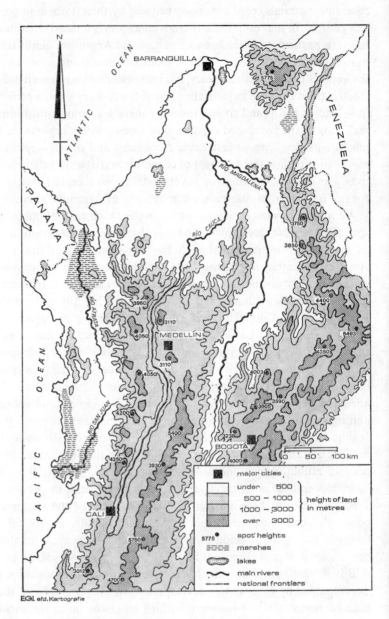

EGI afd. Kartografie

Figure 9–5. Colombia: aspects of the physical and human geography on the location

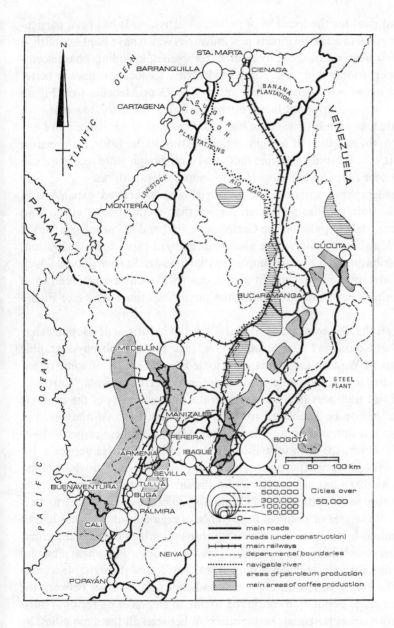

raphy of its core region. Note the control exercised by the physiog-
of economic activities

additional rival for the location of industrial activities. It has been particularly successful in attracting many new industries which have been established for the first time in Colombia by foreign companies, including pharmaceuticals, paper, rubber and other similar industries. Its location gave it better access to major port facilities than either Bogotá or Medellín (see Figure 9-5). This was an important factor attracting foreign industry, together with the fact that, as its industrial sector was less developed, it was hence more susceptible to the adoption of foreign methods. Thus, in the 1950s, Cali became Colombia's most rapidly growing industrial city, though more recently it too seems to have fallen behind Bogotá in its industrial growth rate.

The geographical dispersal of industrial and associated expansion in Colombia, however, has gone even further than to this trio of cities. Two other cities, Barranquilla on the Caribbean coast, and Bucaramanga, in the Middle Magdalena valley, have also both enjoyed rapid industrialization, thus contributing to a rather complex spatial industrialization pattern which also includes some components in smaller centres like Cartagena, Pereira and several other towns located between the main cities themselves (see Figure 9-5).

Why is it that this contrasting spatial pattern of industrial development has emerged in Colombia? It is certainly true that the difficult physiographic conditions of Western Colombia contributed to the ability of some of the lesser centres to maintain a degree of independence from Bogotá. Thus, as a result of bad transport facilities between the different parts of the country, industries had to be orientated to local rather than national markets. But Colombia was not exactly unique in Latin America in these respects. Elsewhere, however, the transformation from small-scale to larger-scale industry—with one firm often given a monopoly for supplying the whole of the national market—has meant location in the single, central core region. The fact that this has not happened in Colombia appears in large part to be a reflexion of the greater political importance of regionalism. This has had to be recognized by successive national governments which did not, therefore, as in other countries of Latin America, create conditions in which a capital city location for industrial development was made almost inevitable. It also reflects the longer period during which bad transport facilities between the major centres of population continued to put an emphasis on regional satisfactions of market potential. Interconnexion between all the main cities, by transport facilities other than air, has only been achieved since the mid 1950s.

Thus, Colombia has already had experience of a pattern of an industrial dispersal to second-order cities that we now predict for Latin America more generally. Paradoxically, however, the major improvements of transport facilities in Colombia in the last decade appear to be having some centralization effects. This is arising presumably because entrepreneurs are now finding that the national market, relatively dispersed through several centres though it is, can be most profitably served by the concentration of production activities in one centre. By such a policy economies of scale in manufacture produce large enough savings to offset additional transport costs to other parts of the country now that these have been reduced through better and more reliable facilities. This argument would appear to offer a reasonable explanation for the most recent ability of Bogotá to secure the most rapid expansion of activities. However, not all industries designed to serve the national, rather than a regional market have, in fact, located in Bogotá. Some have selected one or other of the alternative centres of industrial significance. This suggests that a multiplicity of centres may now be accepted as the 'norm'. Each of the five main individual centres is, moreover, sufficiently large that it should be able to sustain continued growth. If these conclusions are valid, then the dispersed geographical pattern of secondary and tertiary industries in Colombia will continue to set an example for the rest of the continent. However, recent studies of Colombia's economic geography have suggested that positive government action is urgently required to maintain the relatively dispersed pattern of industrialization. Second-order cities elsewhere in the continent may also need such government action to help them to achieve a continuing propensity for self-sustaining industrial growth.

At this stage one needs to point out that the phenomenon of a national territory divided into a 'core' and 'periphery' occurs at strongly contrasting geographical scales in Latin America. For instance, it will be noted that Brazil's core area triangle of Rio, São Paulo and Belo Horizonte extends over an area which is almost as great as the area covered by the more complex system of growth towns and cities in Colombia. Whereas the former can still be described as a core region, in that it leaves most of Brazil's occupied territory outside its limits, the latter involves a system of centres geographically dispersed over almost all parts of the country which are populated to any large extent. (Compare Figures 9-3 and 9-5.) This situation is even more clearly demonstrated in the cases of Puerto Rico and Venezuela. The small Caribbean island territory of Puerto Rico has a total area which fits easily into the Caracas/Maracay/Valencia 'core' region of Venezuela (see Figure 9-6). Thus Puerto Rico, by the geographical standards of the Latin American countries which we have examined so far, could hardly be considered as having a regional development problem of any great significance! However, in spite of

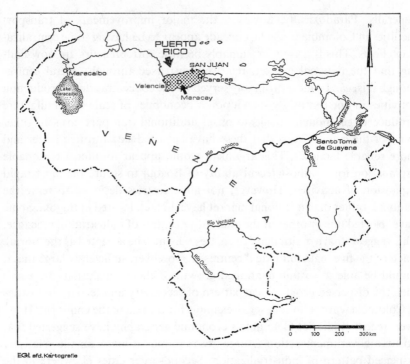

EGI. afd. Kartografie

Figure 9–6. Venezuela and Puerto Rico: contrasts in geographical scale which carry implications for approaches to spatial analysis and planning

this, even Puerto Rico does consider itself to have a regional problem arising from the propensity of San Juan, the capital, to attract most of the new developments at the expense of development everywhere else in the island.

Puerto Rico's rapid economic development in the period since the early 1950s has been based on industrialization under particularly favourable circumstances: viz. a position inside United States tariff barriers but without U.S. tax and other obligations. Though this has meant a speed and ease of development which is unmatchable by other small nations of Latin America, the latter are, nevertheless, almost with exception, aiming at the same end of diversification into manufacturing industry to increase employment and to raise per capita income. Its experience of spatial problems associated with industrial expansion, therefore, is not without importance for another dozen or so nations and territories of Latin America, most of them in the Caribbean area. One can, for example, compare Puerto Rico, and its recent emphasis on the geographical dispersion of new economic activities around the island, with Jamaica, which has many similarities, in both environmental and cultural terms, but which has so far failed to establish any effective programme of comprehensive and co-ordinated spatial development planning with a consequential continued marked concentration of activities in Kingston, its capital city.

The decision to industrialize Puerto Rico at first seemed certain to enhance further the already dominant status of San Juan, which enjoyed a virtual island monopoly of central city services and amenities. This was because few investors would wish to look, or even think of looking, beyond its metropolitan area as a location for their factories, in a situation in which the industrialization programme was based essentially on the importation of raw materials and semi-manufactures and the export of the finished products to the markets of the United States. Such trade to and from Puerto Rico could only be handled through the port of San Juan as the smaller ports of the island could offer neither the capacity nor the facilities (e.g. container berths) required by the traffic. Thus, to locate a factory elsewhere in the island would increase transport costs above the level incurred in a San Juan location and in addition would isolate the enterprise from the professional, technical and other services available only in the metropolitan area. Thus, in the first few years of the industrialization programme over 55% of all new jobs created in manufacturing industry were located in the San Juan area which at that time, in the early 1950s, contained less than 20% of the total population. The jobs created indirectly as a result of the growth of manufacturing (in trade, transport, other services, government etc.) were even more heavily concentrated in the metropolitan zone, which thus seemed set to become a classic example of a core area. Its further development would then have the effect of gradually denuding the rest of the island of economic growth potential as it attracted population in increasing numbers from the provincial towns and the country areas whose inhabitants sought better opportunities in the capital. (See Figure 9-7.) Such a developing geography of economic activities was, of course, fully in keeping with the general model for Latin American countries as presented in chapter 8.

However, in 1953 the government recognized the need to establish a positive industrial location policy designed to contribute to the 'orderly' regional development of the island. The policy as first defined laid principal emphasis on establishing as many factories as possible in the smaller and more remote towns where, it was argued (from the sort of evidence presented above) people had not been getting a proportionate share of the new industrial jobs. Thus, an Industrial Decentralization Programme was formally launched and

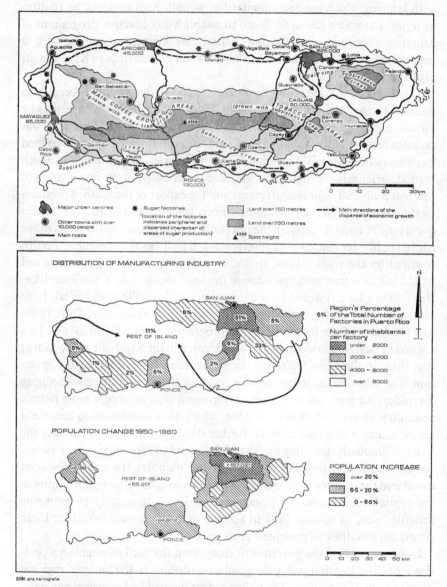

Figure 9–7. Puerto Rico: spatial concentration in the economy is indicated in the lower map while the upper map shows aspects of a more dispersed geography of economic activities

has since remained the basic tool for guiding the development of Puerto Rico's spatial economy. A variety of means were selected to implement the programme. In the early stages most attention was given to the improvement of the infrastructure outside San Juan, but such physical planning developments (for example, new and improved roads and a factory construction programme) are effectively only disincentive-minimization measures. In themselves they could do nothing to ensure that a factory's profits would be at least as great when it is located away from San Juan as when it is in the metropolitan area itself. Thus, positive financial inducements were necessary to persuade industrialists to accept that profit maximization could arise from the choice of an alternative location.

Three forms of financial incentives designed to decentralize industry were evolved and are illustrated in Figure 9-8. In general, the incentives are inversely proportional to the probability of a location securing industrial development and thus reflect the early aim of the programme to secure at least one factory in each municipality. This aim was recognized as one which would not necessarily secure an optimum economic solution to the spatial pattern of secondary economic activities, but was considered desirable in order that all parts of the island could be positively involved in the growth sector of the economy and thus ensure the programme of the widest possible support. Though politically attractive, however, it was soon recognized that such an approach to industrial location was economically untenable.

More recently, therefore, a second aim of the programme has become the dominant element in the government's decentralization efforts. This second aim involved securing major industrial expansion in the island's main regional centres: viz. Arecibo, Mayaguez and Ponce. This effort has proved to be much more successful, and the success now provides the basis for a more balanced geography of Puerto Rico's economic progress and one, moreover, which appears likely to offer net gains to the economy when compared with both other alternatives; viz. concentration in San Juan, on the one hand, and dispersal to all municipalities, on the other. This is the case because the relatively small provincial cities can be expanded cheaply; when compared, that is, with the high marginal costs of expanding the infrastructure of San Juan and the high social costs inherent in further growth of industrial and associated traffic in its already overcrowded streets. Expansion of the provincial cities not only has the effect of giving increasing returns on the funds invested by the government in infrastructure improvements, but it also enables the industrialists themselves, on locating in one of the regional centres of concentrated development, to count on some, at least, of those external economies which

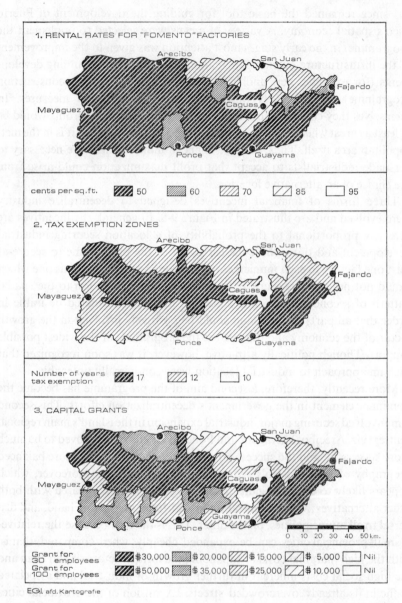

Figure 9–8. Puerto Rico: government incentives for the decentralization of industry

they could have expected to achieve by a location in San Juan. In such a situation, the additional financial help given by the government to industrial investors through the incentives is more than sufficient to offset the extra costs to an industrialist of a location away from the metropolitan region. Thus, the enterprise is more profitable in the out-of-San Juan location. At the same time the additional finance made available to the private investors by the government appears to have been less than the additional amounts of public investment which would have been required in expanding the capital city's infrastructure and other services had all the plants concerned opted for a San Juan location. In other words, there is good prima facie evidence that the Industrial Decentralization Programme has been of net overall economic advantage to the economy.

In terms of the actual developments which have resulted from the decentralization policy, the most significant was the initial establishment of an oil refinery at Ponce, on the south coast, in 1962. This has since provided the basis for the post-1963 development of an associated petrochemical complex which is now in a period of strongly self-sustaining growth. The fact that this development represents a major success for the Industrial Decentralization Programme is seen in the fact that without financial incentives to locate elsewhere, the oil refinery would almost certainly have gone alongside an earlier refinery on the outskirts of San Juan. Its location at Ponce and the subsequent other developments around it have created a viable south coast complex which is important not only in itself, but also as a counter-magnet to the San Juan/Caguas node at the other end of the main north–south route across the island. Arecibo, Mayaguez, Guayama and Fajardo (See Figure 9-7) provide other nodes for development. Their potential, which is now being realized, will ensure that most of the island's working population lives within daily commuting distance of job opportunities in the growing secondary and tertiary sectors of the economy. The development will certainly reduce the incentive for migration to the capital and lay the basis for reorientating Puerto Rico's spatial economy so as to produce a better 'balance' between San Juan and the rest of the island. Significant social, as well as economic, advantages will flow from this new pattern, for the population will also be within reach of centres on which an island-wide extension of educational, cultural and medical facilities can be effectively based.

It should perhaps be made clear that none of these developments imply that San Juan itself will not continue to grow, for, quite apart from its industrial functions, it is the centre of the island's expanding tourist industry and it remains the centre of administration and government and the highest-ranking commercial and professional services. Because of these service functions there is inevitably some new growth of job opportunities in San Juan no matter where on the island a factory is established. All the Industrial De-centralization Programme is doing is take away from San Juan the additional industrial growth element that it would otherwise almost inevitably have had. This, of course, makes the problem of metropolitan growth that much easier to handle: a development which seems to be an advantage in itself.

In the meantime, the direct and indirect job opportunities created in the second-order centres through their effective industrialization will eventually bring these towns to a size and degree of affluence at which they can begin to offer competition to San Juan in the provision of a widening range of services. Their speed and ability to do this, and thus to create an ordered and integrated hierarchy of central places in Puerto Rico, depends essentially on the degree of success of the Industrial Decentralization Programme, for only a significant industrial sector in the economies of the towns concerned can secure the economic base on which a development of their other func-tions will follow.

And what is true in this respect for Puerto Rico, applies in general to most other Latin American countries. The need to get industry into the second- (and third-) order cities and towns is a pressing geographical need which is gradually being recognized in most parts of the continent and the examples of Colombia and Puerto Rico on this issue are not without importance for other parts of the continent. This is starkly demonstrated in the case of Uruguay.

There, structural economic change, involving industrialization and an expansion of tertiary activities, started much earlier than in most other Latin American countries. Since then, continued centralization of devel-opment has produced an entity more like a city-state than a nation (Figure 9-9). Thus, today, so many of the country's available resources have to be devoted to the economy of Montevideo that too few are left to secure any effective development of the periphery, much of which remains almost devoid of activities other than an insufficiently capitalized agriculture making less than optimum use of the land's capabilities and from which migration to Montevideo still continues. In light of this, one is perhaps justified in hypo-thesizing some relationship between the willingness of successive govern-ments to allow Montevideo to secure almost all the development that the country has achieved since the commercialization of agriculture, and the country's poor economic performance over the last 30 years. It certainly appears possible that an alternative spatial structure for the Uruguayan

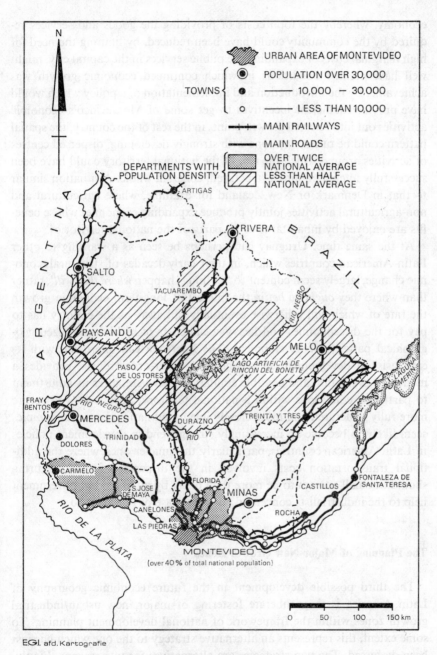

Figure 9–9. Uruguay: a country with a spatial socio-economic system dominated by Montevideo

economy, whereby the total costs of providing the goods and services required by the community could have been reduced, by limiting the need for high marginal costs of expanding the public services in the capital city, might well have created conditions in which continued economic growth was achievable. By the introduction and implementation of a policy which would have provided sufficient incentives to get some of Montevideo's economic activities out into selected growth points in the rest of the country, the spatial pattern could be turned into one with strongly developing, dispersed centres of activities around which the rest of the national territory could have been successfully integrated into a structured, coherent whole. A situation similar to that in Denmark or New Zealand for example, where agricultural and non-agricultural activities jointly produce expanding economies whose benefits are enjoyed by inhabitants of all parts of the national territories.

At the same time, Uruguay can perhaps be seen as a warning to other Latin American countries which, in their early decades of structural economic change, largely seem content to 'let things happen *where they will*', rather than where they *ought to be*, in the interest of long-term economic growth the rate of which will otherwise eventually fall away as the country has to pay for the diseconomies and heavy social costs of highly centralized geographical patterns of development. The Puerto Rican approach, with its emphasis on development in second and lower-order towns, provides a model for evaluation and possible emulation elsewhere, after its adjustment to particular conditions within a national territory. Such moves to secure more fully structured and more closely integrated national space economies seem likely to become an increasingly strong trend in development policies in Latin American countries, particularly the smaller ones, where the additional transportation costs involved in the dispersal of manufacturing should be small enough to be more than offset by quite modest government help to the industrialists concerned, as in the case of Puerto Rico.

The Planning of Major New Growth Zones

The third possible development in the future economic geography of Latin America is the deliberate fostering of major, new urban/industrial growth zones within the framework of national development planning. To some extent, this represents an alternative strategy to the one which has just been discussed. The two strategies are alternatives for two reasons. Firstly, because investment funds are limited, both in the public and private sectors, such that there is choice between financing either one major new growth centre or the development of some or all of the second-order cities: and secondly, because the choice of the one or the other involves different attitudes and outlooks towards spatial aspects of development. Neither of these reasons necessarily makes the two strategies mutually exclusive; in that available funds could be divided and in that differently persuaded pressure groups could each be partially successful. To date, however, in Latin America the two strategies have in practice turned out to be alternatives and so they appear likely to remain. There are certainly strong possibilities that one or two more Latin American countries will follow the major, new growth zone philosophy so whole-heartedly embraced by Venezuela and Brazil over the last decade or so.

Both Venezuela and Brazil have been persuaded of the compelling need to incorporate into the spatial structure of their economies a development representing a marked break with the past in terms both of its nature, and of its location with reference to the previously effectively-used part of their national territories. Out of their persuasion in these respects have emerged the cities of Brasília and Santo Tomé de Guayana. Though the latter name is probably one hundred times less familiar than the former, its significance is probably several times greater and hence will be considered here in somewhat more detail. But first we must present an evaluation of Brasília in terms of its relationship to the existing and the future economic geography of Brazil.

In chapter 8 we excluded the area in which Brasília is located from our consideration of the 'empty heart' of the continent. Nevertheless, Brasília's location was remote, and quite deliberately so, from the pre-existing centre of gravity of Brazil's population and economic activities (See Figure 9-10a where, on the right-hand map, is shown the relationship of Brasília's location to that of all state capitals). The intention in this choice of location for the new city was quite openly and deliberately to switch the country's focus of attention from the coast and the world overseas to the interior of Brazil; but not so far in the interior as to make the whole project ludicrous and impracticable. The project can, therefore, be differentiated geographically from the idea of Brazil's 'manifest destiny' which will be considered later in this chapter.

Brasília might have been conceived and built 'merely' as a major new city on the fringes of the effectively settled part of the country. As such it could, in the long term, have been expected to achieve an important role in various central place functions and to serve as the new centre for a develop-

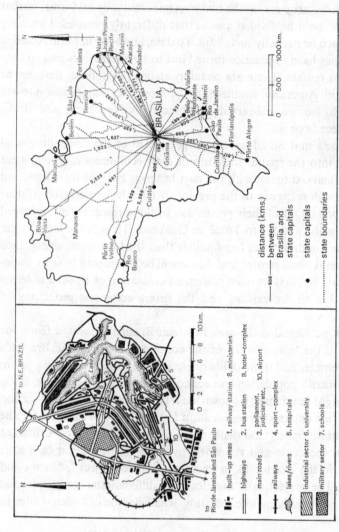

Figure 9–10a. Brasilia: its planned urban structure and its national location. In the urban structure map note the very small area allocated for industrial use and on the national location map note Brasilia's position relative to the developed S.E., the heavily populated N.E. and the undeveloped and unpopulated west and north of the country

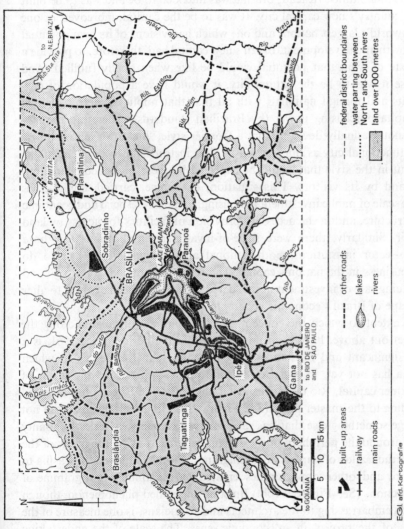

Figure 9–10b. Urban and transport developments in the Federal District, the extent of which is approximately 120 km × 75 km, or roughly the size of S.E. England

ing west. But the 'west' was not really developing very strongly, and in as far as it was, it already had its own central places of a size, and with ranges of functions, appropriate to the level of development achieved. These included towns like Goiania, Goias and Uberaba, each of some 50,000 to 100,000 inhabitants. Instead, Brasília was intended to be and was to be built as the country's new capital city. It was to be the capital, moreover, of one of the world's largest nations and one which had visions of its own potential for growth and development. Brazil's new capital had, therefore, to provide a foretaste of what that potential would be like when finally fulfilled. And because it was to be the capital city, it would have a population of civil servants and foreign nationals with all that that implies in terms of high per capita purchasing power (by Brazilian standards). Therefore the city could not gradually develop from a frontier style, 'hicktown' entity into a multi-functional city as time passed by, but instead had to be planned and laid out in the style that would be expected by these high-income inhabitants, and by its visitors. This situation, of course, carried implications for the scale of public investment in housing, in the city's social and economic infrastructure, and in the necessary provision of facilities for access by land and air. Similarly, there were scale-of-investment implications for those private-sector institutions, both national and foreign, which had to do their business in the nation's capital. The scene was thus set for a high and continuing rate of investment in the 'device' which had been evolved to alter the shape of Brazil's economic geography.

The extent to which the concept and the plan, as formulated along the lines set out above, have been implemented in the period since 1961, is a more significant and outstanding phenomenon than the degree to which Brasília has not yet, in social or cultural terms, approached the status of the former capital, Rio de Janeiro. In a physical sense Brasília has emerged according to the master plan. (See Figure 9-10a.) Though this plan did not envisage something else that has also emerged; namely, a series of shanty towns around the periphery of the designated area, serving the needs of the tens of thousands of unplanned immigrants who have moved to Brasília to find jobs and other opportunities created by the immense programme of construction. (See Figure 9-10b.) But this unplanned phenomenon, though perhaps embarrassing to the architects and politicians, is one measure of the success of the project in an economic sense. The scale of the undertaking has been so great that a self-sustaining economic entity has quickly been created and as a consequence has attracted migrants who would otherwise have moved to the south-east of the country. Brasília, in other words, has already succeeded in deflecting away from the core area of the country around Rio and São Paulo, part of the population flow into it that would otherwise have occurred.

At the same time Brasília's connexions with the rest of the country have gone ahead as planned. As Figure 9-10 shows, a national highway network, which is well on the way to completion, will link Brasília with all the other populated parts of the country. These highways have also enhanced the value of land with access to them and, in spite of an undue indulgence in land speculation rather than in serious efforts at effective land-use, they have created the beginnings of what could turn out to be powerful corridors of economic growth. Even agricultural activities have developed in response to the opportunities presented by the rapidly developing markets of Brasília and by the lower transport costs on foodstuffs made possible by the highway development programme.

Brasília has, moreover, even started to fulfil the functions for which it was planned, and both law-makers and the civil servants have begun to participate in the relocated activities of government switched from Rio de Janeiro. Again the pressures against change have been turned by the magnitude of the forces for change which have been created in the building of the new capital.

But it is too soon yet to evaluate the likelihood of Brasília becoming a second Canberra which, having relatively quickly reached a level of activity and of size consequent upon the relocation of governmental activities, then achieved little further growth, from the multiplication of activities and functions, for several decades. Such a 'fate' for Brasília is still possible and if it occurs it will inevitably make the city an isolated enclave of modern activities within an area of stagnation whilst 'all the action' remains in Rio and São Paulo. Should this happen, then Brasília, in spite of all its architectural splendours, could only be described as a failure.

However, at the beginning of the 1970s the odds seem to be weighted against such a failure, whilst there is a somewhat higher probability that Brasília will become an active component in the spatial ordering of the Brazilian economy. It will function in this respect as the counter-magnet to Rio and São Paulo and thus create the chance of firmly establishing long, and strong, corridors of economic growth between itself and the older centres. All this will, of course, serve to reduce the pressure of population and industry in the core area. This type of development has, however, yet to start and will be dependent upon the establishment of manufacturing industry in Brasília. Such an effective start to the industrialization process of the new capital may well necessitate positive financial penalties to inhibit the location of industries in the Rio/São Paulo/Belo Horizonte triangle of growth. The possibilities of such penalties being introduced seem, at the moment, to be rather remote and thus Brasília will have a much harder task to achieve self-sustaining growth in this sector of its economy.

A similar concern for the lack of a manufacturing industry component in its economy cannot be expressed about the other major Latin American example of a deliberately fostered, new growth zone: Santo Tomé de Guayana in Venezuela. Its establishment and expansion has, by contrast, been predicated precisely on the basis of the development of manufacturing industry and it stands therefore as a markedly different kind of project from that of the better-known Brasília.

Santo Tomé de Guayana has emerged out of a fundamental restructuring of what was originally a 'resource frontier' type of development based on the exploitation of iron ore (for export) and the production of hydro-electricity, at first intended mainly for transmission to the Caracas Metropolitan region. These developments, coupled with a high-cost iron and steel plant in its embryonic stages in the eastern part of Venezuela (see Figure 9-11), gave the post-revolutionary government of Acción Democratica, which was elected to power in 1958, a chance to redeem one of its electoral pledges. In that the party had sought and obtained its main support outside Caracas 'by courting the regional forces that had always been latent in Venezuelan history', the new government stood committed to the development of provincial resources rather than the further accumulation of wealth and power in Caracas: the chief concern of governments for the previous 30, or even 300 years!

Acción Democratica's decision to redeem its promises in this respect, or rather to show that it was attempting to do so, persuaded it to make the so-called Guayana project the cornerstone of its regional planning policy. This emerged, in the first place, simply because it was the obvious thing to do, and secondly, because of a deliberate political calculation that the Guayana project presented a somewhat easy (though certainly a bold) initial step towards effective regional planning in Venezuela. One is entitled to describe it as a 'somewhat easy' first step because the resource base for its development was so outstanding and its long-term economic viability was so apparent. In addition it presented a 'growth point' unhindered by pre-existing social and economic problems in that it is located in what was virtually an empty area. Guayana development could therefore be handled from the politico-economic centre of the country as a Caracas-based and controlled

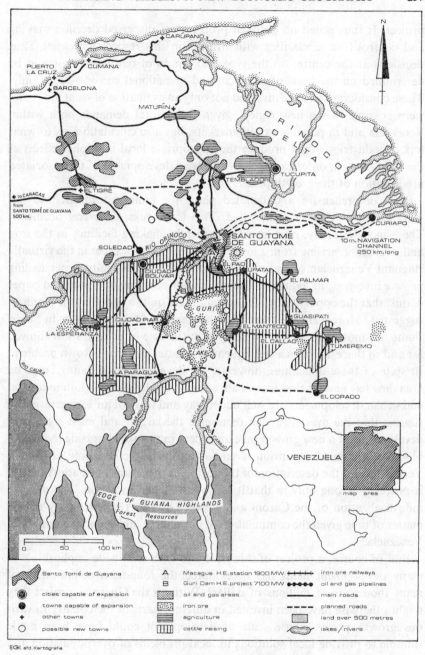

Figure 9–11. Venezuela: the development of the planned new growth region of Santo Tomé de Guayana

project. It thus posed no political problems of dispersed decision making and control (the similarities with Brasília in this respect are clear). Thus decisions at the centre, on the type and tempo of development, could be determined on the basis of technical and/or national considerations only. These considerations have involved not only an evaluation of what industries were possible in the new region, given the market demands both within Venezuela and in possible export markets, but also calculations as to what mix of industries would produce the appropriate local multiplier effects at the right times in order to match the planned development of the associated urbanization of the growth pole.

The comprehensive and detailed plans for industrialization have not worked out entirely as anticipated. This is because of several problems. These include, firstly, over-investment in tube-making facilities in the iron and steel plant, arising from a lower rate of demand for pipes in the virtually stagnant Venezuelan oil industry, and secondly, the difficulty in persuading private investors, in industries like aluminium smelting and pulp and paper plants, that the opportunities at Guayana were quite as good as the planners suggested. Moreover, as at Brasília, the demand for living space in Santo Tomé has moved ahead more quickly than the rate of urbanization allowed for and so there has been a consequential squatter and shanty town problem. In spite of these difficulties, however, the development of Santo Tomé de Guayana has nevertheless moved ahead very rapidly indeed. Both industrial and urban developments are well under way and it is not an exaggeration to suggest that the overall project represents the largest and most significant development of a new growth pole anywhere in the world outside the Soviet bloc. Its continued expansion is set to transform the economy of eastern Venezuela and the description of the region as the 'Ruhr of South America' is probably wrong only in that it has been applied too soon. The massive industrialization of the Caroni and Lower Orinoco rivers is surely only a matter of time given the continuation of population and economic growth in Venezuela.

But, of course, a project of this scale and with such wide implications in many development fields has necessitated the long-term commitment of many thousands of millions of dollars. Without the Guayana project they might otherwise have been invested in different parts of the country in various growth points whose scale of development could have been made suitable to provide local solutions to local problems of overpopulation and underdevelopment. The scale of the spending on the Guayana project has not gone unnoticed in the Andean states of Venezuela with their problems of access, of population pressure on land resources and of the out-migration of their most active citizens. Nor has it been ignored in the State of Zulia which has been suffering from the relative stagnation of the oil industry and its run-down of employment (due to the increasing mechanization and automatization in the industry). These are areas with large populations, many problems and also astute politicians and for them the Guayana development programme has had a demonstration effect. Why not, they argued, get it copied in every part of the country where additional economic opportunities are required for rapidly growing populations and work forces?

How to deal with these areas and their claims represents the problems arising from Venezuela's approach to the question of regional development. Guayana cannot be repeated elsewhere in the country. Not only is it too expensive—even for Venezuela—but it also demands centralized decision taking of a kind which is impossible for areas with both people and politicians. In one sense the concentration of Venezuela's regional development efforts on the Guayana project has meant that these other areas have been left as unaided as it was possible to leave them without running the risk of a major local explosion. Calculations that an expanding Guayana will ultimately be able to absorb the surplus resources of labour that exist elsewhere in the country have produced a relatively high-risk strategy which may not succeed because pressure of population elsewhere builds up too quickly. It also implies that those Venezuelans lacking opportunity elsewhere will be prepared to move to Guayana to better themselves and to leave behind, in their areas of origin, local populations whose reduced size is more appropriate to local opportunities. This is also a high-risk strategy in that it tends to assume that people behave in an economically rational way. If not, then the massive development of a new growth pole is not going to solve the spatial problems of all Venezuela, or even present much more than a second-best alternative to the expansion of the Caracas metropolitan region which may well be preferred by people from elsewhere in the country who have to move to find jobs anyway. On the other hand, the Guayana project has given the national planners some feel for the spatial component in national economic planning and it has brought them up against the need to employ appropriate techniques in dealing with this spatial component. Even forecasts for the future of the Guayana region have necessitated forecasts of what will happen elsewhere in Venezuela, so that the flow of information on regional planning throughout the country has been significantly increased. Thus, perhaps somewhat ironically, the Venezuelan decision to go for a major new regional development project has produced a situation in which the interest in spatial planning throughout the country, and in ways of carrying it out, has been greatly increased.

Brasília and Santo Tomé de Guayana thus represent a type of development in the changing geography of Latin America's economic activity the validity of which has still to be finally proven. However, neither of them can be described as failures and there are possibilities of the approach being emulated elsewhere in the continent, most notably in southern Argentina and in Eastern Peru. In the former case, with an industrial complex approach reminiscent of Santo Tomé and based on the oil and gas resources of Patagonia, and in the latter with a frontier development along the 'Marginal Highway', to which reference has already been made (see pages 172 to 173). The concept of the 'Marginal Highway' leads us on to the fourth possible development in Latin America's economic geography: that of the 'opening up' of the continental interior.

The 'Opening-Up' of the Continent's Empty Heart

We have already, in chapter 8, noted the types of effort made to open up greater Amazonia. We saw then that, with the exception of recent large-scale agricultural colonization development schemes in Brazil based on cattle raising, little impression has so far been made on this massive region. We also hypothesized previously that economic motivations for increasing levels of food production in rapidly industrializing Brazil, whose population is now approaching 100 million, and still increasing at about 3% per annum, could well provide sufficient incentive for massive clearance and development schemes; especially if the promotors of such schemes continue to enjoy favourable fiscal incentives. The 'jungle' will, in other words, become profitable. Thus, given the continuation of a social and political structure in Brazil which not only accords status on entrepreneurs but also guarantees them the right to keep the profits they make more or less intact (without too large a slice being taken by government), then the rate of exploitation of this frontier region may well become a surprising feature of Latin America's economic geography in the 1970s and 1980s.

The likelihood of similarly inspired transformations elsewhere of the interior are remote, with the possible exception of the northern fringes of the region which lie immediately to the south of the growth zone of Guayana in Venezuela (see above pages 236 to 240). Here, in response to the market openings created by successful establishment of metallurgical, chemical and pulp and paper industries etc., we may well find quite soon privately financed exploitation both of the region's forest reserves and of its probable mineral resources. It is also conceivable that those large parts of Amazonia which are potentially petroliferous may become worth exploiting by companies requiring oil supplies for international markets. However, sufficient incentive for such costly operations can, at the moment, only be envisaged as a consequence of some major upheaval in the Middle East which would eliminate large quantities of currently known reserves from the world's total marketable supplies. Ironically, and this also demonstrates well how the scale of development efforts depends on exogenous factors, the successful exploration for oil in another of the world's few remaining frontier regions, viz. the Arctic reaches of Alaska, Canada and the U.S.S.R., has probably had the effect of postponing the likelihood of a really major search for oil in the Andean forelands of eastern Colombia, Ecuador, Peru and Bolivia beyond the next decade. In the 1970s, therefore, Latin American petroleum developments, such as those in the Putamayo region of Southern Colombia, and in adjacent areas of Ecuador, seem likely to remain rather small-scale and only develop at a very modest speed.

The alternative method of tackling the interior frontier is by government-sponsored and financed projects. As explained previously, however, there are good reasons why most such projects to date have not been successful. The probability that these reasons will diminish in significance is low. In particular, it is impossible to envisage the economies or the political structures of any of the nations concerned becoming strong enough in the next decade to enable them to face up to the awe-inspiring amount of capital investment needed to bring about the incorporation of their eastern provinces into their nationally integrated spatial economic and social systems. The former Peruvian President, Fernando Belaúnde Terry, nailed his political future to the development of his country east of the Andes. As an architect/ planner by training he had the ability to conceive the concept and to see the immense implications of the Marginal Highway running from north to south linking the Andean countries in their regions of more or less zero development (see Figure 9-12). He was also able to demonstrate that the scheme was 'practical', in a physical sense, and that it would, when implemented, fundamentally change the economic geography of the nations concerned.

Unfortunately, however, neither the political nor economic motivations for its implementation brought it anywhere near the point of really serious consideration. Politically not even the Peruvians, and especially not

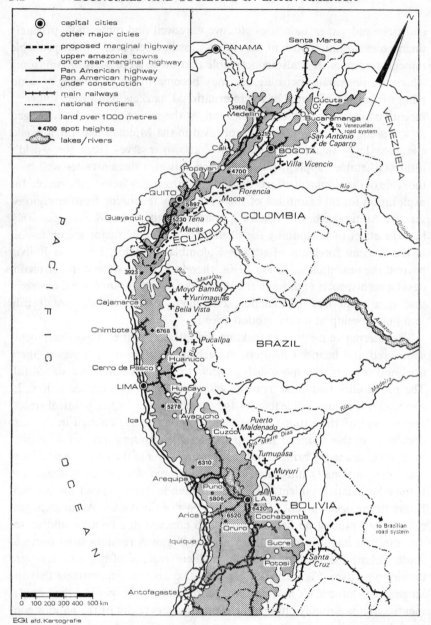

Figure 9–12. Andean South America: the Marginal Highway project. Note how this proposed road runs from Venezuela to Bolivia between the high Andes and the Amazon/Orinoco basins, linking a series of cross-Andean routes and providing possible development points

the largest sections of Peru's population living in the barriadas of Lima and other coastal cities or eking out an existence in the altiplano, saw the concept as being of much more than theoretical validity. In their ranking of priorities for investment funds they put it far below investment which would bring some shorter-term improvement to their lot. Similar attitudes prevailed in the other countries concerned, though elsewhere not even minorities as large as that in Peru saw the Marginal Highway as an attractive proposal: possibly because the idea came from a neighbouring country with, no doubt, an eye to the chance it would give for national aggrandizement! The overthrow of Belaúnde has enabled the Peruvian politicians to dismiss it from the range of alternative possibilities for capital investment: though the chances of its being taken up again by some aspiring politician always exist. Moreover, it does seem one of the obvious starting points for the economic development programme of the internationalists of the Group of Andean Countries. However, the political reality of this international Group's programme and recommendations have yet to be tested against the strength of diverse national forces.

Economically, the development of the interior by means of a capital-hungry marginal highway, or some other similar project, appears likely to be permanently postponed by two factors: firstly by the size of the capital requirement. This is estimated at a minimum of $500 million spread over 10 years—equivalent to about 10% of the total anticipated rate of availability of public investment funds in the four countries affected. Given the many other demands for capital resources, the project is fairly obviously a non-starter without an agreement to get it financed overseas. And this introduces the second factor working against the possibility of implementing the project. This is the high degree of probability that the investment will produce a very unsatisfactory rate of return given the discounting of future revenues (which are much more remote in time than the associated costs) at a rate approximating to the opportunity cost of capital in Peru and the other countries: say a rate of the order of 15%. In as far as overseas investment in these countries is always likely to be concerned with financial returns on capital and not on intangibles like social and political benefits, then it seems likely always to be able to find better investment opportunities than that presented by the Marginal Highway Scheme. Yet without a Marginal Highway, or some equally big public investment in the area, the chance of opening up the interior appears remote. Hence the low-order status which we have conferred on the fourth set of developments, the possibilities leading to a more dispersed geography of Latin America's economic activities.

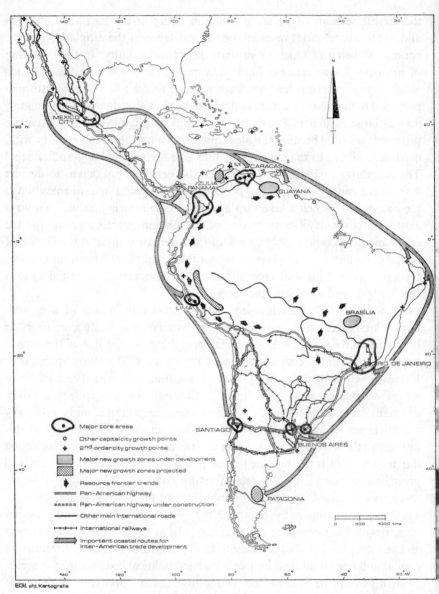

Figure 9–13. Latin America: a summary of the main development trends in its economic geography

Figure 9-13 is an attempt to represent cartographically the four trends that have been suggested in this chapter as ones which could lead to important generalized changes in the continent's geography. But there is one important proviso that we must attach to our presentation of these possibilities. They have all been made on the assumption that Latin America will remain made up of a series of sovereign nation-states, each fully in control of its own affairs. In the light, however, of all the discussion of economic integration in Latin America, both of the whole and of various parts, it would be wrong to conclude this predictive essay without indicating the geographical implications of such economic and political integration. However, our consideration of it does not imply more than a recognition that there is some probability that economic integration will take place and, if it does, that it will contribute to the continent's geographical patterns of development.

The Geographical Impact of Economic Integration in Latin America

Economic integration is, in a legal sense, already a fact as far as Central America is concerned. The nations from Guatemala to Costa Rica inclusive (see Figure 9-14) signed a Treaty of Economic Integration as long ago as 1960 and in various ways since then have been working towards making the five national economies into one unified economic system. The economic, social and political problems, and the difficulties of forming the Central American Common Market (C.A.C.M.), do not concern us here, but we need to look at the geographical background to, and the spatial implications and results of, economic integration.

In the first place, its formation has given a great stimulus to studies and evaluations of the area's problems as a geographical whole, whereas previously studies tended to be made within the framework of the watertight political compartments of the individual countries. This has been particularly important for considerations of infrastructure development, notably in the field of transport. This has already been reflected in an enhanced degree of attention to those facilities—roads, ports, railways, telecommunications, air services etc.—the improvement of which could mean a higher degree of opportunity for the five separate economic systems, as a result of their being able to make physical contact with each other at a much lower cost than hitherto. In that the U.S. has been the main provider of funds for such projects, and in that the U.S. has the integration of Central America

as one of its policy aims, then the reason for the importance of this consideration is easily appreciated. Priority by the U.S. in providing funds for
transportation and communication facilities which have Central American,
rather than just national, significance may thus confidently be expected to
continue. Dependence on American aid in this respect means that, in a real
sense, decisions in this sector are beyond the competence of the national
governments to determine; unless, of course, they are prepared to forgo the
foreign grants and loans which are essential for the successful financing of
all major projects.

In the second place, there are, or rather could be, geographical implications flowing from the decision to integrate, into a common market, the previously five separate national markets for industrial products (agricultural
products are, by and large, excluded from the provisions of the common
market arrangements). Each of the five countries has typically developed a
small range of industries consisting, apart from those concerned with the initial processing of primary products, of import-substitution developments. By
and large these industrial developments have been located in, and immediately
around, the five capital cities concerned. Thus, each capital has functioned as
the core element in a typical core-periphery situation (Figure 9-14). However, had Central America been integrated at an earlier stage, preceding this
degree of industrialization, and, as a result, been better served by transportation facilities, then it is highly probable that most industries would have
selected a single location for serving the whole of the central American
market. The consequence of this would have been the emergence of a single
core region for the whole of the isthmus, with the unlucky other four capitals
becoming the equivalent of provincial cities in a nation-state and thus, on
the evidence from most Latin American countries, likely to find themselves
lacking industrial components in their economies.

A fear that a locational pattern along these lines, as far as newly established
industries were concerned, could be a consequence of economic integration
clearly lay behind the protocol on 'Integrated Industries' attached to the main
treaty. In this protocol an integrated industry was defined as an industry
which could only be attracted to Central America because the existence of
the larger, integrated market made production possible at or above a minimum scale of operation. The industry could not have established itself previously in any one of the national markets because no single one of these offered a large enough demand to make the minimum scale of operations possible. The protocol then went on to specify a locational restraint on such industries. It said that no one member country of the Central American Com-

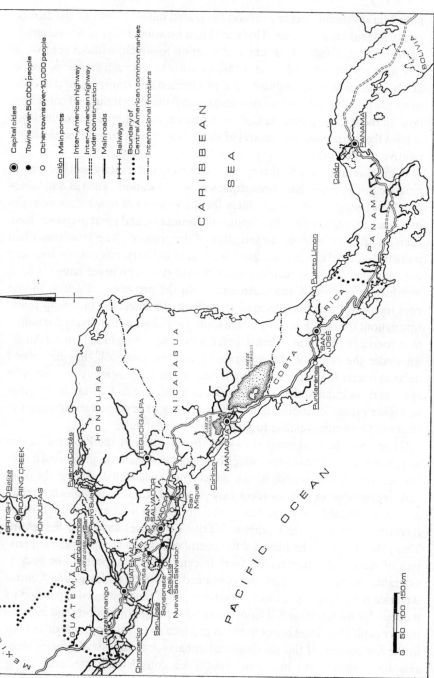

Figure 9-14. Central America: its network of cities and towns and its transport facilities. Note the lack of integrated national spatial systems in all the countries except El Salvador and the non-existent or, at best, tenuous links between the Pacific and the Caribbean coastlands

mon Market should secure a second integrated industry until all the member countries had attracted one. This was thus a measure designed to prevent the centralization of industry at any one location to which, without control, all new industry would tend to gravitate in order to take advantage of particularly favourable cost conditions for production and transport and in order to secure possible external economies arising from such industrial concentration. In theory, therefore, the Common Market has set up a system in which at least the five pre-existing centres of industry should maintain their positions relative to each other.

What was intended in theory has, however, not exactly worked out in practice for, as might have been expected, some locations, such as San Salvador, have been preferred over others for the location of new industrial activities, such as Tegucigalpa, the capital of Honduras, and great pressures have been set up to circumvent the intention of the protocol. The avoidance of an industry's formal designation as an integrated industry was one obvious way out, and many new industries, which would probably never have found it worthwhile going to Central America with the prospects of selling in one country only, have been located there with the intention of selling freely throughout the region under the free trade provisions of the Treaty for industrial goods. In that these industrial plants have not come in to Central America under the rules of the integrated industries protocol, they have been quite at liberty to choose their own locations. In as far as many of them have apparently calculated that San Salvador and Guatemala City are better (that is, higher-profit) locations than elsewhere, they have started to enhance the status of these cities relative to that of the other capitals.

Quite apart from attempts to avoid the intention of the Protocol in this way, however, other industries which have been designated as integrated industries nevertheless appear to have been accepted and located without the original regulations of the protocol being applied. Guatemala, which already has an integrated industry, has secured a second one, even though other member countries of the Common Market do not yet have their first plant. Thus, the ability of the Protocol to control effectively the geographical pattern of industrialization arising from integration now appears to be in considerable doubt. As a result, the continued ability of an integrated Central America to attract new industries (arising out of the continued expansion of markets for industrial goods from the rapidly rising populations and increasing per capita incomes) seems likely to produce an unbalanced rate of growth in the five centres. If this geographical imbalance in industrial development gets too strong, then one can hypothesize considerable pressures being brought to bear against the whole idea of the economic and political wisdom of the Common Market arrangements by those member countries which find themselves losing out in competition for new activities with more favoured localities. Figure 9-15, on the other hand, illustrates the rather complex pattern of infrastructure and trading developments which, it is thought, could inhibit such a tendency towards the centralization of development. To date, there is little evidence to suggest that the countries concerned have either the means or the will to create such possibilities for a spatially more dispersed pattern of development.

But, of course, an integrated Central America, in terms of its geographical area and its total population, amounts to no more than a small to medium-sized Latin American country. This fact has been recognized in the proposal that only an integrated Central America, and not individual Central American countries, shall be eligible to become a member state of an economically integrated Latin America. Steps towards Latin American economic integration date back to the mid-1950s but so far the only concrete institution to emerge out of the countless dicussions is the limited-in-scope, and even more limited in practice, Latin American Free Trade Area. Its efforts to stimulate intra-Latin American trade, particularly in industrial goods, have so far been only very modestly successful. The continued hope, however, that it, or a successor organization, will eventually begin to work effectively, makes it necessary that we evaluate possible geographical implications of continental-wide economic integration.

A prime motivation for economic integration between sovereign nations is the greater opportunity that it gives for industrialization. This is because it introduces possibilities of reductions in unit manufacturing costs as producers take advantage of increasing economies of scale and of interdependencies between industries given the existence of larger markets for their products. Thus many studies have been, or are being, undertaken to determine the most appropriate industrial structure for an economically integrated continent.But within the framework of the evaluation of the continental requirements for, and the possibilities of, industrial growth by sectors (iron and steel, non-ferrous metals, motor vehicles etc.), little official attention has been given to determining the most likely, or the most appropriate, spatial patterns of industrial development. Until the late 1960s advice on location was largely restricted to comments such as, 'industrial expansion should take advantage of suitable siting' and that 'regional investment policy for industry should concentrate on the countries that are relatively less developed'. These comments were more than inadequate. They were also contradictory in that it is

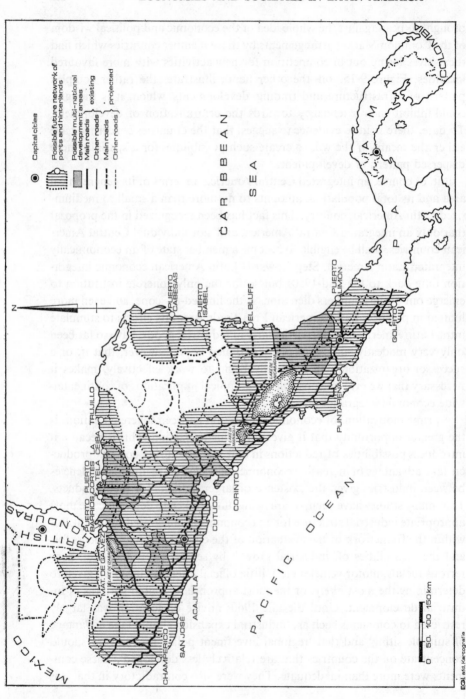

Figure 9-15. Central America: a possible spatial structure for an economically integrated region

highly unlikely that the most suitable sites (determined presumably by the relative economic advantages of alternative locations) will be found in the relatively less developed countries of the continent. More realistically, the present pattern of the geography of economic activities in Latin America and the determinants of this pattern (see chapter 8) suggest that economic integration will well serve to act as yet another cause for the further concentration of activities on existing core areas, in the absence of any positive measures to prevent this happening.

The existing coastal, or near coastal, locations of almost all the main centres of economic activity (see Figure 8-12) seem likely to act as magnets for any new investment in industrial activities. This is not only because these areas are immediately recognizable as industrial growth centres, equipped with the kind of economic and social infrastructure required, but also because these locations provide access by sea to the main markets for industrial goods located at or near the coast in other member countries of the economically unifying continent. The advantages of sea transport over land transport for trade between the various centres of activity are largely self-evident for, in many cases, land transport facilities are either inadequate or non-existent or even provide less direct routes than coastal shipping.

Thus, Buenos Aires will have its existing advantage over Córdoba and other inland locations in Argentina further enhanced (see Figure 9-4). In Brazil, the existing industrial centres of the south-east will be more advantageously located, in respect of transfer distances and costs, in relation to most of the main market areas of Latin America, than will the north-east of the country and inland locations. Mexico is geographically eccentric to the main areas of demand in Latin America anyway, and thus, with a view to minimizing additional costs which are incurred in getting goods to the point of export offering the lowest cost and most frequent shipping services to the rest of Latin America, it is unlikely that any industrialist would look far beyond the Mexico City–Veracruz axis of development (see Figure 9-1). This reduces the chances of success for the proposed economic growth zones to the north and north-west of the capital. There is a similar difficulty for the smaller west coast countries, where any industry aiming to serve the Latin American market as a whole suffers a cost penalty because of the distance involved in shipping goods to the major markets of Argentina, Brazil and Mexico. Thus, it is unlikely that entrepreneurs in these countries will seriously look beyond the existing centres of manufacturing activity in the Lima and Santiago areas, for there at least they can achieve economies in processing costs through linkages with other firms and by taking advantage of the existing infrastuctural developments in these areas. These areas' claims on public funds for infrastructure improvements will thus be even further strengthened to the detriment of claims from other, less well-developed parts of the countries whose relative ability to attract industry will thus fall even further in competition with the core areas.

On the basis of these arguments it can be argued that the moves towards Latin American economic integration have possible adverse consequences for the spatial ordering of economic activities in most countries. The traditional economists' answer to this argument would be that the stimulus to economic growth arising from economic integration will be so great that the favoured, and geographically limited, industrialized 'core' areas will distribute the benefits of integration to other parts of the national territories of the member countries. Any tendency for a prolonged division of a country into expanding and depressed areas will, so they would argue, be remedied by the economic pressures which arise in the processes of rapid development in the expanding areas. Such pressures include the economic and social effects of congestion in the cities of the core region and the requirement for economic policy makers to take a clear look at the development potentials of the depressed areas when it becomes clear that the country is failing to utilize the resources in such areas.

But the evidence to date of the effects of congestion and of the 'clear looks' of economic policy makers is not very encouraging, as we have seen in a previous chapter. Most of the empirical evidence so far suggests, in fact, exactly the opposite. Economic pressures are still producing concentration. And the impact of free trade in industrial goods seems likely to accentuate further the pressures in favour of concentration at most of the existing growth centres. These pressures come from the cost savings secured by plants in such concentrated areas of development through economies of scale in production, by external economies through linkages and infrastructural development and through locational advantages which give lower transport costs to and from existing industrial areas. In that congestion costs are not internalized to the firm—but remain a charge to the national economy as a whole—there is no reason why individual entrepreneurs should worry at all about them in their decisions to locate in the core areas.

A Latin American common market involving free trade in industrial goods could, moreover, also have an adverse effect on the chances of geographical dispersion of economic activities in another way. This could arise from the effect that a common market has on the size of the market available to an industry. Within an individual nation-state, an important factor ultimately leading to a decision to do 'something' about underdevelopment and low-living standards in the periphery of the nation is the curb on the continuation of industrialization in the core area which results from the insufficient size of the home market. In order to stimulate the effective demand for nationally manufactured goods, and to ensure the continuation of the industrialization process, it ultimately becomes necessary to increase the purchasing power of the population in the areas of the country away from the core region. This increasing economic pressure from the industrial sector implies a need for a country to face up to the problems of adjusting economic and social policies, such as taxation and land tenure, so as to ensure that a larger and geographically more dispersed part of the total population could be converted into effective consumers of the goods that the core areas are increasingly able to produce. Some Latin American countries had arrived at that point in their industrialization programmes and others were approaching it. Now, the idea of a common market produces a strong possibility that these economic pressures for reform are reduced, even though its protagonists argue that integration is not an alternative to reforms in the economic and social structure of member countries. The danger arises because economic integration of many nation-states ensures that the capital-city-orientated industrial sectors can survive somewhat longer on the basis of new export opportunities opened up in the markets of the other member countries of the integrating area.

Thus, though it is certainly not intentional on the part of most of the proponents of Latin American integration, most of whom recognize the need for change in the structures of Latin American societies as part of their general dissatisfaction with the existing politico-economic system, the economic integration of the continent could well present an easy way out of the economic, political and social dilemmas involved in the process of creating sufficient new domestic demand for the increasing industrial output of the 'core' areas among the populations of the depressed peripheries of the Latin American countries. Overall, there is a danger that an economically integrated, or even a merely free-trading, Latin America will become little more than a series of interconnected 'core' areas feeding on and having close economic and political relationships with each other. As an inevitable concomitant of this development, each core area will even more effectively turn its back on the opportunities for mutually beneficial contact with the remainder of the national territory within which it is situated. Recognition that such a danger exists in the Latin American moves to economic integration is the first step to formulating appropriate counteraction to inhibit its development.

An understanding of the fundamentals of Latin America's economic geography, as it has developed over the last 400 years under first political, and later, economic colonialism and, most recently, within systems which have sought to secure greater economic independence for the individual countries of the continent, seems to be a necessary prerequisite for an understanding of the most effective ways in which an efficient and, at the same time, a socially just geographical structure of society can be evolved.

Bibliography

The extensive bibliography at the end of the previous chapter provided much of the material from which the ideas set out in this chapter initially emerged. Careful attention to that literature list should persuade the reader of the reasonableness or otherwise of these ideas. There are, however, some other items which must be mentioned.

a) The author has benefited from and enjoyed the stimulus of many discussions (and even arguments) with a group of graduate students that he had the opportunity to supervise at the London School of Economics. Each of these former students has since produced a Ph.D. thesis which, in their more preliminary stages, helped in the preparation of this chapter. The titles of these theses are given below not because many readers will have an opportunity to make use of them, but because articles and papers based on them are certain to appear in the near future and these should be viewed as essential further reading for an understanding of the developing economic geography of Latin America. They are:

GILBERT, A. G., *Industrial Growth and the Spatial Development of the Columbian Economy 1951–64*. University of London, Ph.D. thesis, 1970.

LAVELL, A. M., *Industrial Development and the Regional Problem: a Case Study of Central Mexico*, University of London, Ph.D. thesis, 1971.

SLATER, D., *Spatial Aspects of the Peruvian Socio-Economic System, 1925–68*. University of London, Ph.D. thesis 1972.

b) Other material which provides either further background to the ideas set out in this chapter or which is itself concerned in part with trends in the economic geography of Latin America includes:

BELAUNDE, T., *Peru's Own Conquest*, Lima, 1965.

The case for the development of Peru's oriente.

BROWN, R. T., *Transport and the Economic Integration of South America*, Brookings Institution Washington, 1966.

CASTILLO, G. M., *Growth and Integration in Central America*, Praeger, New York, 1966.

CURRIE, L., *Accelerating Development: the Necessity and the Means*, McGraw-Hill, New York, 1966.

ODELL, P. R., 'Economic Integration and Spatial Patterns of Economic Development in Latin America', *Journal of Common Market Studies*, **6**, 1968.

POSADA, A. J. and DE POSADA, J., *The C.V.C.—Challenge to Underdevelopment and Traditionalism*, Bogota, 1966.

POLEMAN, T. T., *The Papaloapan Project, Agricultural Development in the Mexican Tropics*, Stanford U. P., Stanford, 1964.

REY ALVAREZ, R., Planification Régionale et Intégration en America Latina, *Tiers Monde*, **VI**, 1965.

RODWIN, L., *Planning Urban Growth and Regional Development: the Experience of the Guayana Program of Venezuela*. M.I.T. Press, Cambridge, Mass., 1966.

STÖHR, W., The Role of Regions for Development in Latin America, *Regional Studies*, **3**, 1969.

VELASCO, C. *et al.*, A Preliminary Scheme for the Economic Regionalization of Cuba, *Soviet Geography*, **VI**, 1965.

VOLSKY V. V. *et al.*, Regional Problems of Multipurpose Utilization of National Resources in Latin America, *Soviet Geography*, **VI**, 1965.

Index

257